Somerset and District Friendly Society
POLE HEADS

Designs found in Somerset, East Devon, Dorset,
West Wiltshire and South Gloucestershire

Henstridge Friendly Society anniversary 1912 – outside Inwood House

Michael Ferguson

HALSGROVE

Published in 2024

A CIP catalogue record for this book is available from the British Library.

ISBN: 978 0 85704 370 2

Halsgrove
Halsgrove House,
Ryelands Business Park,
Bagley Road, Wellington,
Somerset TA21 9PZ
Tel: 01823 653777
Fax: 01823 216796
email: sales@halsgrove.com

Part of the Halsgrove group of companies
Information on all Halsgrove titles is available at: www.halsgrove.com

Printed and bound in India by Parksons Graphics

Contents

Acknowledgements

Permission is gratefully acknowledged to reproduce photographs taken by the author of objects from collections in the following museums: Blaise Castle House Museum, Bristol; The Box, Plymouth (formerly Plymouth City Museum and Art Gallery); Dorset Museum, Dorchester; The Holburne Museum, Bath; The Museum of English Rural Life, Reading (MERL); Radstock Museum; Royal Albert Memorial Museum and Gallery, Exeter (RAMM); The Salisbury Museum; Sherborne Museum; The Museum of Somerset, Taunton (South West Heritage Trust and Somerset County Council, acknowledged in the text as Somerset Heritage Centre or SHC); Torquay Museum; Trowbridge Museum; Wells and Mendip Museum, Wells; Wiltshire Museum, Devizes.

Permission to reproduce the copyright image of item M 181.1930 (F 146/2), belonging to the V and A Museum, is gratefully acknowledged.

For assistance with retrieving both the museum collection artefacts and their related accession archives, the author wishes to thank the following past and present museum officers: Jonathan Brown; Thomas Cadbury; Barry Chandler; David Eveleigh; Estelle Gilbert; Christopher Hawkes; Bethan Murray; Judy Nash; Will Phillips; Peggy Rowe; Rachel Smith; Jane Standen; David Walker; Roger Watson; Matthew Winterbottom; Peter Woodward.

To the many owners of collections who have so generously allowed me to see their pole heads and to share their knowledge and enthusiasm I owe a huge debt of gratitude, and especially to P H, T R, R de P, and I M.

Introduction

Friendly societies were voluntary associations providing financial benefits for members in cases of sickness, or death, and were the fore-runners of Britain's 1912 National Insurance scheme. They operated between about 1750 and 1912 and were found over most of Britain. Initially they were locally based, with up to 200 or so members, but from around 1820 affiliated orders (larger combinations with greater financial reliability) replaced many smaller independent societies. There were also the huge, but impersonal collecting friendly societies, where agents would call for the weekly subscription. Most societies were for men only, but there was a small proportion of women's societies. Today most of the small friendly societies are all but forgotten, as too are the great orders such as the Ancient Order of Foresters, the Manchester Unity of Oddfellows, the Druids, the Shepherds and the Rechabites. Also largely forgotten are the majority of the great collecting societies such as the Royal Liver Friendly Society: they have either merged or become commercial insurance providers. For too long the existence of friendly societies has been overlooked, their function in combatting poverty, and their role in the social and economic history of the working class movement understated.

The more locally based friendly societies often had a fraternal element, involving regular meetings for paying subscriptions and benefits. Members generally met at a local public house, or else at a school. Usually they held an annual festival, comprising a church service, a dinner, visits to patrons and festivities such as dances and sports events, although some large societies dispensed entirely with all but the financial side of affairs.

While friendly society anniversaries were celebrated widely over Great Britain (though not so much in Ireland), there were regional variations in some of the formal practices. In a few areas where club walks were held it was the custom for members to carry six-foot long poles to denote membership, or to signify the holding of office. In some of these places the poles were topped with flowers, elsewhere the poles were unadorned, while in other places the poles sported finials of wood or brass. The outstanding county for the latter practice was Somerset. Of some 300 friendly societies nationwide (not counting the Foresters, Oddfellows, Shepherds or Druids) that were known to have carried pole heads, nearly two thirds are from Somerset and a further one sixth are in the bordering counties. These pole heads deserve much greater recognition than is currently the case – they are as iconic to Somerset as well-dressing is to Derbyshire. Their fantastic and curious designs are remarkable examples of folk art and yet far too many museum collections of them remain stored away out of sight.

Well over 600 separate friendly society pole head designs are known. A few were shared by several clubs, but most were unique to just one society and one location. Some pole heads were made of wood, but the majority of surviving specimens are of brass. Some were made in the round, like bed knobs, and some were flat with abstract or figurative patterns, often based on the inn-sign of their headquarters. Even when collectors first started taking an interest in pole heads, especially from the late nineteenth century, many of the clubs that used particular designs had long since gone to the wall, and what was commonplace knowledge of the design of their pole head passed away: we no longer know where many of the surviving pole head patterns were actually used. Contemporary newspaper accounts of mid-nineteenth century feast days, for example, almost never commented on the actual design of the members' pole heads.

The matching of pole heads to particular places is therefore problematic. Margaret Fuller published the first and only widely available identification list in 1964. It was a ground-breaking study and it immediately became the standard source on the subject. It has been slavishly followed ever since. Fuller's work was strongly based on one early collection and the written details that came with it, but unfortunately this information contained many incomplete or unsubstantiated provenances. The present study uses evidence based on a wide range of archival and other material, providing a timely replacement for Fuller's out-dated 1964 text: nevertheless many designs still elude identification. Not only do we know nothing about certain patterns, but alas there are also many others which have a suggested provenance for which no verification can be made. Hopeful suggestions of provenance were passed from collector to collector, and they developed an unwarranted acceptance. This study attempts to peel away the unsupportable. Of course, it can certainly be the case that some suggestions were accurate after all, but in default of evidence they must remain described as unverified.

The present catalogue includes all designs known in the public domain together with many from private collections. All are individually illustrated, with details of their society and verification where proved, and an essay on friendly societies and their pole heads provides a context for the catalogue.

Even in the twenty-first century the occasional hitherto unrecorded design appears. The task of matching a pattern to its location, and to the club that used it, continues.

The Inwood Collection.

1

Friendly societies: a brief history

At the heart of the friendly society movement was the decision by individuals without capital or savings to club together in order to cope with a future loss of income, typically in cases of sickness and the consequential inability to work. By regular payment of a small sum into a common pool a sick member had the right to draw benefit usually for a limited time until able to resume employment. Such payments reflected the fact that an employer only paid a wage earner for time spent working, and not while sick.

The medieval financial provision for the poor took the form of charity provided by the wealthy individuals or the church, while the twentieth century solution to the problem of poverty was the operation of the Welfare State. Friendly societies, together with support from rate-based local funds obtained through the Poor Law provisions, bridged the gap between the two systems. The mutual benefit concept dated back at least to the classical era, but in Britain records of the earliest friendly societies do not appear until the beginning of the seventeenth century. The main period of operation of friendly societies, however, was during the two centuries from about 1750 to around 1950.

Besides providing sickness benefit friendly societies usually also made a payment towards funeral costs following the death of a member, a benefit that was widely regarded as a necessary means of avoiding an ignominious pauper burial. These and any other benefits depended, however, on the rules agreed by members, and might be extended to cover benefits on the death of a spouse, medical attendance, and a wide range of other options. Under friendly society rules the named benefits were obtainable as a right for members, as opposed to benefits offered by benevolent societies, where benefit payments were not automatic, but were considered (usually by a committee) on their merits. Friendly societies were commonly referred to by the alternative name of benefit societies.

The right to receive benefits from a friendly society was achieved first though qualifying to stand for membership. Applicants were typically male. Societies for females were always relatively few in number, while mixed societies were fewer still. In 1803 Somerset recorded approximately 18 women's societies compared with about 270 for men, and while the proportion of female members of friendly societies rose during the nineteenth century, albeit slowly and belatedly, it never matched their share in the total population, reflecting the fact that as males were the main bread-winners it was their potential sickness that had to be insured to retain an income [1].

Applicants for early societies, whether male or female, had to be healthy adults, loyal to the crown, the government, and the protestant religion, and usually to be between the ages of 15 and 40. These were not the only restrictions: applicants could be debarred on the basis of their occupation (if deemed to be insecure or else hazardous to health) or according to any other criteria as defined by a particular society's rules. Such exclusions as the society chose to exercise meant that several sections of the needy population, who in earlier times could have received benefits under the older charity system, were thus forced back onto reliance on such benefits as were available either from the provisions of the Old Poor Law, dating (with later amendments) from the Tudor period, or from its harsher replacement, the new Poor Law of 1834. Once elected to a society, a member had to maintain payments regularly to the central fund to qualify for benefit, should that need arise, but even then a probationary period without right to benefit often had to be served. Failure to make the contributions on time usually resulted in expulsion. It will be clear from these descriptions that friendly societies were not kind-hearted charities, but were organisations strictly run by the members according to their prescribed rules, and generally the poorest and most vulnerable individuals were excluded from their operations.

Early societies generally conducted their meetings at a public house, there being little other suitable local accommodation large enough for meetings, though gradually increasing numbers transferred to school rooms once these were built. Initially meetings for business purposes, whether monthly, quarterly, or otherwise, were conducted with a degree of conviviality. Benefit fund accounts, however, were rarely kept separate from management cost accounts, or from those of expenditure and income for convivial purposes, a state of affairs which, although gradually rectified, persisted in a few societies very nearly throughout the nineteenth century. Almost without exception societies confirmed their fraternal nature by holding an anniversary dinner, in many cases accompanied by other practices including divine worship and a variety of recreational activities open to members' families and other well-wishers.

The adoption of the mutual benefit principle operating through unitary – that is to say independent – friendly societies grew slowly at first but, took off more rapidly in the second half of the eighteenth century. Growth was effected not so much by societies becoming larger, but by the forming of extra new societies. Limits on how far a member would walk to the regular evening meeting after a long day's work in essence meant that a four mile limit around the club head-quarters defined that society's catchment area and represented a walk of roughly an hour long. By 1803 such had been the proliferation of societies that in Somerset, for example, virtually the only parts of the county with poor access to a friendly society lay in the scantily populated upland areas of Exmoor and the Brendon Hills (see MAP). In many areas there was a great deal of choice of several accessible clubs, and much less than a four mile walk was required. In addition the map shows that many areas already offered a great deal of choice of society [2].

Different types of friendly society

Friendly societies were voluntary organisations, run by their members, and for most of their existence were free from state control. The principle of self-government, or voluntarism, was initially very strongly cherished and often ran counter to the idea that the state should introduce controls over their practices with the aim of avoiding mismanagement or financial failure. The notion of the state forcing working people to adopt insurance for sickness or death was generally opposed right up until the end of the nineteenth century. Such friendly society legislation as was introduced was usually of an enabling sort: societies could register to become protected by these laws, or could stand outside the system and retain their total independence. The members could decide.

Early friendly societies were of the unitary class, that is to say they were single clubs without branches and entirely responsible for their own affairs. Their membership necessarily had to be locally based and they were run as independent organisations especially because the lack of effective communication systems meant limited contact between one society and another. It also restricted the effective distance over which they could operate. Thus membership rarely exceeded 200 and more commonly averaged around 70. Such constraints on friendly societies were considerably eased with the development of rail transport, improved roads, and an affordable and reliable postal service. Friendly society organisation on a far larger scale then became possible in terms of both catchment areas and membership sizes, thus enabling large affiliated orders and collecting societies to develop especially from the 1830s and 1840s.

The affiliated orders were based on branches, variously referred to as lodges, courts, or tents, according to the particular order. Here members regularly met for a mixture of business and convivial activities. Branches were overseen by a central body, democratically elected, whose task was to frame and enforce rules which would apply to all sections of the order. Nevertheless, the branches generally retained some degree of autonomy, a situation which certainly over the years delayed the adoption

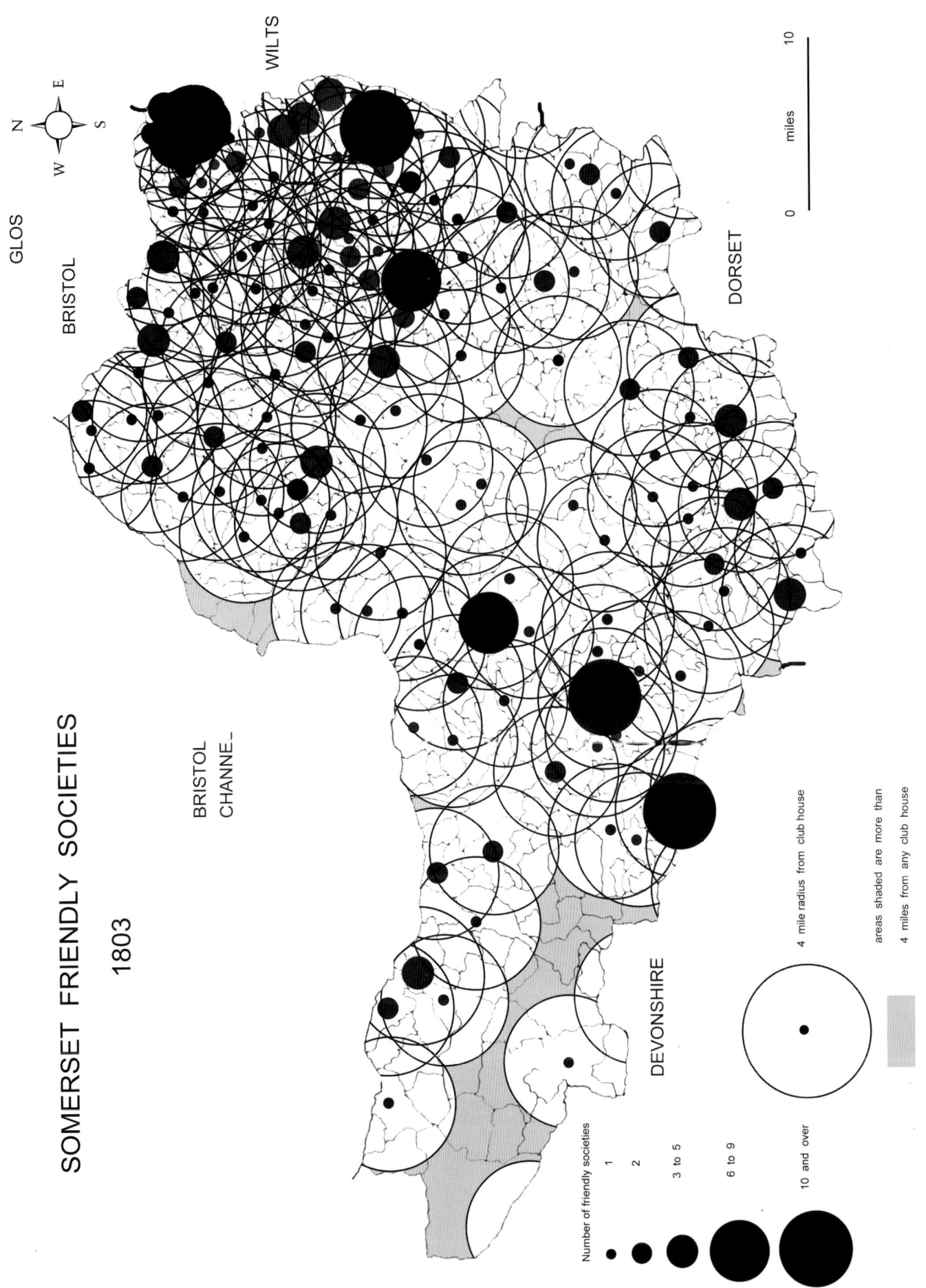

SOMERSET FRIENDLY SOCIETIES

1803

GLOS

WILTS

BRISTOL

DORSET

BRISTOL CHANNE_

DEVONSHIRE

N
W — E
S

0   miles   10

Number of friendly societies

1
2
3 to 5
6 to 9
10 and over

4 mile radius from club house

areas shaded are more than
4 miles from any club house

of reforms necessary for improving the financial security of the organisation as a whole. The largest affiliated orders in Britain came into existence in the early nineteenth century and included the Manchester Unity Independent Order of Oddfellows, the Ancient Order of Foresters, the Ashton Unity Loyal Order of Ancient Shepherds, the Independent Order of Rechabites, and the various orders of Druids: there were many others besides. The main advantage of the affiliated orders over the unitary societies lay in their far greater aggregate membership, which meant that the insurance risk of sickness and death could be spread over a larger base, and so solvency could more easily be achieved. Affiliated orders numbered their membership in thousands: exceptionally large were the Manchester Oddfellows and the Foresters who in 1886, for example, had reached over half a million members each. Small unitary societies, by contrast, could be ruined by an unexpected peak of sickness or death benefit claims or by other unforeseen local factors [3].

By the second half of the nineteenth century the affiliated orders were no longer confined to their core areas, mainly in the industrial north of England, but had spread out and opened branches elsewhere in cities and large towns, and to a lesser extent in villages, sometimes running alongside the earlier unitary societies, but with increasing frequency replacing them. Several of the affiliated orders even extended their net to include overseas branches in America and the colonies.

Another, but quite different, type of mutual organisation, the collecting society, also emerged from the northern industrial areas. It was almost entirely devoid of any convivial element and members did not even meet each other for business purposes, since subscriptions and benefits were paid through home visits by a door-to-door collector, employed by the society. This type of friendly society had a centralised management system but had no branches. To run the teams of collectors there were strategically placed agents, distant from but answerable to the head office. This costly employment was paid for out of subscriptions, so management charges were large in relation to the size of benefits. Nevertheless subscriptions were kept low to appeal to the poorer working classes and these societies thrived by signing up huge numbers of members. The archetypal collecting societies were the giant Royal Liver Friendly Society and the Liverpool Victoria Legal Society, each, for example, with over one million members by 1887. Collecting societies thrived in poorer high density areas, but were less in evidence in rural districts. There was effectively very little difference between the collecting friendly societies and the commercial insurers such as the Prudential Assurance Company, for both systems operated on the collecting principle, save that the latter were not owned by the members, but were run for profit. Furthermore, the commercial insurers were not covered by friendly society legislation but instead were subject to Board of Trade regulation [4].

A further type of organisation, in many respects similar to the collecting societies, developed around the middle of the nineteenth century, and became known as the centralised societies. There were no collectors and generally no branches. Subscriptions were either posted to the head office by members themselves or were paid in to a branch office, to a private address, or to the business premises of an agent, who likewise forwarded them. Benefit payments and subscriptions both made use of the postal order system. There was little face-to-face contact between members, but there were notable exceptions where agents had deliberately made arrangements for social meetings (perhaps thereby drumming up more business) or else where local societies had adopted the financial mantle of the larger body in place of the weaker system of their own failing unitary society. They often then purposely retained the traditional social functions of the original small society. Typical centralised societies included the Hearts of Oak Benefit Society, the Rational Association, and the United Patriots. The National Deposit Friendly Society was similarly centralised, but incorporated a system of savings in its contribution tables. The popularity of these societies grew particularly towards the end of the nineteenth century up to the First World War, as a result of members attaching less and less value to the social meetings of the old societies. Instead, they wanted large, financially reliable friendly societies in order that their benefits could be guaranteed. Nevertheless, since centralised societies were conducted along the mutual benefit principle, members had the right to some input, albeit limited, into the governance of the organisations, through a system of regional delegates to the Annual General Meetings.

The so-called County Societies, associations whose boundaries rarely coincided with those of the historic counties, had elements of both the affiliated order class and the centralised societies. They developed in the 1820s with new ones being formed up until the 1840s. Their origins lay in the concern felt by elements of the upper and middle classes, led especially by clergy of the established church, regarding the way unitary societies in their district were conducted. There were criticisms of mismanagement, fraud, profligacy among officers, and malfeasance by the publicans who often acted as unitary society treasurers, besides widespread disgust at the prevalence of a drinking culture among members. All this was to be changed, it was hoped, when county societies opened their doors to new members. County society branches were to be run not by, but on behalf of, the working class members. County societies were brimming with good intentions, and they attracted copious funds through attracting honorary members. These worthy supporters paid their subscriptions but did not claim benefits. The county societies never achieved a strong measure of popularity among the class whose membership was sought after, the element of patronisation being too much of a stumbling block. Such local meetings for members as took place had conviviality low on the agenda, they were infrequent, and they were mainly for business. Social aspects were generally limited to a single annual tea meeting, with prayers and lectures as part of the programme.

The county societies contrasted strongly with the unitary societies that they were intended to replace. The latter were mainly public house based with their regular and more frequent meetings and their festive anniversaries, all of which provided a degree of social as well as business activity. Even in towns unitary societies had their annual evening dinners, while in rural areas these societies usually celebrated by having a whole day set aside each year not just for the Annual General Meeting and dinner, but also for processions to church and to the homes of benefactors to solicit subscriptions, besides a host of other festive activities to fill the remaining hours. Affiliated order branches also put a high priority on their anniversary day activities. There were no such festivities for the collecting societies or for many of the branches of the centralised societies. In the larger settlements the grand annual public demonstrations, with branches celebrating together, reached a peak in the 1860s, especially in Bristol, but by the end of the nineteenth century the main expression of public activity by the orders became the rather smaller scale Hospital Sunday processions, attended by branches from a variety of affiliated orders and other societies. In the rural areas, however, the annual feast day, or fete as it later became known, persisted up to the First World War and even beyond.

One other type of mutual benefit organisation remains to be mentioned. Dividing societies practised the occasional but regular distribution of surplus funds to their members, at intervals of one, three, five, seven, or ten years, or even longer. At the end of the term, as it was called, the society came to a close, but a replacement, often with amended rules, was formed by agreement, and the whole process was repeated. Sometimes a small balance per member was retained to act as a fund for the new incarnation. Most early unitary societies were of the dividing type. During the nineteenth century, however, middle class public opinion on the practice of dividing funds became very hostile, and well-wishing speech makers from the anniversary dinner high tables would frequently rail against the practice, condemning it as not conforming with the notion of thrift and saving, and blaming members for dissipating their savings promiscuously. They regarded it as senseless to distribute the accumulated capital which should, they thought, be invested, and held as a hedge against possible insolvency. Permanent funds, such as those held by the affiliated orders, were claimed to be a sounder form of financial management. In the wake of such criticism many unitary societies abandoned the practice of periodically dividing their funds, and incorporated the word 'permanent' into their title, thereby suggesting that the society had therefore become financially stable.

The majority of early unitary societies which were run on the dividing principle usually adopted the seven or ten year interval. In the early nineteenth century a few one year societies existed, but they were unusual. Dividing societies had been recognised as a separate type of friendly society in the reports of the Royal Commission on Friendly Societies of 1874, although the commissioners thought that they were declining in importance. They also gave the imprimatur on the view that they were less financially competent than several other types of organisation [5].

Dividing societies have received insufficient attention in accounts of the friendly society movement, because although they were shown to be giving way to permanent societies at the time of the Royal Commission, it is their later revival that has largely escaped notice. After 1874 there was not, as it happened, a wholesale abandonment of the dividing principle, since many seven and ten year dividing societies survived right up to the First World War. More significantly, however, the one year type of society showed an ability not just to survive as a type but actually to experience a revival. A few had already come into existence in the mid-nineteenth century, and there was a slight upturn in the 1870s, with numbers thereafter increasing rapidly towards the end of the century. Of still greater significance was their popularity in the 1920s and 1930s, even after the introduction of National Insurance. Informally (and occasionally disparagingly) these societies were often referred to as slate clubs, as it was held that their accounting practices were so simple that they could be recorded on a slate. Nevertheless, many of these later one-year societies continued to be run along traditional friendly society lines and even took pains to become registered. They had printed rules, elected officers, and an annual dinner. Some even organised annual summer fetes. At the end of the year distributions were made and the results were often reported in the local press. Quite a few had a thrift club operating alongside, although these did not provide any sickness or funeral benefits, but were purely a form of saving, with a useful Christmas pay-out. The major difference between the early friendly societies and these later one-year societies was that the latter were no longer the main form of mutual support: they were designed simply as a supplement to benefits acquired through membership of another society or later through national insurance.

Changes in the proportions of different types of society

The shifting pattern of expansion or contraction of the different categories of friendly society differed from area to area. One factor creating such variations was the local level of wages. Since the affiliated order branches demanded higher subscriptions than the smaller unitary societies they thrived in the high wage urban areas but did less well in the predominantly lower wage agricultural districts. Demography also played a part: Bristol and other large towns experienced continuous population growth in the nineteenth century, fuelled by in-migration, and they saw ready demand for the development of many different types of friendly society, whereas the majority of Somerset, based as it was on an agricultural economy and a textiles industry facing overwhelming competition from the north of England, saw widespread and continuous population decline from around 1850: these were not areas where new branches of the affiliated orders could guarantee strong recruitment.

The first census of friendly societies of 1803 revealed that Somerset had 285 friendly societies with 19,848 members, and these were found in just 150 of its 489 parishes. The members accounted for 7% of the total county population. Most were males, the majority of them supporting several other family members. In Bristol there were just 84 societies with 5,296 members, amounting to 8.2% of the city's population. Allowing for some inaccuracy in the figures it can be said nevertheless that the figures for the take-up of friendly society membership in Bristol and Somerset were broadly similar in the proportion of population with access to friendly society benefits. There was also a strong similarity in the type of friendly society in operation. Although the affiliated orders had already made an appearance in Bristol, the total amounted to just three late eighteenth century Druids' lodges. Somerset had no lodges of any affiliated society in 1803: unitary societies were the only type of friendly society in the county, while in Bristol they amounted to 96% of all societies. Mutual benefit provision was essentially the same in both places: small unitary societies were at first predominant [6].

Whilst the adoption of mutual insurance through friendly societies and commercial insurers both increased through the nineteenth century, Bristol and Somerset showed very different solutions as to the mix of providers that was chosen. The highly patronised county societies admittedly made only a modest impact in Somerset: in Bristol, however, their success was even more limited. By contrast, the affiliated orders went from strength to strength in the city where high subscription levels could be afforded, but in Somerset not only did they become established later, but their market share was considerably lower: new orders made their appearances in Somerset usually only after having been first established in Bristol. Obvious differences in the density of population accounted for there being far more of a presence of collecting society agencies in Bristol than its more rural neighbour: collectors could harvest far more subscriptions and with less effort in the built-up areas. For the centralised societies the case is more difficult to determine, since not only was so much of the business conducted postally and therefore the location of subscribers is unavailable, but also, by contrast, some of the different outlets of these societies were run as if they were branches of affiliated orders. Nevertheless, it is clear that there was a greater centralised society presence in Somerset than in Bristol, partly, it would appear, because some branches were effectively continuations of local unitary societies. The popularity of the annual dividing societies appears to be much stronger in Somerset than in Bristol, but here comparisons based on the numbers of such societies are misleading. In Somerset the societies were small and based on a single venue, almost invariably a public house, and their distribution over the county was uneven. They became more popular in the towns than in the rural areas, probably because the latter areas had less disposable income. There was also a publicity factor at work whereby an element of competitiveness was generated between different inns in a town. The end-of-year dividends payable to slate club members in Wells and Bath, for example, were released in the local press, and inn-keepers, who met regularly to discuss the running of these clubs, were proud to reveal their annual figures. In Bristol, however, a different expression of the one-year dividing society principle had emerged: there was a scarcity of one-year societies but nevertheless there was a large one-year society membership, and it was due to the presence of the monolithic and highly popular Bristol City Sick and Dividing Society, whose end of year distribution figures were also given prominence in the local press. In 1938, for example, the sum amounted to no less than £20,000 [7].

The generalised pattern showing the contrast between Bristol and Somerset can be seen in the table below, where all outlets of the different types of friendly society have been categorised, regardless of date, and expressed as a proportion of the total number of outlets of each place.

Bristol: County Societies <1%; Affiliated Orders 64%; Collecting Societies 7%; Centralised Societies 1%; Annual Dividing Societies 5%; Unitary Societies 23%
Somerset: County Societies 2%; Affiliated Orders 36%; Collecting Societies 2%; Centralised Societies <2%; Annual Dividing Societies 16%; Unitary Societies 42%

Despite these overall contrasts, there was one strongly similar trend shared between the two areas, which was the decline in the proportion of unitary societies in the second half of the century. In Bristol a peak in the formation of new unitary societies was reached in the 1840s, by which time a half of all the city's unitary societies had already been formed: after this time other types of friendly society had become more sought after. In Somerset there was a great growth in unitary societies in the decades immediately following the 1793 Friendly Societies Act, but a secondary peak took place as late as the 1860s. After this fewer and fewer new unitary societies were formed, but also there were fewer new societies being formed of any sort in the county. In Bristol the old-fashioned unitary society principle lost its appeal both earlier and to a greater extent than in Somerset. Bristol, it would appear, was more innovative, and Somerset more conservative, in the adoption of new forms of mutual benefit.

The swing away from unitary societies in Bristol was even more acute than the figures initially suggest, since some of those still active from 1900 onwards were not of the traditional type. Of the 29 unitary societies surviving in Bristol in 1900, nine were schemes for particular company employees (otherwise known as 'shop clubs'), seven others, although legitimately registered as friendly societies, were mutual loan associations; and two were working men's clubs. Only eleven conventional unitary societies were still in business.

In Somerset the near abandonment of the unitary society was by no means as acute as in Bristol – indeed, the old unitary society system showed a great resilience, and many societies lasted far longer than would have been expected by those who had questioned the financial viability of small stand-alone clubs. There is little doubt that voluntary contributions from the better-off helped to keep their finances afloat, a situation made possible in small rural communities where there was more mutual cohesiveness than in the more anonymous environments of the cities and large towns. By 1900 there were nearly 200 unitary societies still operating in Somerset, although only a quarter of them were to survive beyond the First World War, and there were very few in the larger towns.

The growth of government control

The major problem facing friendly societies throughout their entire existence was how to arrange for contributions to be low enough to be affordable yet high enough for the organisation to stay solvent and thus to be able to meet the financial cost of providing benefits. To address the problem new types of friendly society were developed, operating on a variety of principles, some having a savings element as part of the membership commitment. Large numbers of friendly societies and commercial insurers did, nevertheless, run out of funds, not just because of occasional misappropriation by officers, but also because, in the absence of sufficient population data right up until the end of the nineteenth century, even professional actuaries had been unable to calculate reliable life and sickness tables. Members of failed societies could as a consequence eventually be forced back onto reliance on Poor Law relief. A further shortcoming in the mutual benefit system was its lack of consistency: contribution levels, management costs and the worth of benefits varied across Britain from place to place and from organisation to organisation. Even when insurance tables became more accurate the choice of which tables to use, and what benefits to provide, remained with the provider. Despite occasional recommendations for the use of certain tables there was never any guarantee from the government-run Registry of Friendly Societies that by using those tables a society could meet its financial obligations. Insolvency was a constant threat. Moreover, at the same time as actuarial science was struggling to improve, and sickness and life expectancy data were being accumulated, Britain's demographic structure was undergoing change, thus adding to a society's problems since its members were living ever longer. Therefore, not only was there the difficulty of meeting extra demand for age-related sickness benefits, but also the need for old age pensions became more and more critical: but very few nineteenth century friendly societies were able to provide them. Many societies collapsed under the strain of its ageing membership.

Towards the end of the nineteenth century official opinion shifted away from the idea that voluntarism must be preserved at all costs, a principle that had underlain all friendly society legislation up to that point. No society had been forced to register, even though registered societies could benefit from protection by government legislation: it was up to the members of a society to decide whether to enter or to stay out of the pale. But gradually it became accepted that direct state control over the running of the system was both desirable and necessary. The official role would no longer be just supervisory but instead it would undertake the management of the system. National Insurance had been introduced in Germany in 1884 but was resisted in Britain both officially and by the friendly societies themselves for over twenty years longer, despite the topic gaining more and more support. The first stage of government intervention through direct control started with the passing of the Old Age Pensions Act of 1908, which provided a non-contributory pension to a limited section of the population, both men and women, payable through the Post Office. There was only a limited effect from this Act on friendly societies, since they had done little themselves to provide such benefits for members. The 1911 National Insurance Act, on the other hand, generated more of a sea change. Under the new state system contributions and benefits were to be made uniform nationally among the various providers. The government did not, however, set up its own bureaucracy to administer the scheme, but instead arranged to have it delivered through existing systems, including commercial insurers, trade unions, and even the friendly societies themselves. Nevertheless, the individual societies had to be of a certain minimum size to operate the scheme, and so the Act dealt a severe blow to large numbers of small friendly societies, which then voted to cease operations. A few, however, survived by amalgamating to form county associations. By contrast the large affiliated orders, collecting societies, and centralised societies saw a much increased demand for membership, for while members could opt to have their national insurance delivered through their branch and as a part of their normal membership, they could instead, if they so wished, subscribe to a newly formed parallel scheme of state sector branches of the societies. More significantly, many members of the public joined the newly-formed state sector branches of the affiliated orders, simply to comply with their requirement to be part of the system. Such members therefore did not participate at all in the fraternal side of the society activities, which were part and parcel of the voluntary sector branches. Thus friendly societies overall greatly increased their aggregate membership, but the total number of societies took a strong downward turn. Fraternalism and voluntarism were losing their appeal. In any case the business of providing national insurance cast a heavy bureaucratic burden on participating friendly societies. Nevertheless, this hybrid solution survived the entire interwar period.

The greatest blow to friendly societies came not with the 1911 Act, however, but in 1946. The new national insurance legislation of that year took away entirely the handling of the compulsory subscriptions and benefits of the state system by the friendly societies, thus depriving them not only of their state sector business but also rendering the voluntary side largely redundant. This catastrophe was compounded by the further expansion of state control through the National Health Act of 1946, which, when it took effect in 1948, provided free medical care. Thus payment into friendly society health care benefit schemes became largely superfluous to the requirements of most people. Thereafter, only by extending their range of benefits, as a supplement to those provided by the national health service, were the friendly societies able to survive, but despite their best endeavours they also had to face a terminal decline in their membership numbers. The concept of mutuality effectively ceased to have much appeal, and over the ensuing post-war decades most surviving friendly societies abandoned the principle, and members became persuaded that they should turn their societies into demutualised commercial insurance companies. The few very small societies that continued their operations offered either a much reduced supplementary benefits provision, or else became archaic and largely ceremonial affairs, still holding a fete or feast day. A handful in Somerset and a scattering elsewhere even survived in this way into the twenty-first century.

References

(1) Abstract of the Answers and Returns Made pursuant to an Act, passed in the 43rd Year of His Majesty King George III intituled 'An Act for procuring Returns relative to the Expence and Maintenance of the Poor in England', 1804, pp 169 to 188 (Gloucestershire) and pp 425 to 444 (Somerset).

(2) Reports of the Chief Registrar of Friendly Societies for the year ending 31 December 1890, pp 61 and 62. The conclusion to a discussion on the limits for a friendly society in order to allow taking part in business was that a five mile limit appeared to be reasonable, but this seems rather excessive, since most rural members would have had to have walked.

(3) Wilkinson, John Frome, *Mutual Thrift*, 1891, p 237.

(4) Ibid., p 194.

(5) Friendly and Benefit Building Societies' Commission: Reports of the Assistant Commissioners, Southern and Eastern Counties of England, Sir George Young, Bart., [C-997], 1874, pp 21 and 22, 'Class 7 – Sharing-out Clubs'.

(6) Abstract of Answers, op. cit. The three lodges, all of the Ancient Order of Druids, were Mona No 10; Anglesea, No 11; and True Friendship, No 12. All were apparently established in 1789.

(7) *Western Daily Press*, 8 Dec 1938.

2

Events, processions, and the carrying of poles

Processions at large

Celebratory processions and the carrying of poles are typified by the military, with marchers shouldering their weapons, but the practice was also rooted in the symbolic expression of status, power, and identity by other bodies. Royal pageants of many ages demonstrated the pivotal role played by monarchs. Processions with high-ranking clergy were designed to impress by-standers with the crucial role of religion within their lives. In any such processions the exalted rank of the chief person could be emphasised symbolically by the carrying a highly decorated sceptre, crozier, or baton. The practice of a military procession was noticeably recorded in the Triumph on Trajan's column of AD 113, but it extends back even further into the late Bronze Age. The modern expressions of great military processions are still to be seen in China and Russia, while the civilian equivalents can be observed in Britain, whether at Notting Hill during carnival time or at the Mall on the occasion of significant royal events. Since holding a celebratory procession was so widespread among different organisations, and so time-honoured, there was nothing remarkable in the practice being so commonly adopted by friendly societies [1].

Detail of procession on Trajan's column, A.D. 113.

By the time British friendly societies started to come into prominence in the second half of the eighteenth century pole-carrying as a mark of status had long since extended from the most elite strata in society to other less esteemed but still formal groups, whether ecclesiastical, judicial, civic, or fraternal, each of which might process in order to mark some occasion noteworthy to themselves. Throughout the main period of friendly society activity, roughly the two centuries from 1750 to 1950, processions in Britain were commonplace and were the customary way to celebrate a range of events, from those of national interest such as coronations, down to those of more local importance such as electioneering or the opening of a railway or other engineering works. Bristolians, for example, witnessed the opening of the Clifton Suspension Bridge in 1864: it was marked by a massive procession of the military, followed by civic dignitaries, then very many members of trade organisations and eventually some 2000 members of various friendly societies. At the local scale there were happenings of much less widespread interest. These included church festivals, and the weddings and funerals of local gentry. At many of these public events, friendly societies might be invited to take part. In 1835 the local friendly societies at Bala in North Wales, for example, saw fit to process to honour the wedding of R. Williams Vaughan, Esquire, of Nanau. Friendly societies also helped bring the notion of a procession much further down the social scale by organising funeral processions for members of the working class who belonged to their society. Brother William Tudball of Bristol died in 1856: he was the treasurer of the Garibaldi Lodge of the Loyal Order of Ancient Shepherds, and his funeral cortege from his home to the club house, and from there to the cemetery, included nearly 200 members of the order, while the streets were also lined with crowds of onlookers [2].

Different groups in processions proclaimed their identity by the wearing of conspicuous uniforms, while variations of detail within the uniform denoted the status of an individual within the group. The rank of civic dignitaries, court and municipal officials, members of gild and trade organisations, freemasons, and friendly societies could be recognised not just by what they wore but also by what they carried. Weapons, ceremonial or functional, identified the military, while artisans in nineteenth century trade processions sported pole tops with devices denoting their particular trade: potters topped their poles with plant pots and shipwrights with model ships. Friendly societies, whether lodges of affiliated orders or unitary societies, would often carry poles to confirm that they were all part of a particular body linked for purposes of mutual support [3].

Friendly society processions were in evidence from the mid-eighteenth century onwards. Their poles came in a wide range of sizes, and were variously referred to as maces, staves or staffs, rods, wands, clubs, or even just sticks. There tended to be a uniform pattern per society for ordinary members, but there was also some differentiation for officials: the status of the bearer could sometimes be revealed by the length of the pole carried, sometimes also by its colour, and sometimes by the size of the finial at its top. Friendly society poles often had a decorative element, with a pole head peculiar to just that society, or with lengths of ribbon of a specially stipulated colour tied around the tops, all of which display was designed to impress spectators: indeed, not for nothing were the great friendly society processions in Bristol in the 1860s, for example, referred to as demonstrations. One such, in Bristol in 1864, had a procession of 700 members of the Loyal Order of Ancient Shepherds from 36 lodges, who marched with four bands through the streets of the city to the Horfield Gardens, where they were joined for their entertainments by some 8000 members of the public [4].

By the early nineteenth century the affiliated orders of friendly societies announced themselves by their regalia. Oddfellows, Druids, Foresters, Rechabites and Shepherds dressed themselves in particular ways and carried over their shoulders a variety of maces, sickles, axes, and crooks. Maces, often of pewter, and sometimes silver plated on base metal, were carried by Oddfellows, and were around two to three feet long, while poles carried by other societies were about double this length. Druids mainly carried brass sickles on the ends of their poles, the woodwarden officials of the Foresters carried short axes, Rechabites carried a miscellany of long poles with tops resembling those of the Oddfellows and freemasons, while Shepherd society members carried crooks, often of brass and again usually on long poles. In all cases senior officers were identified not just by special clothing, sashes, or collars, but also sometimes in addition by the carrying swords, or other symbolic devices to distinguish what office they held. Officers of Oddfellow societies might be seen in crimson robes and Tudor-style bonnets, while Foresters officers could be seen dressed in green, wearing knee-length boots, sporting Robin Hood pattern hats, carrying bows or sheep's horns, and holding poles topped with stags' heads. The dress of the ordinary members of the affiliated orders was generally simpler, although in Druid societies even rank and file members from some lodges sported white hooded gowns and donned false beards. The Ancient Shepherds were deliberately less showy, but members commonly carried crooks, and rams' heads were sometimes paraded on long poles. By 1900 such displays by the affiliated orders had become rare, although even in 1905 at Washford in Somerset the local Druid lodge processed in full regalia, much to the amusement of by-standers, and when Winston Churchill was initiated into the Ancient Order of Druids at Blenheim in 1908 the whole panoply was still to be seen [5].

Occasions for friendly society processions

In addition to participating in demonstrations of national or local significance alongside other bodies, friendly societies had three particular reasons for arranging their own processions. The first was the celebration of the club anniversary. Processions typically marched from the club-house to church or chapel and back again, often accompanied by a band, and at other times of the day they wended their way around the village or town to solicit donations from patrons and often to indulge in liquid refreshment. For rural societies the yearly celebration very often did not coincide with the date of establishment, but instead took place on or around May 29th (Oak Apple Day), or on one of the days following Whit or Trinity Sundays. Urban societies, however, tended to hold their anniversary celebrations in the winter months, with November 5th or January 1st being popular choices, although quite a few of these societies chose not to process or to have a religious service. Taunton, around 1850, had at least a dozen men's societies and three women's societies, most of them having their anniversaries on November 5th, and yet there are no records of any of them processing.

Towards the end of the nineteenth century anniversary processions held by just one unitary society or by a single lodge of an affiliated order had largely been abandoned in the towns and cities in favour of joint celebrations. At this period various clubs of either sort would amalgamate to form a procession to attend a church service on the days which became known as Lifeboat Saturday and Hospital Sunday. At such events donations were collected, but they were no longer in aid of the individual lodge or club. Instead, the proceeds were given to local medical charities. By this time, a range of regalia was still to be seen, but with the affiliated orders pole-carrying and mace-carrying had mainly fallen out of fashion in favour of the wearing of rosettes, uniform sashes or collarettes. This change had accompanied the gradual but widespread abandonment by the affiliated orders, from around the 1850s, of their hitherto common practices of arcane and quasi-masonic rituals at their business meetings. By contrast, the rural unitary societies hung on far longer to their habit of parading with poles to mark their summer-time anniversaries, and a small handful continued the practice in Somerset into the twenty-first century [6].

The second opportunity for friendly societies to parade with poles arose from the custom of accompanying a deceased member from home to church for the funeral, and from church to the place of interment. This was never an invariable practice, and it was carried out perhaps most frequently by the affiliated order lodges, but even some unitary societies observed the custom right up to the mid-twentieth century. Sometimes just a few stewards were obliged to be present, and sometimes a considerable number of members. On these occasions the ordinary poles were usually carried, but invariably the tops were shrouded in black crape. Less frequently black poles were substituted, and very rarely specific funerary staves were used with special tops. The mid-century funeral processions through the streets of Bristol were also to be experienced in other towns, and they attracted great local interest. It was all good publicity for encouraging new lodge membership, by showing how brethren cared for their kind even after death. At other times the role of a friendly society at a funeral was less ostentatious, but even as late as 1936, the funeral of the Rev Edwin Chalk of Kentisbeare in East Devon was attended by members of the local friendly society, all carrying their poles and brass pole-tops [7].

The third chance for a friendly society demonstration was occasionally offered when a lodge of an affiliated order opened a new branch, and the validating document (the dispensation) was ceremonially carried from the old lodge and transferred to the new. The practice was more to be seen in towns and cities where the old and new lodges were within walking distance of one another, but sometimes the dispensation party would travel by train, to be met and taken in procession, with a display of ornamental crooks or maces of the officers of the lodges, and with a band playing, to the club house of the new lodge. A typical event was the opening of the Banks of the Avon Lodge of the Loyal Order of Ancient Shepherds at the North Somerset Railway Inn, Bristol, in 1864, by the brethren of the Prince Eugene Lodge from the Greyhound Inn, but similar ceremonies were carried out by a variety of affiliated orders in different parts of Britain, as far apart as Glasgow, Wales, and Cornwall. Little of this survived the end of the nineteenth century, however, for by this time the rate of new lodge creation had slowed down appreciably [8].

Uniformity within the affiliated orders and unitary societies

Over the course of the 1800s the affiliated orders spread from their centres of origin to become national and even international organisations. Although the individual lodges retained some measure of independence, nevertheless shared values, a common ritual, and uniform regalia, all meant that there was a strong degree of similarity between them. Moreover headquarters-based publication of rule books, ritual manuals and in-house journals and stationery, together with the meeting of brethren at annual delegates' conferences, all promoted nationwide conformity. Thus, for example, with the Loyal Order of Ancient Shepherds the carrying of crooks by members was likely to be observed wherever the society had lodges, even though the precise design of the crooks could vary from place to place. Some central provision from headquarters led to a handful of patterns becoming commonplace, but lodges were free to purchase where they pleased. Crooks were also carried by the Ancient Order of Shepherds (the select, higher subscription group of members of the Ancient Order of Foresters), but their choice of design has not as yet been identified. Oddfellows paraded with their masonic-based regalia of aprons, sashes, collarettes and jewels (which were primarily badges of office or of status), together with their maces. The latter were either all-metal or were wooden and topped with metal: both types bore symbols, sometimes painted, such as a model hand with a heart in the palm, crowns, stars, moons, doves, crossed quill pens, crossed keys and so forth, and the same array of devices was to be seen in whatever part of Britain the lodges had been established. Once again, lodges were free to obtain their maces from any available supplier, and the sets of maces of different lodges vary to some degree in their design and manufacture. Since these sets were expensive to buy they were not purchased by every lodge, and occasionally it was possible to loan them from neighbours. Axes and sickles were used by various other orders, and they, too, could vary from lodge to lodge.

The poles used by each affiliated order were also far from standardised and they varied between the different lodges of an order. Some were painted, while others were varnished; some were plain while others had lathe-turned ornamentation; the majority used poles of five to six feet in length, while just a few were only a half of this amount.

Pole-carrying was a feature not just of the affiliated orders, but it was also to be found among some unitary friendly societies. In the eighteenth century almost all friendly societies were of the latter type, but gradually the advantages of better financial stability through a degree of pooling of funds led to the growth of the affiliated orders at the expense of the stand-alone clubs. The independence of the unitary societies, however, was often fuelled by their unwillingness to submit to what they saw as government interference, and many of them never registered to submit themselves to protection under friendly society legislation. Many unitary friendly societies survived right up to the 1911 National Insurance Act and some even beyond that date. What is remarkable is that despite not having the overarching control by a centralised authority, such as was the case with the affiliated orders, the unitary societies, wherever they existed, in most respects showed a remarkable homogeneity.

Friendly society meetings and club rules

In England and Wales virtually all friendly societies with the exception of those operating on the collecting principle, whether of the unitary type or lodges of affiliated orders, adopted the time-honoured annual one-day celebration, comprising a business meeting, a procession to church or chapel for divine service followed by dinner for members, and finally the day would end with festivities such as dancing and sports. Their regular meetings to collect subscriptions and to perform other business varied little between the different clubs, and the roles of their officials and how they were elected, together with the tasks of visiting the sick, were equally repeated from one district to another. Procedures were enshrined in sets of rules, whether hand-written or printed, and the many thousand such sets of rules surviving in the National Archives and other repositories have a strong uniformity, often covering both organisational and convivial matters, together with the requisite financial regulations. Only very late in friendly society history do the rule books tend to confine themselves purely to the core aspects of subscriptions and benefits.

The similarity in sets of rules from one area to another arose for a variety of reasons. Sets of rules were copied from one club to the next, partly because the rules were written by the class of people who were in more or less distant contact with others of their own background, such as local land-owners or clergy, thus allowing ideas to spread far and for norms to develop. Sometimes use was made of commercial writers of rules who would produce very similar documents for their different clients. Thus custom and practice were replicated regionally and nationally, albeit with the right of any society to include rules for its governance peculiar to itself. There were also model rules prepared by the government functionary, John Tidd Pratt, in 1835, but even registered societies did not have to adopt them, and they were by no means universally taken up. In any case, they contained little content about convivial matters, such as were almost invariably included in the rule books of unitary societies.

Rules typically outlined the procedures for election of members and officers, details of how subscriptions and benefits were to be paid and the sums involved, conditions for qualifying for membership and for benefits, information on where and when meetings were to be held, clauses on how feast days were to be arranged, and a host of other detail including how members were to behave at meetings. The latter included not swearing or fighting, removing one's hat when standing up to speak, and addressing remarks to 'Mr Chairman', otherwise keeping one's seat, remaining quiet, and so on, all of them very necessary to be specified given the ignorance of procedural norms on the part of members new to formal meetings, since the majority of the newly elected were youths of 20 or under. In general there was little to differentiate the earliest sets of rules surviving from the eighteenth century from those of even a century and a half later, save, perhaps, for the details of new scales of subscriptions and benefits [9].

The development of friendly societies in Scotland had taken a different path from that of England and Wales. Although there were very early examples of mutual societies, most had soon become linked together as affiliated orders of a quasi-masonic nature, but with only loose ties between the individual lodges. Little use was made of public houses for meetings, and there was little conviviality. In the cities burial societies had been developed from the experience of those providers which had started in Liverpool, and there was some presence of affiliated order lodges of English origin. Unitary societies were rare in the rural areas of Scotland: they were not needed, since employers paid sick benefits. Processions by any of these groups were initially unusual and not much seen until towards the end of the nineteenth century. Here they were almost never held for the benefit of a single lodge, but instead were joint arrangements, typically for celebrating the opening of new public facilities, for support of lifeboat funds, or on the occasions of visits of the Annual Moveable Conferences of the larger affiliated orders. By this time the carrying of maces or poles had been largely abandoned [10].

In Ireland the situation was even more unlike the English and Welsh experience, for friendly societies were rare, largely due to the disinterest of both landowners and clergy. As in Scotland, such limited public display by friendly societies as existed took place under the aegis of English affiliated orders. Except at a very few funerals, friendly society processions were scarcely in evidence [11].

Friendly society pole-carrying in England and Wales

The similarity of sets of unitary society rules in both England and Wales had its practical expression in the resemblance from place to place of the ways in which these societies conducted themselves in matters of a convivial nature. Thus instances of broadly comparable procedures on feast days, for example, were recorded very widely over the two districts of Britain. In both, processions by friendly societies were to be seen to celebrate anniversaries, or to honour funerals. As a corollary to the holding of feast day or funeral processions, whether to church or to chapel, there was the custom of parading with poles.

Sometimes the rules of a unitary society are quite explicit in the matter of pole carrying. In some cases the pole was owned by the club, in other cases by the individual, who had to buy the pole (and its top, if one was part of the regalia) from the club: in any case it had to be kept in good repair. But the rules are not always specific, and even where poles were known to have been used the rules occasionally make no mention of the fact. By far the most accessible alternative source for ascertaining the practice of pole carrying in England and Wales is the local press, but here the unevenness of the coverage means that a thorough systematic survey is not possible. Firstly, local newspapers have a wide variety of starting dates: some areas developed local newspapers as much as a hundred years before others. Secondly, and more importantly, however, is the contrast in editorial policy from one paper to another. Many were quite disinterested in the details of local friendly society anniversaries and other meetings. In as much as they mentioned friendly societies at all they confined themselves to accounts of parliamentary bills and announcements on the subject in general. Many papers cared only to report on the woes of legal disagreements, when members of local societies took their officers to court for non-payment of benefits, or when societies had the misfortune to be the victims of theft or embezzlement. Other newspapers, by contrast, were much more positive, and included copious details of club anniversaries; but even here they did not necessarily or consistently observe the minutiae of whether members were carrying poles – let alone whether the poles were ornamented with pole-heads. Thus, although the newspaper evidence shows that the carrying of poles by friendly societies was practised from one end of England and Wales to the other, the proportion of clubs in any one area that did so is very hard to ascertain: an unequivocal sampling procedure for testing the presence of pole-carrying or, for that matter, any other topic, cannot be obtained, and conclusions have to be guarded.

Despite all the difficulties with newspaper coverage, there is nevertheless an overwhelming indication that the incidence of pole carrying by friendly societies was far more prevalent in one particular area of England and Wales than in all the rest, and the area in question is the county of Somerset, together with those parts of the counties that lie adjacent to it, comprising east Devon, virtually all of Dorset, west Wiltshire, Bristol, and south Gloucestershire: these may be regarded as the core area. Through a variety of systematic trawls in British newspapers using different search phrases such as 'friendly society', 'procession', and the like, the relevant successful mentions of pole-carrying by friendly societies from around 1750 to 1850 produce the following impressive figures: Somerset scored no less than 47% of all mentions, the rest of the core area a further 32%, and the whole of the remainder of England and Wales just 21%. Thus, despite the great similarities in the operation of unitary friendly societies throughout England and Wales, in respect of their carrying poles on anniversaries and funerals, Somerset and the rest of the specified core area stood out as unusually strongly committed to the practice. In the core area some 1,500 unitary societies can be identified – this figure not including the one-year dividing societies otherwise known as slate clubs – and of this total just short of 350 retain some evidence that the members carried poles, and of these not quite 200 are known to have adorned their poles with heads of wood, brass or other metal. The others were unadorned, save in some places where bunches of flowers and streamers were attached when on parade.

Members of women's societies rarely carried poles. Notable exceptions include the Female Friendly Society of Lichfield, Staffordshire, in 1774, whose members paraded in white dresses and carried shepherdesses' crooks. In the same county the two patronesses and ten officers of the Female Friendly Society of the Talbot Arms, Burton-on-Trent, at their anniversary in 1797, all carried wands. So too, in 1834, did each of the ordinary members of the Astbury Female Friendly Society in Cheshire. In Somerset, where pole carrying as a whole was far more common than anywhere else, only one instance can be found of women carrying poles of any sort, namely that of the Female Friendly Society at Montacute. For their processions to church at the club anniversaries in the 1830s their rules stipulated the carrying of wands. Even in the joint male and female societies which were found on the Somerset – Dorset border it was only the men who carried poles, while at the Kingsbury Episcopi Female Friendly Society, where pole-carrying by women has been claimed, it was in fact only the stewards who were so obliged, and these official positions were always held by men [12].

Poles

Friendly society poles were locally made using either coppice wood or other small diameter wooden staves. The material was planed into a square cross section and then generally tapered. The section was then reduced to an octagonal shape. The majority were subsequently rounded, with the pole eventually measuring around an inch in diameter at the base to about half this amount at the top. Often the topmost inch or two would be further narrowed to fit into the socket of a pole head, so that the outside of the socket would be the same diameter as that of the pole where the two were seen to meet. Lengths of poles varied between different societies, but generally measured around six feet. Poles were made and painted locally and formed an occasional but significant item of expenditure in club accounts: at Banwell payments for new and replacement poles, including rounding, painting and gilding, cost the society over £6 between 1775 and 1818, despite a price of just 2d each. Flags and flag poles cost them over £8 more [13].

In some cases the poles were varnished, but this was unusual. In the late eighteenth century many of the poles carried either by officers or by members of the clubs were painted white, but at least by the mid nineteenth century blue was by far the most commonly used colour, while black was by no means unusual. Just occasionally red was chosen, and rarer still was green. Over the years there has been considerable darkening of the paint on surviving poles, making the blue and green colours at first sight difficult to distinguish from black. A few societies chose to have the top foot or so of the pole painted a different colour, often red, and a few had spirals painted down the length of the pole, frequently using both red and white, and occasionally yellow. Some have fanciful embellishments in the form of cartouches around the initials of the member, or, more rarely, around the full name. In a handful of societies honorary members were provided with poles of a separate colour, as, more commonly, were stewards. At Barrington, for example, honorary members carried white poles, stewards had theirs painted red, while members' poles were all blue. Different societies in a town were commonly distinguished by poles of contrasting colours, such as at Langport, where the club at the Admiral Vernon Inn had 'blue rods with a gilded top', while the one at the Black Swan sported 'red poles with a gilt head'. Stewards' poles were often longer than those of the ordinary members, while the poles supporting flags and banners were both longer still and considerably thicker: both could be used to display pole heads [14].

References

(1) Withlington, Robert. *English Pageantry: an historical outline*, vols 1 and 2, 1920, passim. Historical pageants are treated exhaustively here, but the author practically ignores friendly society processions.

(2) Clifton Suspension Bridge opening: *Western Daily Press*, 9 December 1864; Williams Vaughan wedding: *North Wales Chronicle*, 21 July 1835; Tudball funeral: *Western Daily Press*, 12 Feb 1856.

(3) A few traders' poles with tops are held by Blaise Castle House Museum.

(4) LOAS 1864 procession: *Western Daily Press*, 28 June 1864.

(5) Victoria Solt Dennis, *Discovering Friendly and Fraternal Societies*, Princes Risborough, 2005, passim; Affiliated order pole heads: M/Axe/01 to 07; M/Crook/01 to 38; M/Mace/01 to 15; M/Sickle/01 to 11; Washford Druids: *West Somerset Free Press*, 17 June 1905, and photograph of Washford procession outside the Washford Arms (private collection); Churchill initiation: *Somerset Guardian*, 14 Aug 1908.

(6) Many Taunton friendly society records, mainly rule books, are held in The National Archives under the categories FS 1 and FS 3; Charles Hardwick's 1859 account of the rituals, myths and mystification among the early affiliated order practices, and their subsequent debunking from around 1850, is still worth reading: Hardwick, Charles, *Hardwick's Friendly Society Manual*, 3rd edition revised, n.d., c.1892, pp 6 – 11.

(7) There is a collection of six funerary staves at Trowbridge Museum (catalogue no. 1977.897): one is illustrated at F 333/3; Kentisbeare funeral of Rev. Chalk: *Western Morning News*, 28 Aug 1936: Kentisbeare F 278/2.

(8) Banks of the Avon Lodge: *Bristol Daily Post*, 19 May 1864; Lodge opening in Glasgow: *Lanarkshire Upper Ward Examiner*, 16 Oct 1886; Lodge opening in Holywell, Wales: *Silurian*, 28 Dec 1839; Lodge Opening in Ladock, Cornwall: *Royal Cornwall Gazette*, 7 Aug 1885.

(9) Rules on behaviour at meetings were generally applicable to all members, but the rule of 'not running up and down the [meeting] room' (Minehead) was clearly aimed at the youths, as was the injunction not to crack nuts during the anniversary church service (Barrington): SHC, Charles Tite collection, Minehead Union Club Rules, 1775; The National Archives FS 1/614/254, Rules of Barrington FS, 1839; Women's societies also had strict rules of behaviour, including not fighting, not singing immoral songs, and the like: The National Archives, FS 1/624/673, Rules of East Coker Female Friendly Society, 1856.

(10) Friendly and Benefit Building Societies' Commission, Reports of the Assistant Commissioners, Scotland, G Culley, Hon E Lyulph Stanley, E Lynch Daniell, BPP [c.998] 1874.

(11) Friendly and Benefit Building Societies' Commission, Reports of the Assistant Commissioners, Ireland and Wales, E Lynch Daniell, BPP [c.995] 1874.

(12) Lichfield: *Derby Mercury*, 1 July 1774; Burton-on-Trent: *Derby Mercury*, 29 June 1897; Astbury: *Staffordshire Advertiser*, 11 Oct 1834; Montacute Female Friendly Society (Kings Arms) Rules, 1836, The National Archives, FS 1/618/425; Kingsbury Episcopi: Fuller implies that women stewards carried the poles – Fuller, MD, *West Country Friendly Societies*, Reading, 1964, p 133 - males occupied all the officers' posts at this society: see *Western Gazette*, 30 March 1883, and *Langport Herald*, 5 June 1875.

(13) Banwell club accounts: SHC D/P/ban 23/26; Barrington: Rev Hamlet's brief history of the club gives details of its pole: SHC D/P/barr 23/2.

(14) Langport: National Archives, FS 1/610/174, 1791 rules, Admiral Vernon Friendly Society, Langport, and The National Archives FS 1/610/175, 1815 rules, Black Swan Friendly Society, Langport.

3

Poles and pole heads

Poles, maces, and emblems carried by members of the affiliated orders

A simple distinction must be made between the various emblems carried by the different categories of friendly societies: there were the type carried by the Oddfellows, Foresters and Rechabites, and there were those that were displayed by the Druids, Shepherds, and unitary societies.

The former groups had regalia appropriate to the office which one of their members might hold. With the Oddfellows there were maces or poles variously topped with designs based on the ones used in freemasonry, which included a sun, a moon, stars, doves, crowns, and quill pens (besides very many others), and these denoted the position which the bearer occupied. The Rechabites also had sets of finials of a similar range of objects for their officers, but they tended to be mounted on long poles rather than on maces. The Foresters carried bugles, axes, and other items relating to their mythical associations with the Robin Hood legend: again, these were carried by officers. The sets of insignia were very costly to obtain, and if owned by a lodge, court, or tent, or by the higher authority in the hierarchy of these three societies, namely, the district, they might be lent out for special occasions to less well-endowed lodges. The designs and ritualistic use of these sets of regalia underline the fact that early affiliated orders were strongly influenced by masonic practices, not only in what the members wore or carried when they assembled together, whether on private or public occasions, but also how their very meetings were conducted. Since these orders were secret societies their lodge meetings combined their mutual benefit business with a great deal of ritual procedures. Thus their sets of insignia, besides being paraded on public processions, were also used on lodge nights for rituals concerned, amongst other procedures, with initiations of new members, or the passing of members from one degree (a level of seniority) to another.

The Druids, however, tended not to confine their insignia to officials, although there were some special objects such as swords for use just by Senior Guardians. Poles were often carried by all members of the lodge in procession, usually topped by a brass sickle, identical for each member of a lodge, but which might vary slightly between one lodge and another, as they were free to choose their own suppliers. With both the Loyal Order of Ancient Shepherds and the Ancient Order of Shepherds (the latter a sub-group of the Foresters) the carrying of insignia was also chiefly the mark of the ordinary members, who carried crooks which were uniform for that particular lodge. There were nevertheless many different patterns of crooks, the choice of which, as with the Druids, was the responsibility of the lodge rather than the order. In most cases the crooks were plain and made of brass, but a few were of iron, and some sets of crooks were ornamented in a variety of small ways, while others were even cast with patterns in bas relief. While in most cases wooden poles of five to six feet long

24

1881 anniversary procession: Foresters (AOF) in Robin Hood attire and Druids (UAOD) carrying sickles.

were chosen, some lodges employed poles of only a half of this length, and many of this type were elaborately turned and were varnished rather than painted.

Poles and pole heads carried by unitary societies

With the majority of unitary societies poles, where used, were carried by all the members, with a uniform pattern of pole head decided by the club. The pole head was the symbol of mutuality, and its display on public occasions played a part in attracting recruits. It was also a symbol of stability: Glastonbury Friendly and Benefit Society introduced their acorn pole head design in 1817 and it continued regularly in use until the 1890s and possibly thereafter on a few occasions until the dissolution of the club in 1912. Dividing societies, which technically ceased to exist after their term of years was up, tended to carry forward the use of their brass-headed poles from one embodiment of the club to its new incarnation: the societies at Aller and at Lopen, for example, were of this type. Similarly, clubs which moved their headquarters from one inn to another generally kept their original design, though when the Filton Junior Benefit Society moved from the Anchor Inn to the Horseshoe Inn in 1866 they were said to have replaced their brass anchor pole heads with a more appropriate horseshoe motif. A society which was created following the closure or collapse of an earlier one might decide to proclaim its independent existence by selecting a new pole head. When the old society at Meare of 1843 origin was replaced by the new society in 1874, a radically different design for the pole heads was adopted. In larger settlements where more than one society existed a variety of patterns could be found. Halberton in Devon, for example, had two quite different designs, as did Williton and Nether Stowey in Somerset. In Dorset, the case of the Stalbridge Union of Foresters, which simultaneously sported three different designs for members, was unique. The situation came about by three formerly separate societies joining forces. Club photographs sometimes show line-ups with a few non-matching pole heads, but these belonged to visitors who had been invited for the day to join the club walk [1].

If officials were to be distinguished from members at anniversary or other celebrations, whether to honour their status or simply to make them distinguishable when helping to marshal the club procession, they were almost always issued with a larger pole head of the standard club pattern, but there were a few exceptions, where the officers had a quite different design. Merriott officers sported a more ornate pole head than ordinary members, for instance. A few clubs chose to provide just their officers with pole heads, as at Timberscombe, where the ordinary members simply attached large bunches of flowers to the tops of their poles [2].

Contrasts in size: flag pole top and members' tops at Panborough.

Banners and flags often had brass tops purchased from George Tutill or some other London regalia supplier, or else they might have the same brass pattern as the members or the stewards, but larger still, even up to around 18 inches tall as at Meare. The massive 25 inches specimen from Stalbridge, however, seems far too delicate to have been consigned to a flagpole top and may have been used to distinguish the president or chief honorary member of the club [3].

No women's society in and around Somerset carried pole heads. The possible exception that has been suggested comprises a simple small brass diamond-shaped example without a socket, directly mounted on top of a pole. It was said to have belonged to the Kingsbury Episcopi Female Friendly Society and to have been an officer's pole head. Thus, since according to this society's usual practice the officers were men, its existence does not conflict with the general rule. At Montacute the Kings Arms Female Friendly Society regulations of 1836 specify that members should carry a wand in procession, but there is no mention of a top, and no other pointers confirm such a feature. The pole head erroneously claimed for the Nether Stowey Female Friendly Society was in fact used by the male society which met at the George Inn. The error originated in an incorrect amendment to one of the Taunton Museum lists and was unknowingly perpetuated, unchecked. The women's society of Nether Stowey only ever carried posies of flowers on their club walks. In contrast to Somerset and its surrounds, there are, nevertheless, occasional reports in other parts of Britain of women's societies carrying poles or wands and even very occasionally pole heads [4].

The use of ritual and regalia in friendly societies

The affiliated orders eventually spread over all of Britain, albeit with regional concentrations, while some of the smaller orders were often much more confined in the extent of their coverage. By the second half of the nineteenth century, as a result of the spread of the orders and of the measure of control exercised by the headquarters of many affiliated orders over the lodges, their regalia tended to be of a uniform pattern. Thus their sashes, aprons, medals, maces, and staffs could be recognised from one end of the country to the other.

The love of display, however, was not to last, and particularly in the case of the Oddfellows (and their various break-away groups) their acceptance of the mythological invention as to their origins began to wear thin, and the fascination with ritual and secrecy was criticised in some quarters as being a distraction which took away from the core purpose of a mutual benefit organisation. The Oddfellows and Rechabites alike experienced massive crises of confidence in the 1840s, losing many lodges and tents, and under the influence of reformers such as Charles Hardwick these orders soon afterwards underwent modernisation, not only in their financial systems but also in their lodge practices, with the deliberate doing away of much of the arcane ritual and regalia. Nevertheless, it look several decades for the display element of processing with their regalia to diminish. Whereas the wearing of masonic-style aprons gradually fell out of fashion, the use of jewels (which were essentially medals), sashes, and collars remained popular throughout almost all of the existence of the affiliated orders.

There were just a few lodges that still used their sets of maces even in the twenty-first century, by which time the majority had long since ceased to value them. The Druids, Foresters and Shepherds also gradually abandoned the carrying of sickles, axes, and crooks, together with their more outlandish costumes, though again such items were still occasionally to be seen at church parades or annual moveable conferences in the inter-war years. Late examples of display by the affiliated orders included the massive Druids' ceremony at Stonehenge in 1905, when white robes and brass sickles were to be seen in abundance, while the Rechabites in conference continued to parade in the streets with their large symbols of the dove, lamb, and wheatsheaf, even in the inter-war years.

With the unitary societies ritual had rarely gained much of a hold, save for that of the annual corporate visit to church (or chapel) followed by dining together. A few clubs might start their ordinary business meetings with a prayer, but these were very much in a minority. The other ritual that might be carried out was when new members were being inducted, but the procedure was brief and somewhat insignificant. The initiation ceremonies of some of the very earliest unitary societies merely consisted of a catechism of set questions, and they were designed to keep the society out of trouble from the authorities by giving demonstrable proof that every member was not only protestant but also a supporter of the king, and favourable to the government. These practices did not survive much beyond about 1820, and in many cases they had become superfluous since societies which were registered were no longer under much scrutiny from the magistrates, the case of Tolpuddle notwithstanding.

The pole-carrying ritual of the unitary societies, however, which had already taken root in the eighteenth century, by and large remained popular throughout the nineteenth century and beyond, but, as was seen in the previous chapter, the incidence of pole-carrying was decidedly a localised feature of a part of the West Country, rather than being found uniformly in all areas of Britain. Even in Somerset, however, there were certainly some clubs that had never walked – they were often the ones which catered for rather better-off members who did not see any need to process and to pay calls on honorary members or potential sponsors. Similarly there were few town-based societies that carried out an obligatory communal walk on their feast day or anniversary. Thus in Somerset, where 29 Bath societies had processed in 1814 to celebrate the supposed return of peace, the practice of club parades died out soon afterwards. At Frome, Wellington, and Taunton, for instance, despite their having about 30 individual societies between them in the 1860s, no annual club walks or processions to church took place. Their dinners, often on November 5th or at the turn of the new year, would be held during the hours of darkness and after a full day's work. The custom of taking an unpaid day's holiday and parading with poles and pole tops was very much the preserve of the rural villages and the smaller towns. Nevertheless, even in the latter, not all clubs walked. In Crewkerne, contrary to the practice of the other societies, the Crown club celebrated its anniversary by just meeting for dinner, as did Milverton's United Benefit Society and Martock's Farmers' and Tradesmen's Society [5].

Pole heads in the West Country and beyond

The earliest evidence for pole-carrying and the use of pole heads in the West Country comes from the second half of the eighteenth century, with eight Somerset societies requiring the use of poles at anniversaries, Evercreech being the first in 1770. Banwell members from 1788 seem to have had tops for their poles, and it is likely from the early references to gilding or painting that these pole heads were all wooden. Brass is first mentioned in 1807 as a material for pole heads in the club rules for Brislington, but wooden heads were still in use for various other societies long after this date. At Hawkchurch and Beaminster the clubs retained their wooden pole heads throughout their existence, as did Stoke Abbott, which even had identical wooden replacements made in 1929. Other societies, however, substituted brass for their original wooden tops. In 1804, as the London Courier announced, 'brass ornaments for carriages and horses are now becoming the rage' and no doubt this fashion for a bright, shiny metal applied equally to other types of domestic articles, including pole heads. Moreover, 1804 is the very date first seen engraved on a friendly society brass pole head, namely, one from East Harptree. Several others also carry dates from the 1800s, including two from Heytesbury which are both stamped 1807. Caution must be taken with dated brasses: while most dates are proof of when the pole head was used, and often refer to the entry of an individual to membership of a society, in other cases there is less certainty. The inscription of 1778 on the reverse side of one of the Heytesbury specimens specifically also mentions that this was when the society was founded, and thus is no proof of it being used at that time. The introduction of brass and the transition from wood to brass was spread over a long period: at Warminster the changeover occurred in the 1850s, as, too, was the case at Shepton Beauchamp, where the younger members were said to have become too proud to use the old gilt-painted knobs, but bought brasses instead. Nevertheless, the old men continued to use the wooden version for years afterwards [6].

Just as the practice of carrying poles ceremonially by unitary friendly societies was observed to some degree all over England and Wales in scattered locations, but was strongly concentrated in Somerset and the adjacent counties, so, too, the custom of adorning the tops of the poles with an ornamental finial was equally unevenly distributed. In the opinion of early writers of the 1900s on the subject, pole heads were essentially a Somerset feature, with some extensions into the adjacent parts of east Devon, Dorset, west Wiltshire and south Gloucestershire. Despite later admitting to having somewhat ignored other locations such as the Midlands, they were never able to provide any convincing proof that such other areas were anything like as prolific in their use of pole heads as Somerset and the rest of the core area. Nor, since then, has any evidence come to light that the initial claim was all that far from the truth. In 1964 Margaret Fuller recorded 141 Somerset pole heads, a further 66 in the rest of the core area, and just 17 in the remainder of Britain. Subsequent research, however, shows totals of 182 pole heads verified for use in places in Somerset, and 78 for the rest of the core area. The total for the remainder of Britain changes to a mere 16: it includes some new additions, but also some removals from Fuller's list, for want of verification [7].

The most fruitful area to find further evidence of the use of pole heads would seem to be the West Midlands, partly on account of the brass manufacturing of Birmingham and district, and partly from the experience of the early collector, Sir Spencer Ponsonby-Fane. In his illustrated notebooks he referred to using dealers who provided him not only with West Country pole heads, but also many others which were said to have originated from the West Midlands. The totals were thirty from

Warwickshire, six from Staffordshire, five from Worcestershire, three from Shropshire and a few from elsewhere. On analysis, however, the results are far less significant. Several of the specimens turn out not to be friendly society pole heads at all, but are brass ornaments topping such features as andirons, while most of the rest have so far eluded proof that they were actually used in the West Midlands. He appears to have fallen prey to his suppliers. Another collector of the 1890s and 1900s, the Rev Charles Shickle of Bath, equally fell into the trap of misidentifying objects as pole heads, or of being sold fake items created by the marriage of genuine parts with improbable add-ons, and he, too, included in his collection specimens said to be from the West Midlands, but which still elude identification [8].

Even if more places with pole head usage beyond the core area can be proved, with suggested locations being verified, the overwhelming concentration in and around Somerset is very unlikely to be challenged.

References:

(1) Glastonbury Benefit Society: F 298 to F 299/5; Aller: F 208/1 & 2; Lopen: F 004/2; Filton Junior Benefit Society, letter on the removal from the Anchor Inn to the Horseshoe Inn, 16 July 1866 – later the club moved back, and then yet again moved to the Horseshoe Inn: The National Archives, FS 3/82/817. AW Allen claimed that the society changed its pole heads (notes accompanying the Allen Collection, MERL; Meare: F 078 and F 024/1 & 2; Halberton: F 267 & F 278/1; Williton: F 273/2 & F 267; Nether Stowey: F 124 & F 219; Stalbridge pole heads were described by the last club secretary, Sgt-Maj Smallbrook, with details repeated in a letter by Lady Theodora Guest to Sir Spencer Ponsonby-Fane, 1908: Ponsonby-Fane Notebook, opp. p.50, MERL; Group photograph of the Broadway Friendly Society, showing a few visitors with their different pole heads: Parsons family, private archive.

(2) Merriott: F 172/1 and F 235; Timberscombe: F 328 and F 329/1; Commercial banner tops: M/Various/13 and M/Various/14.

(3) Local society banner tops: F 155 (Panborough) and F 024/2 (Meare); the large presidential pole top from Stalbridge, nearly 25 inches tall, is illustrated at F 077.

(4) Reputed Kingsbury Episcopi brass: F 003/1; Kingsbury Episcopi Female Friendly Society: 1912 Rules, Tite Collection, SHC, and Notes accompanying the Allen Collection, MERL; Montacute Female Friendly Society (Kings Arms) Rules, 1836, The National Archives, FS 1/618/425; Nether Stowey Female Friendly Society: there was no expenditure on pole heads shown in any of the society's detailed account books and no images of their use (Account Books, SHC DD/TYL 2 & 3. The pattern mistakenly claimed for the society (F 219) has an example stamped with the date May 29, 1856, which corresponds with the commencement of the George Inn Male Friendly Society (private collection); the Lichfield Female Friendly Society members carried shepherdesses' crooks, *Derby Mercury*, 1 July 1774.

(5) The supposed return of peace was celebrated in Bath by 25 male and 4 female friendly societies, with a procession of 2265 members: *Bath Chronicle*, 23 June 1814; Crewkerne anniversaries: *Pulman's Weekly News*, 7 June 1881; Milverton United Benefit Society: *Western News*, 11 June 1881; Martock Tradesmen's Society: *Pulman's Weekly News*, 21 June 1867.

(6) Evercreech 1770 rules, The National Archives, FS 3/328/91; Banwell Friendly Society accounts (1775 to 1818), cost of rods and gilding, various dates between 1778 and 1816, and 1796 reference to 'cap on the rods': SHC D/P/ban 23/22; Brislington, rule number XXVII, 1807 – 'brass nub': The National Archives FS 1/614/284; Hawkchurch: see F 318 and F 321; Beaminster: see F 170/3, F 170/4, F 170/5, F 317/1, F 317/2, F 330, F 331/1, & F 331/2; Stoke Abbott: *Western Morning News* 10 June 1929; "Fashion in Brass", *London Courier*, 2 June 1804; East Harptree: see F 058/2; Heytesbury: see F 082; Warminster: SHC Taunton Museum archives, letter from WE Edwards to HStG Gray, 10 April 1914, 'brass halberds were substituted for wooden pole heads', Shepton Beauchamp: SHC Day Book 2, 17 September 1909, p.100: note by the Rev. J Hamlet.

(7) Ponsonby-Fane, Sir Spencer: 'This custom of the "Brass Pole Head" was, I believe, peculiar to the county of Somerset alone, and to a few parishes bordering on it', Club Pole Heads in Somerset, *The Connoisseur*, vol XVII, April 1907, p 256; Ponsonby-Fane later modified this view to include Birmingham, Staffordshire, and Warwickshire: Somerset Friendly Society Pole Heads, *The Connoisseur*, Extra Christmas Number, vol XXXVII, 1913, pp. 61 – 70; Kelway, James, 'Pole heads…[are found] chiefly in the West and particularly in Somerset and the counties over [its] borders', Head-hunting: a West Country Hobby, *Country Life*, vol XXVII, no 678, January 1st, 1910, p 27; Fuller, Margaret, *West Country Friendly Societies*, Reading, 1964, p 119 and 133 – 146.

(8) Ponsonby-Fane, Sir Spencer, Club Pole Heads 1 (bound and illustrated with drawings), c.1910, MERL, Reading, and Club Pole Heads 2 (bound and illustrated with drawings), c.1910, The Box, Plymouth; Shickle collection of pole heads (1951 accession), MERL.

4

Pole head design

Society choices

The decision whether a society should carry poles and pole heads is sometimes referred to in its sets of rules, but not in any detail. At Stogumber in 1827, for instance, the opportunity was given for the majority of members to decide whether to have any ornaments, and if so, what they should be – but there is no indication that the society ever took up the option. The majority of members at Langport's Admiral Vernon Inn society in 1791 were to decide on the rods for the clerks and stewards, while those at Martock in 1800 were to decide on rods for both officials and members. In clubs such the Chard New Friendly Society of 1813, under its 1818 rules, it was a committee majority that settled the choices. The subsequent stage in the selection of the colour for the pole or the design and material of the pole head is quite unrecorded for practically every society. Equally, little is known of how a manufacturer was obtained: only Ilchester and Meare have left any clues. With the former, money was paid to a third party to obtain their club pole heads from Birmingham, while with the latter the treasurer himself ordered the pole heads from a Bridgwater foundry [1].

We have no indication that brass founders had illustrations or examples of possible pole head designs to assist choice, or whether those responsible for obtaining the pole heads went to the manufacturers with an idea for a pattern already in their minds. The clustering of certain related patterns in particular areas suggests that much of the selection process was determined by what designs friendly society members observed in nearby clubs. Societies with column brasses of very similar pattern are mostly found close to one another. The column brass topped by large leaves and an upstanding acorn is reputed to have been used at Bawdrip, Goathurst, North Petherton, and Puriton, and all lie within just seven miles of one another. The column brass pattern topped by a small cluster of leaves is said to have been used at Kingsbury Episcopi, Hardington Mandeville, Montacute, Norton sub Hamdon, Odcombe, and Stogursey. Five of these also lie within seven miles of each other. Interestingly, the odd one out, Stogursey, has no proof that the design was actually used there. With the flat style of pole heads the four societies said to have used the halberd design, Chewton Mendip, Farrington Gurney, Litton, and Ston Easton, are all no more than three miles apart. Clusters are also shown in the locations of knob-type pole head pattern: highly similar designs are to be seen In the seven societies at Chetnole, Leigh, North Coker, Sherborne, Stoke under Ham, Thornford, and West Coker, all lying within just ten miles of each other. East Coker, however, was also situated quite within this cluster, and it too had a pole head, but the pattern is unknown. It is tempting to imagine that it resembled those of its neighbours, but such an assumption is unreliable. After all, Sherborne, which is also part of this group, had a second friendly society, and their choice was for a totally contrasted flat pattern. Furthermore, other places such as Martock, Meare, Nether Stowey and Williton all had two societies, and each society chose pole heads of quite different designs. The local copying factor as an element in the choosing process, strong as it appears to have been, should not be exaggerated [2].

Pole heads of wood, iron, and glass

The earliest wooden pole heads were produced locally using lathe turned patterns with varying degrees of elaboration. Their bases were hollowed out to fit on top of a pole. Acorns, urns, balls and spires were popular, and all were easy to produce. Uniquely, at Timberscombe, the stewards were furnished with abstract patterned heads that were painted on thin sheets of wood. Poles were generally decorated with only one colour, while the wooden pole heads of a society more often than not were uniformly painted in a contrasting variety of bright colours, usually a combination of white, yellow, red, and blue, but occasionally black was added to the list. Funeral poles, where mentioned, were always black, and it appears that some clubs may have kept some of these in addition to the normal issue, but only a single set of six black pole heads has come to light, and they are not on their original poles. The rarity of funerary poles and pole heads is explained by the fact that a covering of crape over the standard pole head usually sufficed [3].

Enough wooden pole heads have survived to give an indication of the wide range of chosen designs, although general wear and tear, decay, and later discard, have all meant that their total number is limited. Nevertheless, forty-eight different designs of wooden pole heads in the round are known, and the main museum collections each have a number of different specimens [4].

In a very few cases pole heads of iron were produced. Except for the cast spear reputedly from Drayton, flat metal sheets were used from which the designs were cut or forged, and the products were made by local blacksmiths. Most of them appear to come from clubs in West Wiltshire [5].

Rather rarer are large metal open crowns, ranging in height from around seven inches to over four times as tall. Only eleven have been recorded. Philip le Gros, whose pole heads form the majority of the friendly society collection at Blaise Castle House Museum, managed to acquire four, which were claimed to have been used by a friendly society at Horningsham, but they have no verified provenance. Others were said to have been used at Tintinhull and at Maiden Bradley. Two, at least, mounted on poles, were colourfully decorated and probably made to celebrate the golden jubilee of Queen Victoria, but whether for use by a friendly society or not is unknown [6].

Nailsea glass works were reputed to have produced a few pole heads, but only three survivals have been recorded. They are all different, and seem to be one-offs, produced by members for their own use, rather than uniform batches for all members of the society. Two formed part of the Challicom collection of Nailsea glass, which was bequeathed to Taunton Museum in 1940, but they cannot now be traced in the Taunton catalogue. The location of the third example is unknown [7].

Pole heads of brass

There were many organisations other than friendly societies who from time to time marched with rods or wands topped by brass finials. Thomas Blinman's brass foundry workers attended the 1821 coronation celebration procession in Bristol each carrying a brass crown. The Taunton silk throwsters at the equivalent event in 1838 also had 'wands surmounted by an elegant crown', while reports of both 1823 and 1859 noted that the apprentices sponsored by Bristol's Grateful Society marched through the city with gilt dolphins on top of their poles. While crowns were quite appropriate for professing loyalty to the monarch, the choice of coronets, dragons, swans, and eagles for the tops of wands, all of which were on display at an 1827 London parade organised for some 700 to 800 brass foundry workers, were just a matter of serendipity – the result, it was stated, of using whatever old stock items came to hand in the workshops. Figurative brass ornaments of this nature, together with the more abstract designs such as balls, urns, and spires, and ornate columns with knops, are commonly seen on longcase clocks, firedog finials and brass candlesticks, and the items would have provided readily available patterns, or at least ideas, for transfer by brass founders to friendly society pole heads. The lightweight head for Bishops Hull uses precisely the same thin gauge fluted ball as is found on the tops of long case clocks, and the top of the supposed Middlezoy brass, an upright bird with wings outstretched, is an identical casting to the one also used for clock finials. Heavier duty castings for doves on the tops of brass chandeliers have a great affinity with those reputed to have been used by the affiliated orders, or by unitary societies in the Midlands. Acorns and small brass crowns, which appear in many friendly society pole head designs, are also found, for instance, on tipstaffs or wands used by a variety of officials. A close study of collections of photographs of brass artefacts from the seventeenth century onwards shows that pole head designs, whether flat or in the round, were quite in step with a wide range of other English brassware [8].

About a half of all friendly society pole heads were made in the round, and although many have affinities with other uses, few of them have any obvious clue for suggesting that they belong to one place rather than to another.

Of the flat type, the case is reversed: there is less commonality of use with other organisations or for other purposes, but sometimes their place of use is easier to pinpoint. Many of them at first sight suggest a militaristic origin on account of their resemblance to spears and halberds. Such weaponry, however, had long since been exchanged for more up to date armaments, and yet medieval weapon design undoubtedly provided a rich source for the patterns of friendly society pole heads. There have been fanciful attempts to try to find a continuous historic link between the friendly society spear-shaped designs and the bearing of arms, but such claims have lost currency due to lack of proof. A common favourite was to recall that Somerset villagers had supported the Duke of Monmouth, armed just with pole weapons, and somehow the tradition was carried forward into the friendly society era. While it might be suggested that early friendly societies had some strong proactive function which could be symbolised by adopting a weapon-like pole head, it must be remembered that many late eighteenth and early nineteenth century societies, founded during the period of revolution in France and the later Napoleonic Wars, had rules which required new members to affirm that they supported the government, the monarchy, and the protestant faith. Magistrates were vigilant lest friendly societies became sources of civil disobedience. Nevertheless, many societies in Somerset chose to carry old-fashioned spear-type pole heads. A plausible alternative explanation for this adoption is that it drew on the ceremonial weapons carried by the javelin men, appointees of the High Sheriff, and the customary protectors of the judges when they were passing through a county en route to the quarterly assizes. Long after such weapons had become obsolete elsewhere, halberds and spears, each with tassels attached, were still carried by javelin men, and the practice even

Arabesque design typical of edges of many flat pole heads.

survived in some counties right into the twentieth century, by which time the javelin men's role had been taken over by the police. Thus for a long period the designs would have been highly visible on a regular basis, and available for copying by a friendly society.

In the early nineteenth century the office of High Sheriff changed annually, and each appointee had to provide his own javelin men with uniform and arms. A favourite theme was Tudor dress and accoutrements. In 1828 the new Somerset incumbent furnished his men with 'javelins ornamented with hatchet crosses', while the 1830 High Sheriff provided 'highly polished halberds, elaborately wrought'. The Hampshire High Sheriff of 1846 even chose from his family armoury 'excellently preserved specimens of ancient implements of warfare, consisting of halberds, partizans and battle axes'. The brass halberds of the Farrington Gurney Friendly Society and other clubs nearby, the spears of the West Pennard, East Harptree and the Stalbridge clubs, and the tassels seen at the Westbury-sub-Mendip and Leigh (Dorset) friendly society anniversaries all bear witness to this archaic influence from the javelin men, whether consciously adopted or not [9].

A good many of the other flat brasses which have also been described as spears are based on a pattern for which is no clear precedent. They are formed in a triangular shape, base down, with an arabesque style loop resembling an upside-down tankard handle at the middle of each side, below each of which projects a square or curved foot. There are around eighty variations on this theme, depending on how far the term 'similarity' is stretched. At the pointed top of some specimens there may be an acorn, a crown or a button, while the centre of the triangle may be pierced with letters, diamonds, hearts or other patterns. The face may even have sprigs of brass leaves attached on each side. In the majority of cases there is little meaning behind the choice of design motifs, but pierced letters invariably referred to the name of the society. Unfortunately there is still ambiguity about which societies were signified by the letters S, FS, and BS which are found on at least seven patterns. They are usually interpreted as standing for 'steward', 'friendly society', and 'benefit society', but these definitions are unconfirmed [10].

Another family of patterns takes the spear (or perhaps an heraldic fleur de lys) and adds three or four pointed arms on each side. Beyond this family the designs are even more abstract – with selections of loops, appendages and piercings. There are no obvious origins, but there are shared resemblances, and certain features are repeated in a variety of combinations. Many appear to be the unique design of a particular friendly society pole head, not encountered elsewhere, whether as a pole head or as some other artefact. Again, there is little significance behind the choice of design.

The flat brasses have much more understandable explanations when they represent the inn signs from club headquarters, but even here the designs are not always straightforward. The curious outline of the brass belonging to the Rose and Crown Friendly Society at Nether Stowey is hard to explain, despite the pattern including a piercing in the shape of a rose, and having a crown added above. Two other societies, moreover, have a similar silhouette, which signifies that the outline is simply a stock idea, but suitably differentiated by a piercing and a topknot. The outline of the pole head of the Bell and Crown society at Zeals is also shared by two other societies, and these have nothing to do with inns. With the West Stower (modern West Stour) pole head which depicts a sailing ship, again there is no significance in the ornate silhouette. More self-evident is the use of the Hood family crest, used in its entirety as a silhouette, both as the inn-sign and as the pole head of the friendly society from the Hood Arms in Kilve. Similarly, the design used at the Full Moon Inn at Fishponds is simply a moon, no more, no less. There are around fifty patterns of flat brasses which are probably based on inn signs, and at least seven more in the round, but considerably fewer than a half of these can be fully verified as belonging to an inn at a particular place. The distinctive pole head with a pierced pattern showing five bells is among many other inn-related designs which elude identification – in any case, the designs are sometimes ambiguous. Does this particular pole head represent an inn called the Five Bells, or one called the Ring of Bells? [11].

Suppliers of brass pole heads and their manufacture

Surviving friendly society records are almost completely silent on how each committee obtained its brass pole heads. In the otherwise very full papers from the Stogursey New Friendly Society, which existed between 1845 and 1952, there are references to show that club poles, tassels, and brasses were purchased between 1846 and 1864, but there are no details of quite how they were obtained. The same is true with records of clubs at Odcombe, West Chinnock, and Wookey. At Chilcompton the accounts refer to the payments made for the purchase of brasses, but it is obvious that the named payees are intermediaries in the transactions and are not the manufacturers. Nevertheless, it is undoubtedly clear that the Chilcompton brass spears, large spears, and tassels came from Bristol. These sketchy details appear to represent the only surviving archival evidence on the matter from Somerset clubs. In the case of the Ilchester Old Friendly Society, J Stevens Cox wrote in 1948 that he was able to examine the manuscript accounts of a John Stone, who was paid for 200 brass knobs purchased on behalf of the society in 1867. For these, the cost price was one shilling each, but, more importantly, the accounts reveal that the brasses came from Birmingham, although the name of the manufacturer was not given. The accounts have not resurfaced [12].

Pole head brasses themselves only very rarely carry the manufacturer's name. Only four instances have ever come to light, three from Bristol and one from Bath. The earliest belonged to the society at Evercreech, whose highly elaborate brass spears were stamped 'Blinman & Co – Bristol' in a circular pattern, with a serial membership number in the middle. In a few of this pattern the number is omitted, and some had no stamped detail at all. Thomas Blinman ran an ironmongery and brass-founding company in Bristol, but his partnership was dissolved in November 1825, after which presumably the 'Blinman & Co' description would not have been appropriate. There was a new manifestation of the Evercreech society in 1825, so it would appear that they were just in time to have the 'Blinman & Co' marking and this would therefore be the likely date of the Evercreech brasses. Thomas Blinman remained in business, but as a sole trader, until at least 1831. It is unlikely that he would have used the old company name on his products between 1825 and 1831: perhaps this period was when the unmarked Evercreech brasses were produced. Also carrying a Bristol stamp is an urn-shaped pole head with the inscription 'Golden Lion Friendly Society established 1833 – Wasbrough Hale & Co Bristol'. This firm produced a wide range of goods, including gas fittings, clocks, bells, and large chandeliers for churches, so the making of friendly society pole heads was well within its compass. The company remained under that name until 1848, thus limiting the period when the pole head might have been produced. Where this pole head was used, however, has not been established. Wasborough Hale & Co were also reputed to have produced the pole head used at Donyatt, a brass column supporting a ball, on top of which was the shaking hands motif and, above that, a crown, but the brasses do not have a manufacturing stamp. When extra supplies were needed the society was said to have then used a firm trading as Capnurse, supposed to have been a successor to Wasbrough Hale, but the name seems to have been a transcription error. Another pole head of Bristol make, a chased double-sided flat depiction of a horse, produced in three sizes, was used by the White Horse Friendly Society at Hambrook in the Bristol suburbs. These brasses were all stamped 'Hale & Co Bristol', referring to the Thomas Hale business which is known to have succeeded Wasbrough Hale in 1848 and which lasted until liquidation in 1875[13].

Only one pole head pattern bears a stamp from a manufacturer outside Bristol. The two stewards' brasses from the West Stower Friendly Society that met at the Ship Inn carry the imprint 'G Weedon – Bath', but the members' brasses are not stamped with the name. The production date is uncertain, since although George Weedon became bankrupt in 1823, and his stock was sold in 1824, he is nevertheless recorded as being in business again in 1837, and presumably was in operation for several years before that. Judging from the similarity of design of the West Stower brass to several others on the Somerset – Dorset border, it seems quite possible that Weedon supplied many other societies [14].

Apart from Bristol and Bath, the only other place of manufacture so far verified is Bridgwater, which also had a brass foundry trade, and was well-known for producing some high quality chandeliers still hanging in several Somerset churches. For such manufacturers, just as for their Bristol counterparts, the production of friendly society pole heads, flat or in the round, would have been well within their capability. Margaret Fuller drew attention to an apparent distribution pattern where for flat brasses the centre of origin was Bristol, and brasses made in the round came from nearer Bridgwater, and lay west of the Polden Hills, but she was not able to substantiate the idea. Moreover, the Golden Lion Friendly Society pole head by Wasbrough Hale & Co is in the round, and yet was made in Bristol, as, too, may have been the Donyatt brass, also in the round; so the simplicity of the claim is upset. On the other hand, her proposed link between firms making pole heads and those producing chandeliers has finally been vindicated. The Bridgwater firm of Thompson Brothers, like Wasbrough, Hale & Co of Bristol, could manufacture a wide range of ironmongery and brass foundry products, and in 1860 they made three brass chandeliers for All Saints Church at Huntspill. This was the same firm which as late as 1914 was chosen to make 50 brass pole heads for the newly revived Meare Benefit Society. Which other friendly societies had used their services in previous years is unfortunately still a matter for conjecture [15].

While many pole head specimens from a particular club are identical in shape and dimensions, there are other cases where slight variations occur in patterns which superficially appear to be the same. Newly set up societies did not necessarily have the funds to order large numbers of pole heads all at once. At Wookey, for instance, the society bought 30 spears (almost certainly of brass) in 1819, 24 more in 1826 together with two larger ones for stewards, and a further 10 in 1840, and many other societies also bought their pole heads in batches. It would be quite understandable if there were differences between the batches, even if it were only a matter of slightly altered socket shapes. These minor differences, however, pose problems in identification. The Bishop Sutton variants, however, are certainly from the same club, even though their shapes, proportions and sockets show some discrepancies, and the East Harptree variants both belong to the same place, even though they are of different vintage. In the latter case, the original early nineteenth century specimens have a separate socket into which the blade is slotted and pinned, while with the 36 revival specimens of 1905 the sockets and blades are integral, and cast as just one unit [16].

In the matter of manufacturing processes there is no other evidence than what may be gleaned from close inspection of the pole heads themselves. By the very fact that some flat brasses and practically all brasses in the round were produced by casting, it follows that over one half of all pole head designs were produced by this method. For some flat brasses cutting out from relatively thin sheets of brass around a template would have been quite adequate for the small batches of brasses that a club would have ordered at any one time. Brassware manufacturing techniques were very well established long before the making of friendly society emblems was required. Even the most casual study of earlier brass items from English manufacturers, such as candle sticks and chandeliers, andirons and fire tools, trivets and wall pockets, long case clock and other ornaments, together with many other artefacts of eighteenth or even seventeenth century origin, shows that the production of pole heads for friendly societies must have been a fairly routine business. It would seem that some of the very simple flat brass designs may have belonged to the early period of friendly society patterns while more sophisticated designs with much surface ornamentation cast into the surface came later, but unless further evidence is unearthed, this suggestion must remain conjectural. Nevertheless, the two patterns for the Hood Arms friendly society appear to support the idea [17].

With the application of elbow grease by members and even more strenuous cleaning techniques by antique dealers, surfaces of pole heads have in many instances been worn down, and such detail as the engraving of names, initials, dates, and so on, have in some cases been reduced to feint impressions, but membership numbers were often added with punches and tend to have survived. Brasses in the round are on the whole less well endowed with inscriptions, but there are outstanding exceptions, such as the early Glastonbury members' specimens. Some brasses have initials applied with the aid of dots crudely punched in by the tip of a nail, while occasionally the whole surface of a brass may be engraved with the most intricate patterns. It was partly a matter of marking the pole head with some identifying mark to avoid misappropriation, and partly a matter of artistic endeavour. Pole heads have occasionally suffered the loss of protruding arms, sometimes by accident, and sometimes deliberately: the latter, it is suspected, was by unscrupulous dealers trying to invent a new pattern. Such items are well represented in most collections, but none has ever been proved to have a genuine provenance. To this must be added the practice of fabricating fancy pole heads by marriages of unrelated parts: the Ponsonby-Fane collection had several of these, including the so-called Langport brass, as did most early collections. In a few cases mutilation of the pole heads was carried out by members of friendly societies themselves: the Paulton flat brass topped by a crown very often has the cross at the very top broken off, perhaps, it can be suggested, from some religious scruple, while the Fivehead doves have often had their wings bent down (presumably by rubbing and applying pressure) even to the extent of a wing being fractured or actually broken off by metal fatigue. A few brasses were nailed to pub walls and still bear the nail holes and corroded backs, while others, where breakages have occurred through the delicacy of the pattern, have had the fragments lovingly restored by solder or by rivetted reinforcements [18].

Identification of pole heads: sources of evidence

While ornamental finials at the tops of friendly society poles are generally known as pole heads, alternative terms were often used, including knobs, staff or stave heads, tops, ensigns, or even emblems. Other descriptions, common in newspaper accounts, specified that the poles were brass-mounted or brass-headed. Regrettably there was also a habit among correspondents of referring just to the pole, while actually signifying both the pole and its pole-head, so it is often difficult to know whether or not pole heads were present at an event.

By the late nineteenth century the annual newspaper write-ups had repeated certain anniversary day reports for so long that the correspondents simply fell back on the time-worn phrase that members were 'carrying their indispensable club poles'. The omission of specific references to an actual finial causes even further ambiguity, since there were many clubs, even in Somerset, and particularly in the west of the county, that did not top their poles with any permanent device – though streamers and flowers might be attached temporarily. Flowers could also be attached even when there was a pole head.

In a few cases the pole heads were indeed mentioned in the press, but they were given an over-brief description such as 'spear' (which almost inevitably meant a flat brass design) or 'knob' (which unhelpfully could mean either a flat pattern or else one in the round). Newspapers were rarely more specific than this, but in a few cases the design of the finial was indeed mentioned, albeit in much too simple terms. The Clifton and Hotwells Benefit Society members in 1863 carried 'spear headed staves', but this information is quite insufficient to enable the identification of the precise pattern, and no alternative leads on that particular subject have come to light. The 1875 report of the Evercreech society was a little more helpful by recording 'formidable staves with brass devices'. There were, nevertheless, a handful of rather more useful press references to pole heads, such as the one which in 1871 recorded the designs of the two Halberton societies: each was described as including a ball, the one topped by a swan and the other by a crown. In a few cases the reports are sufficient to identify the pattern despite being concise: in 1843 the members of the Royal Victoria Union Friendly Society at Fishponds had 'a blue staff, bearing a representation of the moon' – a description that only fits the one known pattern of a moon. At Combe St Nicholas the description of 'poles with a star mounting' is equally helpful, as are the accounts with the words 'bell-shaped, brass-topped staves' at Curry Mallet, and the 'representation of the Hood Arms' at Kilve. In only one or two cases, however, do contemporary press accounts ever contain really detailed descriptions, but those of the Sturminster Newton and the Bishops Hull clubs are models of perfection, and provide very precise details, quite sufficient to identify the respective designs with complete certainty [19].

Early Rule Books often contain a wealth of detail about the running of unitary societies. Apart from financial information on the vital topics of subscriptions and benefits administration, details about the arrangements for anniversary celebrations were often included, such as the need to attend the service at church or chapel and to take part in the club walk for visiting patrons, and these regulations often also mention pole-carrying and, less frequently, some indication that a uniform pole head was required. The detail in these rules, however, is always vague. At most a 'knob' or 'spear' might be specified, without indication of the pattern: indeed, the rule of the Evercreech society which specified that a 'spear' should be carried hardly does justice to its complex pattern. A few rule books specify that the material should be brass, but equally common were the ambiguous terms 'gilt' or 'yellow', both of which could refer to a painted wooden head or one made of brass.

Identification from contemporary photographs is one of the most promising sources of pattern identification, but often the scale is too small to be really helpful, especially in those instances when the pole head pattern was produced at a variety of sizes for different villages and where it has been difficult to match a particular size to a particular village. In other cases the club procession shown in the picture is too far away, or the band takes up too much of the original photographer's interest. Several clubs were reported as having posed for photographs, but in a few of them copies have yet to emerge from such sources as family photograph albums. Very occasionally photographs of clubs with their pole heads can be seen in the inns where they once held their meetings. Examples such as the George Inn at Nether Stowey and the Duke of York Inn at Shepton Beauchamp have both provided this useful link with the past. Despite the early advent of this medium, few photographs seem to have been taken of friendly societies prior to about 1890.

Many pole tops are engraved or stamped with the member's initials or name. Initials are almost never of any assistance in identifying provenance, and even full names can be of little help unless some hint of the location is already available, or the name is unusual. In several instances the name cannot even be traced in any of the censuses, the member presumably having died or moved away from the settlement at the date of the enumeration. Names or initials of settlements or societies were rarely incorporated into the pole head design, but there were rare exceptions, such as the SOFS 1761 cut-outs that appeared on the Sherborne Old Friendly Society brass produced in 1861 to celebrate the centenary of the club. The MFS and TCFS cut-outs are equally helpful for confirming the designs of Marnhull and the Templecombe Friendly Society specimens respectively. On the other hand the cut-out letters were not always correctly identified: early owners of the CFS and DFS patterns wrongly ascribed the brasses to Combe Florey and to Donyatt: it required supplementary information to correct the locations to Crowcombe and Dowlish Wake [20].

The design of the brass, especially where it incorporates a reference to an inn sign can be convincing proof of location, as is the case with the Hood Arms pole head from Kilve, but there are several designs where the precise identity of the inn is not apparent: the brass with the Five Bells depicted could have come from any one of a number of inns with those names. In other cases the name of the inn is so unusual that a brass making visual reference to it clearly indicates its provenance: cases in point are the Flower Pot Inn at Kingswood and the Bell and Crown at Zeals [21].

It is rare so long after the demise of most clubs to find reliable evidence of their existence in the settlement where they functioned. In some cases the brasses were discarded or sold for scrap or to collectors, usually without any surviving record. Failure to pass on information between successive generations, especially because of deaths or out-migration, contributed to the loss of local knowledge. Nevertheless, material is still being uncovered, and occasionally even now undoubtable provenance can be proved by people with the requisite roots in a place: verification of two variants of a pattern used in Bishop Sutton, for example, occurred as late as 2022. Unfortunately there are other cases where people's memory is patently incorrect, and elisions of information provide false trails. The tapping of local knowledge has paid dividends in the past, however, none so more than the painstaking enquiries made by Sir John Jardine in the 1930s and 1940s, when he wrote to a great many parish clergy, enclosing sketches of the pole heads which he wished to verify as having come from that place. His respondents at the time were remarkably generous with their attempts to be helpful, and they made many positive identifications by asking elderly local inhabitants for their recollections. In other cases early collectors were occasionally able to obtain their examples of pole heads directly from individuals who had actually used them, thus establishing cast iron provenance, provided that suitable a record of the transaction was kept.

Regrettably, most collectors were by no means sufficiently concerned or even interested in scrupulous recording, and simply regarded their hobby as trophy hunting. Nevertheless, notebooks with sketches and photographs and varying amounts of written detail were put together by Sir Spencer Ponsonby-Fane, H J Hooper, and James Kelway, while Sir John Jardine's carefully recorded data is an invaluable source of information. With other collectors, such as W B Broadmead, Dr T Hopkins and E H Caley, it was often considered sufficient simply to confirm the location where the pole head was supposed to have been used, whereas on the matter of which actual society at that place was involved (and there were often several possibilities) they remained tantalisingly vague. Over the years, museums, too, have been equally imprecise. Furthermore, collectors and museums alike were all too ready to accept unsubstantiated claims for provenance from individuals who had established themselves as authorities on the subject, and who were eager to stamp their opinions on others [22].

References:

(1) Stogumber Union Society, rules 1827, The National Archives, FS 1/619/487; Langport, FS held at the Admiral Vernon Inn, rules 1791, The National Archives, FS 1/610/174; Martock FS held at the White Hart Inn, rules 1800, The National Archives, FS 1/611/191; Chard New FS, rules 1818, The National Archives, FS 1/606/60; Cox, J Stevens, Ilchester Club Pole Heads of the 19th Century, Somerset & Dorset Notes & Queries, vol XXV, part CCXXXVI, March 1948, pp. 81 & 82; Meare: Central Somerset Gazette, 5 November 1915.
(2) Acorn design: F 291, F 292/1, F 292/2, and F 293; Small cluster of leaves design: F 284 to F 290; Halberd design: F 103 to F 106/1; Design used by Chetnole and others: F 198/1 to F 199 and F 202; East Coker pole head: Western Gazette, 22 June 1876; Sherborne designs: F 025/!, F025/2, and F 205; Martock (with Bower

Hinton) designs: F 013/2 and F191/1; Meare designs: F 018, F 024/1, and F 024/2; Nether Stowey designs: F 124, F 219 to F 221/2; Williton designs: F 230 and F 273/3.

(3) Timberscombe: F 328 and F 329/1.

(4 Wooden pole heads are shown between F 300/1 and F 327/2.

(5) Drayton: F 333/1; blacksmith-made pole heads reputedly from West Wiltshire: F 332, F333/4 and F 333/5.

(6) Le Gros crowns: M/Crown/02 to M/Crown/05; Tintinhull (unconfirmed): M/Crown/01; Maiden Bradley (unconfirmed): M/Crown/07 and M/Crown/08; Queen Victoria 1887 jubilee crowns: M/Crown/09 and M/Crown/10.

(7) Nailsea glass pole heads: M/glass/01 to 03, and Gray, HStG, Nailsea Glass, *The Connoisseur*, vol XXX, no. 118, pp. 88 and 95.

(8) Blinman crowns: *Bristol Mirror*, 28 July 1821; Taunton silk throwsters: *Taunton Courier*, 4 July 1838; Grateful Society brass dolphin, F 163: *Bristol Mercury*, 17 November 1823 and *Bristol Times*, 13 November 1859; London brass workers' parade: *Morning Post*, 17 February 1827; Bishops Hull: F 207; Middlezoy: F 281; Doves used by unitary societies or perhaps by affiliated order lodges: F 236/1, 2, and 3, F 237, and F 239; For representative collections of brass artefacts with similarities to brass pole heads see Schiffer, Peter, Nancy, and Herbert, *The Brass Book*, Atglen, PA, USA, 1978, passim, and Gentle, Rupert, and Field, Rachael, *English Domestic Brass*, 1975, passim.

(9) Javelin men and antique weapon design: *Bath Chronicle*, 10 April 1828, Exeter & Plymouth Gazette, 3 April 1830, *Dorset County Chronicle*, 12 March 1846; Halberds and spears of Farrington Gurney and locality: F 103 to F 106/1; West Pennard: F 056 and 057; East Harptree: F 058/1 and F 058/2; Stalbridge: F 060/1 and F 060/2; Tassels below pole heads: Westbury sub Mendip: F 031 and F032, and Leigh (Dorset): F 199.

(10) Unidentified pierced letter designs (S, FS and BS): F 018, F 019, F 020, F 021/1, F021/2, F 046/1, and F 046/2.

(11) Rose and Crown: F 124; Bell and Crown: F 043; West Stour: F 095/1 and F 095/2; Hood Arms: F 159 and F 160; Full Moon: F 164/1 and F 164/2; Five Bells: F026.

(12) Stogursey: SHC D/P/stogs 23/1; Odcombe: SHC DD/X/MNC/1; West Chinnock: SHC D/P/chin.w 23/4; Wookey: SHC A/BTA 1/2/1; Chilcompton: SHC DD/SAS/C/795/PR74; Ilchester, type 3 of the different patterns: J Stevens Cox, Ilchester Club Pole Heads, *Somerset & Dorset Notes & Queries*, XXV, March 1948, p 81.

(13) Evercreech: F 064, *St James's Chronicle*, 10 November 1825 (dissolution of Blinman partnership), and Eveleigh, David J, Brass Founders, Braziers & Coppersmiths, Bristol, c.1650-1890, *Journal of the Antique Metalware Society*, vol 12, June 2004, p.13; Golden Lion FS, F 172/5: the Rev C Shickle, the original collector, believed the specimen to be from Merriott, but no society there started in 1833, nor was there a Golden Lion Inn; Press reports show Wasbrough Hale in business between 1830 and 1847 (*Bristol Mirror*, 18 December 1830 and *Bristol Times*, 11 September 1847); Donyatt FS, F 272 and F 273/1: Burnell, Margaret, Notes on the Donyatt Village Club, *Somerset & Dorset Notes & Queries*, vol XXIV, December 1943, p.65; White Horse FS, F 151, F 152, and F 153/1: *Bristol Mercury*, 17 June 1848.

(14) West Stower FS (modern West Stour), F095/2: *Bath Chronicle*, 11 December 1823, *Bath Chronicle*, 8 April 1824 and *Taunton Courier*, 4 January 1837; Bridgwater and Bristol chandeliers: Sherlock, Robert, West Country Chandeliers and their Makers, *Antique Metalware Society Journal*, vol 10, 2002, pp.1-12; Fuller, MD, *West Country Friendly Societies*, Reading, 1964, p.120.

(15) Thompson chandeliers: *Bridgwater Mercury*, 14 March 1860; Meare Benefit Society pole head purchase (1914) reported in *Central Somerset Gazette*, 5 November 1915.

(16) Wookey FS: accounts, SHC A/BTA 1/2/1; Bishop Sutton: F 051/1 and F 051/2; East Harptree: F058/1 and F 058/3.

(17) Schiffer, Peter, Nancy, and Herbert, *The Brass Book*, Atglem, PA, USA, 1978, passim (this source has a wealth of illustrations of different categories of brassware covering Europe as well as the US); Hood Arms, Kilve: F 159 and F 160.

(18) Glastonbury: F 298; mutilated brasses (selection): F 089;/2, F 091/2. F 094/3; Langport: F 294/1; Paulton: F 013/4; Fivehead: F 280/1; Redlands Union Benefit Society, Bristol: Fuller, MD, *West Country Friendly Societies*, Reading, 1964 - the highly rivetted specimen from the Shickle collection is shown on the dust jacket.

(19) Clifton and Hotwells: *Bristol Daily Post*, 26 May 1863; Evercreech (F 064): *Western Gazette*, 4 June 1875; Halberton (F 276 – crown, and F 278/1 – swan): *Western Times*, 6 June 1871; Fishponds (F 164/1 & F 164/2): *Bristol Mirror*, 10 June 1843; Combe St Nicholas (F 262): *Western Gazette*, 22 April 1892; Curry Mallet (F 250): *Western Gazette*, 9 June 1911; Kilve (F 159 & F 160): *West Somerset Free Press*, 20 May 1882; Sturminster Newton (F 256): *Sherborne, Dorchester and Taunton Journal*, 18 June 1835; Bishops Hull (F 207): *Western Gazette*, 9 June 1865.

(20) Sherborne: F 025/1 & 2; Marnhull: F 092/1; Templecombe: F 093; Crowcombe: F 041; Dowlish Wake: F 042.

(21) Kilve (Putsham): F 159 & F 160; Ring of Bells / Five Bells: F026; Kingswood: F 168/1; Zeals: F 043.

(22) Ponsonby-Fane, Sir Spencer, Club Pole Heads 1 (bound and illustrated with drawings), c.1910, MERL, Reading, and Club Pole Heads 2 (bound and illustrated with drawings), c.1910, The Box, Plymouth; Hooper, H J, The Red Book, entitled 'Village Emblems (Club Brasses) in the Holburne Museum' (bound and illustrated with photographs), c.1920, Holburne Museum, Bath; Kelway, James, The Kelway Notebook, (bound and illustrated with drawings), c. 1930, Taunton Museum archives, SHC; Jardine, Sir John, notes, MERL, D85/12.

5

From society emblems to collectors' trophies

Decline in the use of poles and pole heads

As with the affiliated orders, so too with the unitary societies, the love of display palled to some extent. Club walking started to diminish after the 1860s. Part of this was due to the smaller clubs ceasing to exist, having become victims to financial decline because of the ageing of the membership and the inevitably increasing demands for sickness benefits. Some societies drew to a close because their members had transferred their allegiance to branches of the affiliated orders. Other societies, however, which had abandoned club walking, found that they had underestimated the social value of the whole routine: in 1866 the Puckington and Stocklinch society re-introduced their feast-day, with its associated club walking, many years after having abandoned their 'club poles, brasses, banners, and ribbons'. They found that the revival did wonders for re-establishing recruitment. A similar situation occurred in Yeovil in 1880, and possibly elsewhere, but by this time fewer new unitary societies were being created which could engage in the old ritual of processing with their club sticks [1].

While difficult to prove, it is likely from the frequency of newspaper accounts of club walks that pole-carrying reached its zenith in the 1860s. Thereafter the number of unitary societies gradually declined, with an abrupt drop in 1912 when National Insurance was introduced. Pole-carrying anniversary celebrations had already been reduced to some 30 Somerset societies by 1910, and then to just 14 by 1930, when members of clubs such as Aller, Curry Rivel, Fivehead and Henstridge still polished the brass tops of their poles and processed in the time-honoured fashion. Even after the Second World War just a handful of societies continued to display their poles at club walks: the Westbury-sub-Mendip club resumed its annual walk after its break for the war years, as did the Henton Friendly Society, for a short time. Beyond the Somerset boundary a very few societies had kept up the custom of displaying their brass pole tops at their club walks: the practice was observed in the 1930s at Kentisbeare and Talaton in Devon, and at Bradford Abbas and Litton Cheney in Dorset. Of these, only Bradford Abbas lasted beyond 1950 [2].

The Sidney Vaux collection (dispersed).

40

Even fewer clubs survived into the twenty-first century, by which time their benefit function had become practically insignificant: the custom was maintained essentially for its social value to the village concerned. Examples include the pole-carrying clubs at Henton and Stoke Abbott, but in some cases while the club still walked, the members had no poles. At Wincanton, where pole-carrying had once been commonplace, pole heads had become such a rarity even as early as 1914 that it was seen fit to draw attention to the 'two ancient club spears' that were on parade. Similarly, at Witham Friary the society was reduced to just one 'spear' by 1937, as was Long Sutton. Priddy, too, eventually could only muster one of its bed-knob pattern of pole heads. Only at Westbury were pole heads to be seen in any quantity: in 1951 many members carried 'their spear-headed staves, each of which was surmounted with a red, white and blue tassel'. The nosegay-carrying women's society at Nether Stowey also kept up an annual walk, but this was long after it had ceased to function as a benefit club. In the rest of Britain beyond Somerset very few societies adhered to the pole carrying tradition after the Second World War [3].

Friendly society pole head collections.

Many societies which had carried brass pole heads came to an end several decades before enthusiasts started their collecting habit. Although the final year for a club is often very difficult to establish, a rough idea of the demise of the carrying of brass pole heads can nevertheless be suggested. From the scant data available a trend can be discerned: in Somerset and the core area up to the middle of the nineteenth century when one unitary society in a settlement collapsed it was generally replaced by another of the same type. After this time, however, the combined effects of population stagnation in much of Somerset and the growing popularity of the affiliated orders meant that many unitary societies came to an end without revival. At least two brass pole head carrying societies ended in the 1840s, three in the 1850s, fourteen in the 1860s and 15 in the 1870s.

Fortunately for collectors, families which had been connected with the failed clubs often retained their pole heads out of sentiment, although gradually many of them parted with these heirlooms to collectors and dealers, for a price. Collecting brass pole heads would seem to have coincided with the progressive abandonment of the once more widespread practice of carrying them in procession. The first hint of what became a popular collecting hobby was recorded in 1887 when Dr Frederick Porter Smith, president of the Shepton Mallet Natural History Society, gave the members a short talk about friendly societies and their pole heads. He had on display at the meeting 'a number of village club spear heads' from his own collection, including the magnificent specimen shown at number F 099/2. Dr Smith travelled widely around the area in his professional capacity and amongst other roles he was the elected surgeon to six local friendly societies. It seems that some of his pole heads were subsequently bought by the Wainwright family, estate agents also of Shepton Mallet, and in 1971 this collection, too, was sold and dispersed.

A second medical practitioner, Dr Thomas Hopkins of Burnham, was starting to build up a collection at about the same time as Dr Smith, having been introduced to the hobby by yet another professional colleague, Dr Charles MacVicker of Street. Dr MacVicker's collection of well over 100 items was sold and dispersed after his death in 1927, but Dr Hopkins himself had given up collecting many years previously, and in 1907 sold the bulk of his collection, amounting to 164 pole heads, to Taunton Museum. For a long time they formed the major portion of the museum's large holding of pole heads. By around 1910 Taunton, together with Wells, had the largest collections in the public domain. It appears that the none of the three doctors published anything about their collections, nor did they leave any manuscript notes [4].

Doctors evidently had the means and opportunity to collect pole heads from around the rural areas, but so too did those who possessed the finance for such a hobby and the facilities for hunting down their quarry. WB Broadmead of Enmore Castle, landowner, magistrate and local politician, was a late nineteenth century collector, and he generously donated 34 pole heads to Taunton Museum in 1906, thus anticipating the Hopkins purchase and forming the museum's first holding in this field. At Brympton, near Yeovil, Sir Spencer Ponsonby-Fane, landowner, courtier and diplomat, must have started his collection in the 1880s and eventually his haul ran to nearly 400 specimens. Around 100 of his collection, essentially the duplicates, were donated in 1936 to Plymouth Museum by one of his sons, while the remaining major portion was sold at auction by his heirs in 1951. Fortunately this part of the collection was not entirely scattered: nearly 100 of the Ponsonby-Fane hoard were kept together and in 2018 were obtained by Taunton Museum under the Sir Edward Du Cann bequest. Ponsonby-Fane was one of the earliest popularising writers on the subject of local friendly societies and pole head collecting, having contributed two articles to the 'Connoisseur' in 1909 and 1913. His two hand-illustrated note books are a most helpful source of information on the pole heads that he had acquired. He and his family lent these books to other collectors such as CR Wainwright and AW Allen for inspection, thus circulating his particular claims for the provenance of his items [5].

By 1908 Taunton Museum, with its two large display cases of brasses, had acquired a reputation as a centre of information for verifying and identifying pole heads. Its reputation in this respect was greatly enhanced when William Wyndham of Orchard Wyndham, landowner and philanthropist, purchased the entire 200-strong collection of James Kelway in 1932. He presented it to the museum on the understanding that duplicates would be shared with other museums. Kelway, a nurseryman from Langport, had been obliged to sell his pole heads when in financial difficulty due to foreign competition in his business. Unlike the slow accumulation of some of the other collectors of his era, he had managed to pick up his specimens in under two and a half years, between 1907 and 1910, and by his own admission 'this quest has carried many people during the last few years to the quaintest of old places'. Kelway, too, helped to spread knowledge about pole heads, through his 1910 article in 'Country Life', and his valuable annotated and hand-illustrated catalogue of his collection was lodged with Taunton Museum [6].

In Bristol the antique dealer HJ Hooper was a source for several of the early collectors, but he also collected on his own account, and was clearly interested in provenance, since his amendments found their way into museum lists such as at Taunton and the V & A. His notebook, illustrated with photographs of his collection of some 136 items, has survived at the Holburne Museum at Bath, which bought his pole heads in 1922: Hooper had been collecting for about twenty years [7].

In Bath by 1911 the Rev Charles Shickle had already assembled, exhibited and lectured on friendly society pole heads and had written articles on the subject. Unusually, he appears to have had little contact with other enthusiasts. In 1928 his collection of over 250 was bequeathed to the Victoria and Albert Museum where for some time it was put on display. In 1951, however, it was at first loaned and later transferred by the V & A to the newly formed Museum of English Rural Life at Reading. While the collection has many rare specimens it also includes some very dubious items [8].

The Reading museum soon afterwards purchased the A Wydville Allen's collection of around 400 pole heads, which had been assembled between the 1920s and the 1940s while Allen was living in Butleigh Wootton, and where he was well-known to the majority of other serious collectors. Allen had an extensive knowledge of the subject, he helped to catalogue the Wells Museum collections, and he had a hand in amending the records of most other museum collections as well. Nevertheless, his notes are less illuminating than they should have been, since they omit proof of provenance in the majority of cases [9].

The circuit of collectors was tight-knit, and Allen was in touch with most of them, including Sir John Jardine, who ran factories for lace-making machinery and typewriters in Nottingham and later in Shepton Mallet, and who in 1908 had moved from the Midlands to Glastonbury with his father, who was about to become MP for East Somerset. Jardine proved to be the most thorough of the early collectors in trying to establish provenances for his collection of over 250 specimens, particularly in the 1930s and early 1940s. In many cases he was just in time to glean accurate first-hand information from Somerset sources. He systematically wrote to a great many local clergy for information and received some valuable pieces of information in return. More significantly, he recorded his findings meticulously. Jardine eventually moved back to Nottingham and donated his pole heads to the museum there in 1947, but they were later transferred to Reading in 1961 [10].

The Jardine family were known to the Le Gros family of Frome, who had taken over their Shepton Mallet factory in 1928. Like the Jardines, they were also manufacturers in the textile industry: the founder's son, P Edgar Le Gros, built up an array of over 200 pole heads, probably from about 1900 to 1930. Prior to his death in 1931, Edgar had bequeathed his collection to the Society of Somerset Folk in Bristol, who in turn first loaned and then transferred them to the Blaise Castle House Museum. Although usually ascribed a location, the items in the Le Gros listings have virtually no proof of provenance, which is unfortunate, given the uniqueness of many of the specimens [11].

Le Gros had dealings with many other collectors, including the Wainwrights, father and son, auctioneers, of Shepton Mallet. CR Wainwright, the father, had started the collection in small way, and his son, also CR Wainwright, added to it, mainly in the decade before the First World War. The collection of around 200 had some unusual specimens. In 1971 it was for a very short time on display at Frome Museum, and later for two months in the autumn at the short-lived Phillips Museum at Brokerswood. Some research done by the museum organiser claimed to reveal some provenances, but these only amounted to sixteen out of the whole collection, and in any case the details and proof were not given. The collection was auctioned in 1974 and purchased as a single lot, but the subsequent destination of the items has not come to light [12].

In 1895 P Edgar Le Gros had been a groomsman at the wedding of another significant collector, E Harold Caley, who was a bank employee at various Somerset locations, eventually retiring as a branch manager at Clifton. His frequent career relocations provided him many opportunities to make useful contacts in the county – and it is on record that he knew not just Le Gros, but had come across other collectors including Wainwright and Hooper. In 1907 he had sufficient to show a few of his pole heads at a meeting in Shepton Mallet and eventually his collection topped the eighty mark. His widow presented eighteen of the rarest ones to Taunton Museum in 1940 in his memory: the destination of the remainder is not recorded [13].

There were a few other collectors of late-nineteenth to mid-twentieth century, many of whom donated several pole heads each to local museums, but almost without exception the items were presented with little helpful information as to their origin. Whereas the early collectors were mostly well-known to each other, and acquired and swapped brasses among themselves, they nevertheless were still able to obtain several of their trophies from primary sources. Later collectors, however, were simply recycling pole heads which had long since left their place of origin, and though several of them donated to museums, the provenances were mostly unstated, and few of their gifts were anything other than duplicates of material already in the public domain. Nevertheless, there remain a few extant private collections which include important pole heads not seen elsewhere, and very occasionally these holdings include bona fide evidence linking the items to their original place of use.

It will be seen from the foregoing accounts of the early collectors that the museum acquisitions of their friendly society materials were essentially a matter of receiving in their near entirety the collections of enthusiasts, not all of whom had kept reliable records. Except for the efforts of the first curator of Taunton Museum, Harold StG Gray, no museum officials systematically set out to fill the gaps in their holdings, but simply relied on what came through their doors. Moreover, since the aim of each of the private collectors was to find one of as many of all the different types of pole heads as were available, the result was that when a museum received a second or third donation or purchase there was bound to be a very great number of duplicates. The museums at Taunton and Reading both have collections approaching one thousand pole heads, but their unique items form only a minority of their holdings. The problem was compounded when in the 1980s there was a vogue for inter-county swaps, so Taunton museum, for example, was given back many of the already duplicated Somerset specimens which it had so carefully dispersed to other locations in 1932.

By around the mid-1960s the major collections had already come into the public domain, but it was unfortunate that several museums were far from meticulous in their keeping of detailed records of what was known about each specimen. All too often an assumed village location was recorded on a pole head label, simply because another similar one was already so described, and little information was included save the name of the location: the titles of the actual societies which had used them were given scant attention. The temptation to transfer a name to a specimen which did not have any accompanying details of its own was seldom resisted. The V & A list of the Shickle collection, and the many-times revised Taunton list, mainly updated by Harold St George Gray, were generally adopted as guides in this process: both had sets of accompanying photographs. When a far more exhaustive list was produced in Margaret Fuller's 1964 publication, it soon replaced the other two sources as the standard reference text. Nevertheless even this source did not solve the problem of properly identifying pole heads. Its main shortcoming was its over-reliance on the items in the Allen collection, many of which had suggested provenances, but too many of these were unsubstantiated [14].

Displays of large numbers of pole heads were once to be seen in the museums where the early collections were lodged, but the changing fashion towards a more concise presentation of ideas has resulted in the packing away of the bulk of museum collections of pole heads.

Lists of pole heads with their provenances

The earliest systematic attempt to make lists of the provenance of pole heads and to ensure that the results were open to inspection was undertaken by Harold St George Gray, curator of the Taunton Museum. In 1907 Dr Hopkins' collection of 164 brasses had been purchased, and with it came suggested identifications for some of the specimens, besides seven sheets of photographs. This collection formed the source for the Taunton list which was made available to collectors on request. Over the years the contents were revised many times, almost always with no indication as to the basis on which amendments and new identifications were made: some archival material, however, has survived in the museum, enabling limited checks to be made. A W Allen, whose collection was bought by the Museum of English Rural Life at Reading, was one of those who had a hand in updating the Taunton lists. Allen himself left a few notes of his own research, but while he may have had adequate proof of provenance of the items in his collection to his own satisfaction, unfortunately his claims cannot all be substantiated and must be treated as unproven [15].

Another list available for consultation came from the Reverend Charles Shickle of Bath who, like Hopkins, had amassed one of the largest early collections. His notes were subsequently lost, but the list accompanied the collection when it was bequeathed to the V and A in 1928 . At some later stage the collector and antique dealer H J Hooper was allowed by the V and A to amend their accession copy of the list – which was done without any indication of the proof behind the amendments, nor of which alterations had been made by Hooper. The list was held at the V&A and from 1951 could also be seen at the Museum of English Rural Life [16].

The Fuller catalogue of 1964

Up until 1964 there was no published listing of friendly society pole heads and searchers had to rely on copies of the lists from Taunton and the V&A. The situation changed when Margaret Fuller became involved in the subject in the 1950s. The Allen Collection had been exhibited at Reading University Library in 1951, and was purchased by the Museum of English Rural Life in 1955. It subsequently formed the focus of study by Fuller for her 1958 MA thesis and she published her findings in 1964, with few changes, as 'West Country Friendly Societies'. It was undoubtedly a pioneering study at the time: there were no other systematic accounts of unitary societies available, nor any published account to record their pole heads [17].

Unfortunately the Fuller illustrated list of 333 different specimens is very far from complete. Her catalogue was largely based on items from the Allen collection, yet she ignored 43 quite distinct varieties of pole head from this source which should have been included. Despite the transfer of the Shickle collection in 1951 from the V&A to MERL, where Fuller was later employed, and despite the museum's further acquisition of the Jardine collection in 1961, she only used some of their different varieties of pole heads, and omitted a further 33 from the two sources; she stuck to the Allen collection for four fifths of her total specimens. She also incorporated 18 pole heads from other museums which she visited, and 25 from private collections, but once again there were a great many unusual designs which she did not include: she omitted 77 such specimens from the museums, and 6 from the private collections. With the inclusion of specimens omitted by Fuller, and with the addition of those from new sources, the current list of different patterns of pole heads has been expanded from Fuller's 333 items to a new total of 687. It is likely that there are still others to be revealed.

As for the identification of where all these specimens were used, Fuller seems to have almost entirely relied on the locations as suggested by the lists accompanying the various collections. Consequently, since the majority of Fuller's selection came from the Allen collection at Reading, with its general lack of proof of provenance, the validity of many of the claims in her catalogue is open to question. Those which she included from other museums were hardly any better in terms of reliable provenances, with many specimens having over the years lost their labels or in a great many cases having been donated without any recorded background detail.

Since its 1964 publication Fuller's book has formed the only reference source readily available for museums and collectors alike to identify where the pole head specimens were used, and in a few cases, the actual society to which they belonged. To such an extent did the work subsequently become a standard that in some museums the specimens bearing their original labels and provenances were even relabelled with the Fuller identifications, while other specimens, which had been furnished with no provenance at all by their original donors, were labelled with the Fuller identification as if this were the true origin of the brass.

More of Fuller's suggested identifications might yet prove to be correct, but since she did not cross-check many of the unconfirmed opinions of Allen and others, their reliability must be challenged. Unfortunately, also, a few actual errors have crept in, and these have been spread and perpetuated through their inclusion on the specimen labels of some public collections.

The Portobello collection (dispersed).

The need to make available a more inclusive list of friendly society pole heads and to improve their identification is the reason behind the present catalogue.

The Fuller listing revised

Since the Fuller classification of patterns and her numbering system have become so widely accepted, the current listing keeps the Fuller numbers intact. Specimens not recorded in the original list have been examined to find the most similar pattern, and then inserted immediately following. Thus, to give a hypothetical example, in the Fuller series, between numbers 10 and 15, the figures are first redesignated F 010, F 011, F 012, F 013, F 014 and F 015, and then, supposing there were one extra specimen similar to F 011, and three extras similar to F 013, the new series would be amended to read: F 010, F 011/1, F 011/2, F 012, F 013/1, F 013/2, F 013/3, F 013/4, F 014, F 015. The original Fuller numbers have thus only been slightly modified. If an item has been inserted after Fuller's number 11, for example, this number is first restated as F 011 and then it is further distinguished by an additional identifier, thus becoming F 011/1. In this way the integrity of the original scheme has been retained.

Where a design has been verified for a particular society, the entries in the current catalogue show the society and its location in bold type. Where only the location can be proved for a pole head, but which society used it is unknown, the location alone is shown in bold type. Unconfirmed suggestions are shown as 'not verified' for that place, while specimens with no background information at all are also shown with the phrase 'not verified'. Further details, including the basis for verification, are included.

The original Fuller lists excluded pole heads used by the affiliated orders: these, and a handful of others which resemble friendly society pole heads are added at the end of the current list, and are in the miscellaneous categories labelled M/Axe, M/Crook, M/Crown, M/glass, M/Javelin, M/Mace, M/Sickle, and M/Various. These entries are not intended to cover all the pole head designs of the non-unitary societies, but they include a wide range of items found in various collections. A representative sample of generic flag pole and banner tops used by friendly societies, trade unions, or other organisations is included in the miscellaneous section.

References:

(1) Puckington and Stocklinch: *Western Gazette*, 20 July 1866; Yeovil: *Western Gazette*, 21 May 1880.

(2) SHC Tite papers, 1910 and 1930 lists of friendly societies; Westbury-sub-Mendip *Wells Journal*, 25 May 1951; Henton: *Wells Journal*, 14 June 1946; Kentisbeare: The National Archives, FS 15/1626; Talaton: *Western Times*, 2 June 1939; Bradford Abbas: Garnett, Eric, *Bradford Abbas, the History of a Dorset Village*, Sparkford, 1989, pp 222 – 228; Litton Cheney: *Western Gazette*, 6 August 1848.

(3) Wincanton: *Western Chronicle*, 12 June 1914; Witham Friary: *Bath Chronicle*, 23 January 1937; Long Sutton: Smith, EA, *The Story of Long Sutton*, n.d., p.34; Priddy: Thompson, Albert, *The Book of Priddy*, Tiverton, 2000, p.132; Westbury-sub-Mendip: *Wells Journal*, 9 June 1950; Nether Stowey Female Friendly Society: *Taunton Courier*, 24 June 1950.

(4) *Shepton Mallet Journal*, 16 December 1887; Wainwright Collection of Friendly Society Brasses: Christie's Sale Catalogue, 14 November 1974; *Taunton Courier*, 1 April 1914; *Wells Journal*, 2 March 1945; Somerset Heritage Centre, Day Book 2, January and March 1907.

(5) Somerset Heritage Centre, Day Book 2, 2 November 1906; Carter, Charles, Village Pole Heads, *The Bazaar Exchange & Mart*, 4 August 1936, pp. 1 & 2; Sale Catalogue, Yeovil, 1956, Museum of English Rural Life, D 35/11 no.4; Somerset Heritage Centre, Sir Edward du Cann collection of friendly society brasses, accessioned 2018; Ponsonby-Fane, Sir Spencer, Club Pole Heads in Somerset, *The Connoisseur*, vol XVII, April 1907, pp. 256 to 262, and Somerset Friendly Society Pole Heads, *The Connoisseur*, Extra Christmas Number, vol XXXVII, 1913, pp. 61 to 70; Ponsonby-Fane, Sir Spencer, Club Pole-Heads, book 1, Museum of English Rural Life, D 35 No 11, and book 2, The Box, Plymouth, no catalogue number; Letter from Charles Wainwright, 25 June 1915, acknowledging the loan, also from AW Allen, 1914, Museum of English Rural Life, D85/11/1.

(6) Taunton Museum report for 1907: *Taunton Courier*, 15 January 1908; Somerset Heritage Centre, Club Brass Collection Accession note books, vol III, 1932, p.162: '224 brasses: 96 retained and 128 sent to other museums'; Kelway, James, Head-hunting: a west country hobby, *Country Life*, vol XXVII, no.678, pp.27 to 29; Somerset Heritage Centre: The Kelway notebook.

(7) Hooper, HJ, Collection of Friendly Society Brasses, *The Red Book*, Holburne Museum.

(8) Shickle Rev CW, Lecture: *Bath Chronicle*, 24 March 1910, and Exhibition: *Bath Chronicle*, 28 September 1911; Shickle collection: V & A Museum catalogue, register numbers M 555 to 809 - 1928, pp 178 to 185, Collection of 255 Brass Staff-heads received 27 June 1928.

(9) Purchase of AW Allen collection, *Reading Standard*, 5 August 1955; Letter to AW Allen from AT Wicks, 18 November 1937, Museum of English Rural Life, Classified Information / Societies and Associations / AW Allen.

(10) Notes accompanying the Jardine Collection, Museum of English Rural Life, D/DX 993 and D/DX 1783; Jardine collection purchase: the items were accessioned in 1961 but not finalised until 1999.

(11) PE Le Gros exchanged brasses with Taunton Museum in 1907: Somerset Heritage Centre, Taunton Museum Accessions Book, vol II, pp.88 & 89; *Western Daily Press*, 4 March 1931.

(12) Overend, Eunice, ed., Catalogue of the Wainwright Collection of Friendly Society Brasses, The Phillips Museum, Brokerswood (defunct), Autumn 1971, p.1; The Wainwright collection was exhibited in Frome Museum in 1971: *Somerset Standard*, 11 June 1971; Sale of the Wainwright collection: Christie's, Auction catalogue 'English and Continental Oak, etc.', 14 November 1974, pp.23 – 26; The auction price was just over £4000: *Bristol Evening Post*, 15 November 1974.

(13) *Clifton Society*, 19 September 1895; At the Shepton Mallet Natural History Society meeting in July 1907 Caley exhibited some pole heads: present at the meeting were Wainwright and Hooper: *Shepton Mallet Journal*, 12 July 1907; Caley donation: *Taunton Courier*, 10 Aug 1940.

(14) Fuller, MD, *West Country Friendly Societies*, Reading, 1964.

(15) Taunton Museum Day Book 2 (dated entries of acquisitions), and St George Gray, H, lists of club brasses (initially handwritten and later typed: all undated), Taunton Museum archives, SHC; Allen, A W, The Allen Collection of Friendly Society Emblems, (typescript essay, and list of 304 items with subsequent additions, c.1955), MERL.

(16) Shickle collection: V & A Museum catalogue, register numbers M 555 to 809, pp 178 to 185, entitled 'Collection of 255 Brass Staff-heads', received 27 June 1928, with accompanying photographs, and comment indicating that Hooper had made alterations.

(17) Fuller, M D, *West Country Friendly Societies*, unpublished MA thesis, University of Reading, 1958; Fuller, M D, *West Country Friendly Societies*, Reading, 1964.

Catalogue

F 001

F 001   8.3″   SHC / OSFS / 097

This pattern is verified for **Kilmersdon Friendly Society (Old Club)** (1840 or earlier to 1876) (unregistered), which met at the Gauntlett Inn (*Frome Times*, June 12th, 1861). Details of the club are given in the notes of S Lloyd Harvey, March 22nd, 1926 (SHC Taunton Museum archives), who included a drawing of a specimen engraved 'H' (for Henry Hill, a former member). This actual brass was presented to Taunton Museum by the latter's son. Another two specimens were seen in Kilmersdon by Lloyd Harvey c.1926. The design is illustrated in *Down Hoame*, Barney Hodges, Folk Press, n.d., title page. The inside of the socket is tapped.

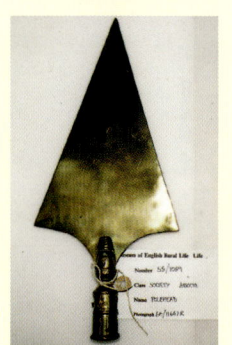

F 002/1

F 002/1   11.1″   MERL / Allen / 551059

Allen, the original collector of this specimen, stated that it is a flag pole top from Stoke St Michael (Stoke Lane), but he offered no evidence. The pattern, however, more closely resembles a member's brass from Kilmersdon (F 001), and may be a steward's version from that society.

F 002/2   23″   SHC / OSFS / 726

This unique specimen is verified for **Kilmersdon Church Friendly Society** (1856 to 1913: registered in 1861) (SOM 709), which met at the School Room. It was designed for the Church Club by Charles F Evans, son of the Master of Kilmersdon Endowed School, and was last carried at Queen Victoria's Diamond Jubilee celebrations on June 27th, 1897 (SHC Taunton Museum archives, letter and drawing, S Lloyd Harvey 1927). The top part was based on the Kilmersdon Old Friendly Society design (F 001).

F 002/2

F 002/3   7.5″   MERL / Allen / 551137

Allen attributed this design to Paulton, but without evidence. One side is inscribed 'RB', suggesting a member's brass and not a flagpole top. The Taunton example (SCH OSFS 149), plain on both sides, is attributed to Paulton, but again without evidence.

F 003/1   3.8″   MERL / Allen / 55105

Allen, the original collector, attributed this specimen to Kingsbury Episcopi Women's Society, but there is no evidence. There are no rule-book references nor any newspaper accounts of women members carrying poles. As only this one example has been found, it is therefore unlikely to have been an ordinary member's brass, and may have been a flagpole- or banner-top, or a stewards' brass. In this women's society the stewards' roles were occupied by men, and Allen claimed that it was they who carried brass pole heads (MERL: Introductory essay to the Allen Collection). The design and mounting of this pole head is very simple: it may be a one-off locally made item.

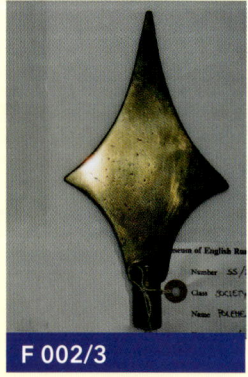

F 002/3

F 003/1

Seavington Friendly Society, c.1910: F 004/2.

F 003/2   7.6"   MERL / Allen / 550942

No evidence has been seen for this specimen, which may possibly be a cut-down brass. One face is inscribed 'JPP', suggesting that it was not originally a flagpole top, despite its appearance.

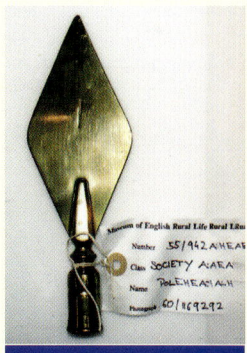

F 003/2

F 003/3   9.25"   Wells and Mendip Museum / Box 196

No evidence has been seen to associate this specimen with Clutton. Identical examples are in the SHC (OSFS 703) and in MERL (Shickle 510893), where the design is tentatively ascribed to Clutton, but without any evidence. It may not be a member's brass, but on account of its shape it may instead be a flag pole top from Clutton or from any other club.

F 004/1   9.2"   MERL / Allen / 55086

This design was used by **South Petherton Labourers' Friendly Society** (established 1786, re-established in 1843 and 1852, and ceased after 1912) (unregistered), which met at the Bell Inn and the Crown Inn. The Ponsonby-Fane notebook at MERL, p 47, no 3, states 'from Mrs Hoskins, who had it from the man who carried it [at South Petherton]'. The SHC (Taunton Museum) Day-Book 2, July 2nd, 1907, states 'given by Hugh Norris, Hon. Member of South Petherton Labourers' Benefit Society, established 1852' (specimen OSFS 505). Both of these sources indicate the same pattern as the one shown here. Allen attributed this brass to Seavington, but Fuller (1964) also includes South Petherton and Lopen. Allen had a second, near-identical specimen of 9.4" (551046), which he attributed to Lopen, but without any evidence. *The Chard and Ilminster News*, June 2nd, 1877, referring to the Seavington St Michael Friendly Society, reported that: '[the] club pole tipped with a brass spear shone brightly'.

F 003/3

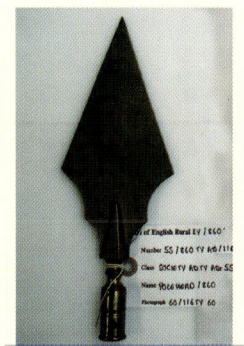

F 004/1

F 004/2   8.8"   Holburne Museum / VE050

This design was used by **Lopen Seven Year Society** (1852 to 1911) (unregistered). A brass similar to the one illustrated is stamped 'Noah Long 1863' (MERL Forster 55234). This member lived at Lopen, was 16 in 1861, and was a sailcloth labourer. The Lopen society members were recorded as each carrying a 'blue pole with a spiked head' (*Western Gazette*, June 4th, 1880). **Seavington Friendly Society** (1820 to c.1911), which met at the Volunteer Arms, had 'poles with brass tips' (*Somerset County Gazette*, June 2nd, 1900), and they are seen indistinctly in fig 107, *Victorian and Edwardian Somerset from Old Photographs*, David Bromwich and Robert Dunning, 1997, and more clearly in the corresponding glass negative photograph from the Vaux collection (SHC). There are many variants of F 004, ranging from 8.75" to 10.5" high and with a wide variety of sockets. The major distinction is the blade shape. F 004/2 has a concave lower edge where the blade joins the socket.

F 004/2

F 004/3   10.5"   Dorset Museum, Dorchester / R.1991.273.10

This variant may be from Lopen, South Petherton, or Seavington, but there is no clear evidence. South Petherton Labourers' Friendly Society was established in 1786, re-established in 1843 and 1852, and ceased after 1912 (unregistered). Lopen Seven Year Society existed between 1852 and 1911 (unregistered). Seavington Friendly Society lasted from 1820 to c.1911 (unregistered). Lopen members each carried a 'blue pole with a spike-shaped head' (*Western Gazette*, June 4th, 1880), while Seavington had 'poles with brass tips' (*Somerset County Gazette*, June 2nd, 1900). The Seavington design is indistinctly shown in illustration no.107, *Victorian and Edwardian Somerset from Old Photographs*, David Bromwich and Robert Dunning, 1998, and more clearly in the corresponding glass negative photograph from the Vaux collection (SHC). There are many variants of F 004/1, 2, and 3, from 8.75" to 10.5" in height, and with a wide variety of sockets. The major distinction is in the pattern of the blade. The design shown here has the scalloped edges on each side in the lower third (rather than half) of the blade, and an extended straight upper edge. This type tends to be taller than most others.

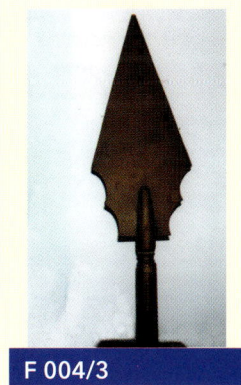

F 004/3

F 005/1

F 005/2

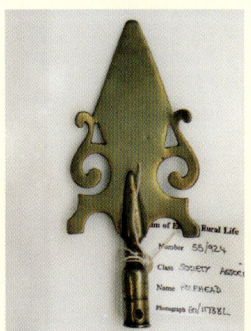

F 006

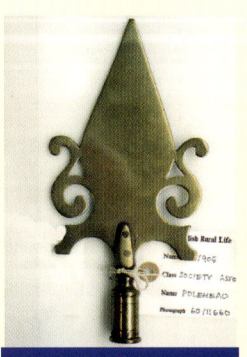

F 007/1

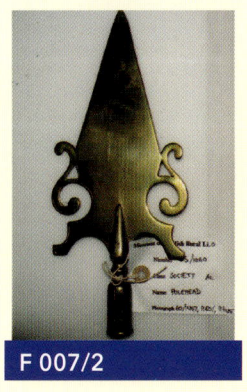

F 007/2

F 005/1   6.9"   MERL / Allen / 550916

This design is verified for **Stourton Caundle Union Friendly Society (Blues of the Vale)** (1836 to 1911) (DOR 028), which met at the Trooper Inn in 1861 (*Sherborne, Dorchester and Taunton Journal*, June 6th, 1861) and later at the Parish School Room. In a letter to AW Allen dated January 18th, 1937, AT Wicks wrote: 'my father (who dealt in antiques) got dozens of this small head from Stourton Caundle'. The Stourton Caundle pole head is the smallest type of this pattern (F 005/1 to F 009/5) (MERL Classified Index of societies and associations). Twenty-eight nearly identical Stourton Caundle brasses have been recorded, ranging from 6.75" to 6.9". This general pattern, with arabesque arms and splayed 'feet', was a most popular design, with specimens from other clubs measuring up to 17.2". Distinguishing stewards' from members' brasses is a major difficulty.

F 005/2   7.2"   Private collection

No evidence has emerged for this pattern. This is the most common of the flat brass designs, and it comes with various heights. Early collectors and museums suggested many places for which no satisfactory proof has emerged, including Clutton, Dunkerton, Henton, High Littleton, Longwell Green, South Brewham, Wanstrow and Wells. Rule books, documents and newspapers offer no clues. The heights of the brasses of this general pattern tend to cluster at certain values, suggesting that a particular height is associated with a particular club or clubs. In this instance, for example, there are five brasses recorded that cluster in the range from 7" to 7.2", but they have so far not been definitively linked to just one society.

F 006   7.4"   MERL / Allen / 550924

This design is verified for **Portishead Friendly Society** (1824 to 1885) (SOM 472), which met at the Anchor Inn. The writer A.E.S., 'More Somerset Brasses', *Somerset Year Book*, 1936, vol XXXV, p.100, illustrates a specimen, carried c.1850 by W Crease, native of Portishead, grandfather of VJ Davis, the owner, and a letter from AE Stephens, Chewton Rd, Keynsham, gives the same provenance, but a height of 7.75". Ten examples have been seen between 7.2" and 7.8". Whether the Portishead stewards had larger brasses is difficult to determine, as such brasses would perhaps have been of similar size to members' brasses of a different club. The stewards' brasses may, however, have been distinguished in some manner other than by size.

F 007/1   8.6"   MERL / Allen / 550905

Allen suggested Dunkerton for this design, but he provided no evidence. There were two Dunkerton societies, Dunkerton Friendly Society (1794 to pre-1813) (SOM 073) and Dunkerton United Friendly Society (1823 to after 1860) (SOM 078), but neither of these has evidence for the use of poles. Four 8.6" brasses have been recorded, all having the same breadth to height proportions. Characteristic shapes can be distinguished: this particular type shows a relatively large breadth to height ratio, which is obvious even despite small differences in dimensions attributable to hand crafting.

F 007/2   9.9"   MERL / Allen / 551060

Allen did not suggest any particular location for this specimen. This general design was ascribed by early collectors and museums to many places but without sufficient proof, including Clutton, Dunkerton, Henton, High Littleton, Longwell Green, South Brewham, Wanstrow and Wells. Rule books, documents and newspapers offer no clues. This design is the most commonly found flat brass and it occurs in a range of heights from 6.75" to a massive 17.2". There is also a large variation in the height to width ratio for the various sizes. Most of the different sizes are unidentified. A few are probably stewards' brasses similar to the smaller brasses used by members. To distinguish pole heads belonging to different clubs the height frequencies can be analysed, and clusters appear at a variety of different values.

F 008   10.8″   MERL / Allen / 550831

This design has been verified for **West Cranmore** but not for Wanstrow (as was suggested by Allen). **The Friendly Society of Sundry Trades and Callings at West Cranmore** (1798 to 1812 and possibly to 1855) (SOM 441), later called **Cranmore Provident Society** (1855 to after 1908) (unregistered), initially met 'at Mr William Brown's, and later at the Schoolroom. A specimen in a private collection is inscribed 'WCC' (West Cranmore Club) and is described in the SHC Hopkins catalogue end notes: 'height c.10½ inches'. It was also described by Alfred W Lintern, of Dean, Shepton Mallet, as 'W Cranmore, defunct', and by Arthur Stubbs (letter, c.1932, MERL Jardine Index). The design feature that distinguishes this type, apart from the height (10.5″ to 10.75″), is the relatively short socket, at the top of which (but below the flat face of the brass) is a waist, on which the usual included knop is lacking.

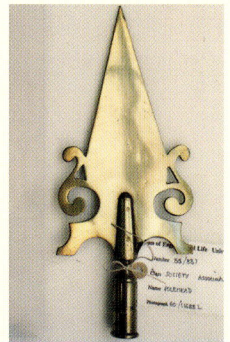

F 008

F 009/1   11.8″   MERL / Allen / 550828

This design is verified for **Farmborough**, but no satisfactory evidence has emerged for Allen's suggestion of High Littleton. **Farmborough Friendly Society** (1794 to 1839) (SOM 099), (1839 to 1864) (SOM 617), (1864 to 1893) (unregistered) met at the Bell Inn. A second unregistered club of unrecorded duration also started in 1864. There is evidence that brasses of this outline and size were used at Farmborough: on December 17th, 1929, S Lloyd Harvey wrote to Taunton Museum, and included a tracing of the brass belonging to Mr Fred Viner of Farmborough, of the **Bell Inn Village Club** (established in 1839 and ceased in 1893) (SHC Taunton Museum archives). The specimen is inscribed 'James Wiatt', but his name has not been traced in the 19th century censuses.

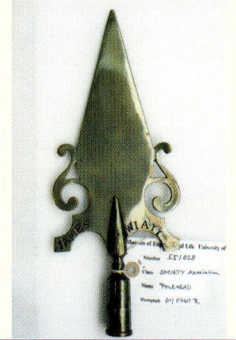

F 009/1

F 009/2   12.3″   MERL / Allen / 550822

No evidence has been seen for this specimen, and Allen did not suggest any provenance. It is unclear whether this is a member's brass or a steward's brass.

F 009/3   12.9″   Wells / Club brass 699

The photograph in the Wells and Mendip Museum display of Club Brasses confirms this pattern as the one used by the Henton Club, but the size of the pole head cannot be determined. Henton Friendly Society was revived in 1882, and lasted until after 1939 (unregistered). In 1934 the members of the Henton Friendly Society were recorded as 'carrying spears' (Western Gazette, May 25th, 1934). The large height of this specimen suggests that it is a steward's brass. Only two larger examples are known.

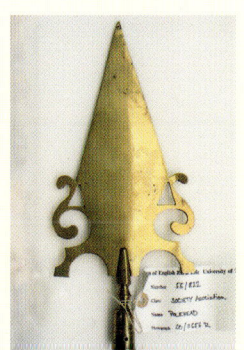

F 009/2

F 009/4   13.5″   Private collection

No evidence has been seen to identify where this pattern with this particular height was used. Apart from the provenances which have been proved for Stourton Caundle, Portishead, West Cranmore and Farmborough, this general pattern is also claimed for Clutton, Dunkerton, Henton, High Littleton, Longwell Green, South Brewham, Wanstrow and Wells. This design is the most common of the flat brass patterns, and it comes in a range of sizes: at 13.5″ this specimen is almost certainly a steward's brass. Only one larger specimen is known (F 009/5).

F 009/3

F 009/4

F 009/5

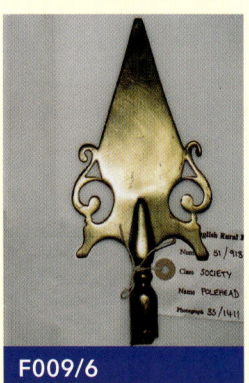

F009/6

F009/7

F 010

F 011/1

F 009/5   17.2"   Blaise Castle House Museum / T7598

This exceptionally large specimen is clearly a steward's or flag-pole brass, but it has no verifiable provenance. In the collection from which it came Wanstrow was suggested. It was originally owned by Philip Le Gros of Frome, but is now in Blaise Castle House Museum. Le Gros left no notes on his sources.

F009/6   8.5"   MERL / Shickle / 510918

No evidence has emerged for either Wanstrow or North Brewham. Shickle suggested Wanstrow, while in the Ponsonby-Fane notebook at Plymouth City Museum and Art Gallery the suggested provenance is North Brewham. This version of the common pattern was not included in Fuller's 1964 list. The identifying feature is the joining of the lower side scroll to the foot by a small spigot. Only four examples of this plain pattern are recorded, and they vary only slightly in height, from 8.5" to 8.6".

F009/7   8.5"   Private collection

No evidence for provenance is recorded. The pierced outline of a cockerel would suggest that the design was associated with a society meeting at an inn called 'The Cock', 'The Black Cock' or 'The Old Cock'. Several societies were so located, but other than the Cock Club at the Cock Inn, Warminster (F 085), there is no recorded evidence of pole carrying. Four variants of this design with the conjoint scroll and foot exist, all with the same shaft pattern and almost identical height, suggesting a manufacturer in common. F 009/6 is plain, while the others have the blade pierced: F 006/7, here, with the cockerel; F020 with the letters 'FS'; and F 028 with a miner's pick.

F 010   9.3"   MERL / Allen / 550859

The pattern is verified for **Blagdon Friendly Society** (Mendips) (1806 to c.1875) (SOM 578), which met at the George Inn, and for **Iron Acton**, Gloucestershire, for an unknown society, perhaps the Iron Acton Benefit Society (1823 to 1892) (GLOS 0128), which met at the Lamb Inn, but there were other possible users. The design was verified for Blagdon Friendly Society by the Rev E Merriott (letter, September 17th, 1932, MERL / Jardine DDX/993). An example is in the church. A second Blagdon society had a different design: see F 013/1. Iron Acton was verified by the Rev SJ Handover, but not for a named society (letter, December 10th, 1943 [he bought twelve, c.1923], MERL Jardine DDX/993). Apart from Iron Acton and Blagdon, the design may have been used elsewhere as well.

F 011/1   10"   MERL / Allen / 550899

Yatton New Friendly Society (1837 to 1872) (SOM 346) was suggested by Allen for this design, but he offered no evidence. The society met at the Prince of Orange Inn. Poles were certainly carried by the Yatton New Friendly Society as both the 1837 and the 1852 rules specify, but they do not mention tops, brass or otherwise (The National Archives FS 1/617A/346). This pattern is distinguished from others of a similar outline by having two cut-out hearts, and a diamond, and a disc at the top of the crown in place of the more usual cross.

F 011/2　　12.8″　Private collection

The design of the pole head for the Yatton New Friendly Society (1837 to 1872) (SOM 346) is unconfirmed. The society met at the Prince of Orange Inn. No provenance details have emerged for this specimen, but it appears to be a steward's version of F 011/1. Poles were certainly carried by the Yatton New Friendly Society, as both the 1837 and the 1852 rules specify, but they do not mention tops, brass or otherwise (The National Archives FS 1/617A/346).

F 011/2

F 012　　9.5″　MERL / Allen / 550903

The design is verified for **Henstridge Friendly Society** (1799 to 1944), which at various times was based at the New Inn, the Fountain Inn, or the Virginia Inn. On a photograph of the club visit to Inwood House dated 14th June 1912, presented to Taunton Museum (SCH) by Lady Theodora Guest, the pole heads are clearly visible, and even the thick upright portion of the cross at the top of the brass is distinguishable. This stem of the brass cross at the top of the crown is much thicker (1/3″) than the equivalent portion on specimens from other clubs, such that it can usually be identified at a distance in group photographs.

F 012

F 013/1　　9.6″　MERL / Allen / 550849

The design is verified for **Blagdon** (Mendips), but which particular society used it is unknown. Specimens of each of the two different Blagdon pole heads are held by the Church at Blagdon (Mendips): for the first of these societies see F 010. Besides the church specimen of F 013/1 no evidence has emerged that any Blagdon societies used this pattern, save that Allen told Jardine that he saw two of this pattern in the village (MERL Jardine DDX/993/1). This pattern was adopted elsewhere by more than one club.

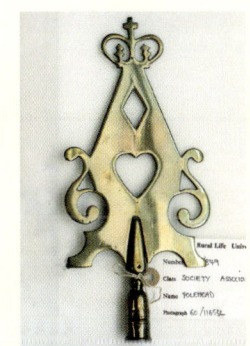

F 013/1

F 013/2　　9.6″　MERL / Jardine / 6124407

The design is verified for **Bower Hinton Male Friendly Benefit Society** (1845 to 1912) (unregistered), which met at Goose Hill Farm Barn (*Western Flying Post*, June 3rd, 1881). In a letter to Jardine dated September 24th, 1932, the Rev GW Saunders identified the pattern and wrote: 'Bower Hinton - met at Goose Hill Barn and walked on the last Tuesday in May' (MERL Jardine DDX/993/1). Also, a specimen belongs to the church at adjacent Martock. This pattern was adopted by more than one club.

F 013/2

F 013/3　　9.6″　Private collection

The design has been verified for **Long Sutton**, but it is not known which of the manifestations of the society used it. Long Sutton New Friendly Society (established in 1837 and registered in 1845) (SOM 496) may not have an unbroken link to the most recent society (extant in 2005). A photograph of what is claimed to be an original staff head is shown in Redvers Burt's *Long Sutton as 'twere*, private publication, 1997, Bradford-on-Avon, p.77. There is no indication, however, of how long the staff head had been owned by the society. This pattern was adopted by more than one club.

F 013/3

F 013/4

F 014

F 015

F 016

F 017

F 013/4   9+" (cross missing at top of crown) Private collection

This design is verified for **Paulton Friendly Society of Coalminers, Tradesmen and Others** (1784 to 1855) (SOM 452) or its successor, **Paulton New Club Benefit Society** (1856 to 1890s) (SOM 925), which met at the Red Lion Inn. This specimen is engraved 'W Crees'. Mercy Crees, a Paulton woman, and sister-in-law of William Crees, was involved in fighting during a Paulton Feast Day. The account came from the recollections of John Watts, b.1844, of his boyhood in Paulton, and was sent by the Rev JA Beazor to Jardine, September 24th, 1932 (MERL Jardine Index). The story was repeated by Margaret Fuller, *West Country Friendly Societies*, 1964, Reading, p.114. Another pole head with an identical pattern was owned and carried by a patient of Dr Bulleid, the Paulton club surgeon (SHC Taunton Museum lists of pole heads in the Hopkins collection, various dates). In the Tite notes (SHC) the club pole was described as having red, white and blue spirals, with red, white and blue ribbons attached, and woollen tassels quartered pale blue, yellow, purple, and red. In common with many others of this pattern, this particular specimen lacks the small cross which should be at the top of the crown. Whether the stem of the cross was weak, and so tended to snap off through normal handling, or whether it was deliberately removed for sectarian reasons, is open to question.

F 014   12.4"   MERL / Allen / 551134

There is no evidence to link this pattern specifically to any of the clubs at Blagdon (Mendip), Bower Hinton, Long Sutton, or Paulton. This particular example is a larger version of F 013, and is an officer's brass, but it has no known provenance. A similar example at Taunton is shorter, as, like some of the smaller members' brasses, it has lost the top part of the crown (SHC OSFS / 22A) (see notes for F 013/4). The Blaise Castle House specimen is engraved 'CLERK' across the centre of one side (T 7529) and it measures 12.6".

F 015   11"   MERL / Allen / 55080

This pattern is almost always ascribed to Frampton Cotterell, Gloucestershire, but no evidence has emerged to support the claim. Several clubs operated in Frampton Cotterell, but their rules do not mention poles, and there are no clues in the newspaper accounts of their meetings. Many of this design are stamped with a membership number.

F 016   8.6"   MERL / Allen / 550861

This pattern was not identified by early collectors or museums and no evidence has emerged subsequently. The design has several surviving examples, but none with a provenance. This specimen does not appear to be a cut-down version of the similar F 013/1-4 without the top crown.

F 017   8.7"   Private collection

This pattern has been verified for **Westbury on Trym**, Gloucestershire, but it is not known which particular society used it. Westbury on Trym Junior Benefit Society (Westbury Young Club) (1839 to 1903) (GLOS 0424), which met at the White Lion Inn, is invariably suggested, but neither its rules nor newspaper accounts shed any light on pole-carrying. The evidence for the location, as distinct from the club, is provided by the specimen illustrated, stamped 'A Rowles, 1857'. Alfred Rowles lived at Westbury on Trym (1861 census - age 27). In 1861 there were no others named A Rowles in whole of UK. '1857' may record his date of entry to one of the two clubs which ran simultaneously at Westbury. Westbury old club was said to have carried the pole head numbered F 119, but again there is no evidence.

F 018   9.5″   MERL / Allen / 55113

No evidence has emerged for this design. The pierced letters 'BS' may indicate 'Benefit Society'. It is also possible that the 'B' stands for the name or location of the society. Several examples are known. The SHC version is stamped '19' (OSFS 701).

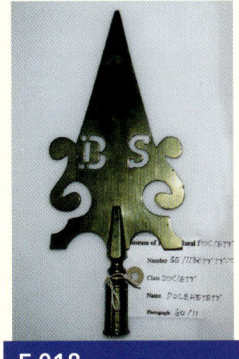
F 018

F 019   17″   MERL / Shickle / 510938

No evidence has emerged for this design. The pierced letters 'BS' may indicate 'Benefit Society'. It is also possible that the 'B' stands for the name or the location of the society. This is one of a pair of much larger versions of F 018. From their great size they are probably banner tops. The tips are deliberately squared off, probably from the start, for safety reasons.

F 019

F 020   8.5″   MERL / Allen / 551037

No evidence has emerged for this design. The pierced letters 'FS' may indicate 'Friendly Society'. It is also possible that the 'F' stands for the name or the location of the society, while the 'S' may refer to 'Steward' rather than 'Society'. There may be some connection with F 009 / 6, as the height and pattern are identical except for the pierced letters.

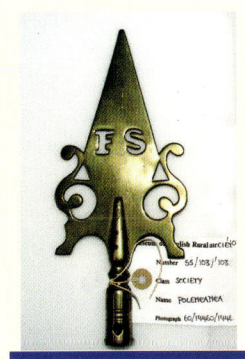
F 020

021/1   7.5″   MERL / Allen / 551135

No evidence has emerged for this design. The pierced letter 'S' may refer to 'Steward', a device to distinguish stewards when in procession (some rule books suggest that the pole heads of the stewards or committee members should be distinctive). The outline and size of F 021/1 strongly resemble the Portishead brass (F 005/1). This particular specimen is also stamped 'SF'.

F 021/2   11.5″   MERL / Shickle / 510924

No evidence has emerged for this design. The pierced letter 'S' may refer to 'Steward', a device to distinguish stewards when in procession (some rule books suggest that the pole heads of the stewards or committee members should be distinctive). This is a considerably larger version of F 021/1, but there may be no connection between the two specimens.

021/1

Pole head of William Crees, Paulton: F 013/4.

F 021/2

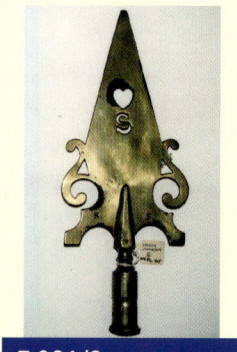

F 021/3

F 022

F 023

F 024/1

F 024/2

F 021/3   11.2″   SHC / OSFS 705

No evidence has emerged for this design. The pierced letter 'S' may refer to 'Steward', a device to distinguish stewards when in procession (some rule books suggest that the pole heads of the stewards or committee should be distinctive). This is a considerably larger version of F 021/1, but there may be no connection between the two designs. This specimen is similar to F 021/2, but with a cut out heart as well as the 'S'. It is also stamped 'S S'.

F 022   11″   MERL / Allen / 551157

This pattern is verified for **Sturminster Newton Castle Friendly Society**, Dorset (1811 to 1844) (DOR 201), which met at the Swan Inn and later at the Crown Inn (1855). Newspapers record the members' new brasses in 1835, the gift of the vicar (*Sherborne, Dorchester and Taunton Journal*, June 18th, 1835) (see F 256). The pierced initials almost certainly stand for 'Sturminster Newton Society'. Two examples exist and they were probably stewards' pole heads.

F 023   14.5″   SHC / Du Cann collection / 2018

This pattern is verified for **Sturminster Newton Castle Friendly Society**, Dorset (1811 to 1844) (DOR 201), which met at the Swan Inn and later at the Crown Inn (1835). Newspapers record the members' new brasses in 1835, the gift of the vicar (*Sherborne, Dorchester and Taunton Journal*, 18 June 1835) (see F 256. The pierced initials almost certainly stand for 'Sturminster Newton Society'. This example is of a unique design and was a committee pole head, engraved on the socket 'John Imber, Clerk - James W Elliott and John Ford, Chief Stewards - 1833'.

F 024/1   10.6″   MERL / Allen / 550908

The design is verified for **Meare Friendly and Benefit Society (Meare Benefit Society)** (1843 to 1874) (SOM 402), which met at the Vestry, the Schoolroom, and later at the Ring of Bells Inn. The club restarted (unregistered) in 1874, and again in 1890. In 1911 it closed, but restarted once more in 1914. Charles Tite's photograph with the caption 'Benefit Society, Meare, "Club Walk", Whit-Tuesday (c.1912)' (SHC) shows both the ordinary members' pole heads and the much larger stewards' versions, which are of a similar pattern. The 1843 rules refer to a 'blue pole' and a 'brass head' (The National Archives FS 1/717A/402), but this is probably the design at F 078. This pole head probably dates from 1874: the earlier society started in 1843, and its pole head is probably the one shown at F 078. When the society was restarted in 1914 new 'spears' were bought at 3/8d each, but it is not clear what design was chosen (*Central Somerset Gazette*, November 5th, 1915).

F 024/2   17.4″   Wainwright collection (dispersed): (location untraced)

The design (a steward's brass) is verified for **Meare Friendly and Benefit Society** (1843 to 1874) (SOM 402), which met at the Vestry, the Schoolroom and later at the Ring of Bells Inn. The club restarted (unregistered) in both 1874 and in 1890. In 1911 it closed but restarted once more in 1914. Charles Tite's photograph with the caption 'Benefit Society, Meare, "Club Walk", Whit-Tuesday (c.1912)' (SHC) shows both the ordinary members' pole heads and the much larger stewards' versions, which are of a similar design. The 1843 rules refer to a 'blue pole' and a 'brass head' (The National Archives FS 1/717A/402), but this is probably the design at F 078. This pole head probably dates from 1874: the earlier society started in 1843, and its pole head is probably the one shown at F 078. When the society was restarted in 1914 new pole heads were bought at 3/8d each, but it is not clear what design was chosen (*Central Somerset Gazette*, November 5th, 1915).

F 025/1   7.1″   MERL / Allen / 550868

The design is verified for **Sherborne Friendly Society**, Dorset (later called **Sherborne Old Friendly Society**) (1761 to 1950) (DOR 221), which met at the Town Hall.

The design has the piercing 'SOFS 1761', which confirms the provenance of the brass as the Sherborne Old Friendly Society. These brasses date from the centenary celebrations of the society in 1861 (*Frome Times*, June 5th, 1861).

F 025/1

F025/2   11.5″   Sherborne Museum, on display (banner tops).

The design is verified for **Sherborne Friendly Society**, Dorset (later called **Sherborne Old Friendly Society**) (1761 to 1950) (DOR 221), which met at the Town Hall. The design with the piercing 'SOFS 1761' confirms the provenance of the brass as the Sherborne Old Friendly Society, established in 1761. These brasses, however, date from the centenary celebrations in 1861 (*Frome Times*, June 5th, 1861). These large specimens are probably banner tops.

F025/2

F 025/3   6.4″   MERL / Allen / 550863

No evidence has emerged for this design. At least two examples exist, but they have no provenance. The design seems to suggest that they served as plain flagpole tops, but not necessarily that they were used by a friendly society.

F 025/3

F 025/4   9.3″   Private Collection

No evidence has emerged for this design, which is made of steel. There is no indication that this pole head, which appears to be ornamental, was actually used by a Friendly Society.

F 025/4

F 026   8.8″   MERL / Shickle / 510913

There is no recorded provenance for this brass, which is sometimes attributed to Frome. The design clearly refers to the inn where the society met, for example the Ring o' Bells, or the Five Bells, but which of the many contenders is unknown. In 1866 (*Kelly's Directory*) there was a Five Bells Inn at Crewkerne, and there were nine inns called Ring o' Bells in Bristol and Somerset.

F 026

Detail of SOFS pole of T Adams: F 025/1.

F 027

F 028

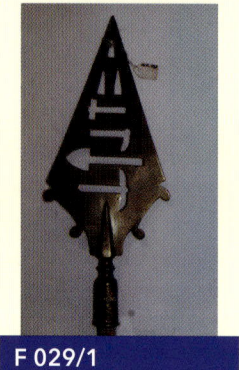

F 029/1

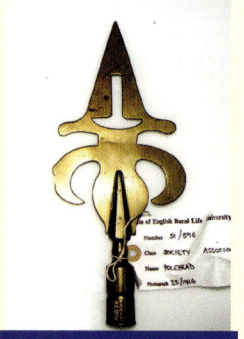

F 029/2

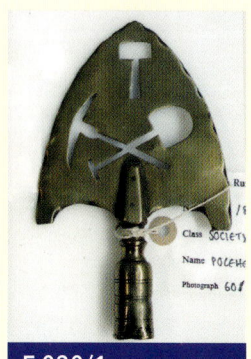

F 030/1

F 027   10.2″   MERL / Allen / 55085

This design is often attributed to a society that met at the Seven Stars Inn at Winsley, Wiltshire, but no evidence has emerged to support the claim. In 1866 (*Kelly's Directory*) two further Seven Stars inns were listed, one in Bristol and another in Bath, but again there is no evidence to link this design to either location.

F 028   8.6″   MERL / Allen / 551098

Allen suggested that this design was used by a club at Caerphilly, Glamorganshire, but he produced no evidence in support. Even if his specimen was found at Caerphilly, it is quite possible that it had been taken there by a miner migrating from the Somerset or South Gloucestershire coalfields. The existence of a pole-carrying friendly society in Caerphilly has yet to be proved. On the other hand, a brass-mounted pole was used in the coal-mining district of Monmouthshire by the Ebbw Vale New Town Benefit Society (also known as the Fireman's Club), but the pattern of the pole head is unknown (*Merthyr Telegraph*, August 19th, 1865).

F 029/1   10.3″   SHC / OSFS / 158A

The design has been verified for **Radstock**, and was probably used by a society that met at the Bell Inn, although little evidence is available concerning the Bell Inn (5 year) Friendly Society (unregistered), save for accounts of Whit Tuesday club anniversaries (*Bristol Mercury*, 16th May 1894 and SMJ 31st May 1901). A letter in SHC dated January 1st, 1927, from S Lloyd Harvey includes a scaled drawing of one of these designs, height 10.3″, and showing the inscription 'RP'. The brass itself was given to the museum by Wallace Treasure, 16 Frome Hill, Radstock (SHC OSFS / 158A). It belonged to the father of his father-in-law, Levi Seymour, of Radstock, who was a member of the 5 year Bell Inn club (1858 to 1872) (SOM 686). The brass is thought to have been acquired c.1840. An image of the pole head appears on a painted sundial above the porch of St Nicholas Church, Radstock.

Radstock pole head design on sundial, church of St Nicholas.

F 029/2   9.6″   MERL / Shickle / 510896

No evidence has emerged to identify this specimen. Only one museum example is known to exist, but there is also at least one modern copy. The older brass is a mutilated one-off specimen. Whether it was legitimately made for use in a society, or made for a collector, is unknown. The specimen is a cut down and pierced version of F 085 (Warminster).

F 030/1   6.1″   MERL / Allen / 550879

Allen suggested Shipham as the provenance, but gave no evidence to support his claim. From its design the brass clearly belongs to a society for of miners. The Shipham connection is reputed to refer to a club associated with the Miners Arms Inn there.

F 030/2   10″   Private collection

No provenance has emerged for this specimen, but almost certainly it is a steward's brass of the same society as F 030/1, for which Shipham has been suggested, albeit with no proof of provenance. The outer edges of this specimen are smooth, whereas on the smaller members' brasses they are lightly cusped. A further possibility is that this is an example of the brass-mounted pole that was used by the Ebbw Vale New Town Benefit Society (also known as the Fireman's Club), but the pattern of that pole head is also unknown (*Merthyr Telegraph*, August 19th, 1865).

F 030/2

F 031   9.9″   MERL / Allen / 550917

The design is verified for **Westbury sub Mendip Society of Tradesmen and Others** (1795 to present) (SOM 307), which met at the Railway Hotel. *The Wells Journal*, June 16th, 1881, reported that members were 'carrying their spears with tassals [sic] attached'; Ethel W. Gunn, 'Somerset Club Brasses', *Somerset Year Book*, 1922, has a Bristol Times and Mirror photograph with members on their 1922 club day, holding brass-headed spears of this design, and the *Western Daily Press*, June 9th, 1936, p.9, shows 22 spears also with pole heads of this design. The same pattern of members' brasses has been claimed for the Street and Walton Friendly Society (F 034/1), and for Wick (Gloucestershire) (F 034/3), but there is no supporting evidence for either. A copy of the 1922 Westbury sub Mendip photograph is in the Du Cane Photograph Album (private: Inwood collection), where the name 'Westbury' may be seen on the banner.

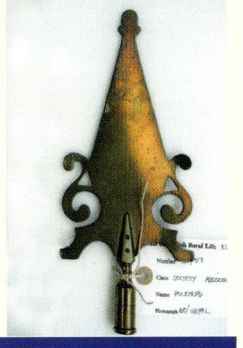

F 031

F 032   13″   MERL / Allen / 55091

This design is verified for **Westbury sub Mendip Society of Tradesmen and Others** (1795 to present) (SOM 307), which met at the Railway Hotel. Allen left no evidence for the provenance of this large specimen, but two examples can clearly be seen, held by stewards, in Fuller (1964), plate X, where the members' smaller brasses are also visible.

F 032

F 033   9.1″   MERL / Allen / 55087

This pattern is verified for **Shirehampton Benefit Society**, Bristol (1781 to 1886) (GLOS 0109), which met at the George Inn. The provenance was verified in a letter from S Lloyd Harvey to the Curator, Taunton Castle Museum, July 1928, with a drawing of a specimen owned by Thomas Yeeles, a former member (SHC Taunton Museum archives). A letter from George A Collins, resident of Shirehampton, dated September 9th, 1932, confirmed that the headquarters were at the George Inn and the details of the dissolution date (MERL Jardine Index).

F 033

F 034/1   10.1″   MERL / Allen / 550856

No evidence for pole carrying has emerged for the Street and Walton Friendly Society (1833 to 1863) (SOM 494), the society to which Allen attributed this design. It is more likely to have been used by the Walton Ten Year Friendly Benefit Society (1843 to 1863) (SOM 304) and its successor the Walton Ten Year Friendly and Benefit Society (1864 to 1874) (SOM 769), both of which met at the Globe Inn. The society rules of 1843 specified 'a white rod, brass spear and red ribbon' (The National Archives FS 1/615/304, rules): its pattern, however, was not described. F 031 and F 034/1 are virtually indistinguishable from each other. Even the heights are practically identical within the limits of hand-crafting. The F 034/3 version is distinctive, however, due to the serial numbers stamped on the brasses.

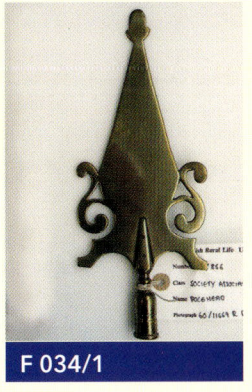

F 034/1

F 034/2

F 034/3

F 035

F 036

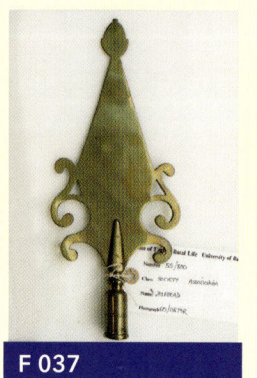

F 037

F 034/2   12.6″   SHC / OSFS / 185

Taunton Museum ascribed this design to the Street and Walton Friendly Society (1833 to 1863) (SOM 494), but there is no evidence that the society carried poles. More likely is the Walton Ten Year Friendly Benefit Society (1842 to 1863) (SOM 304) or the Walton Friendly and Benefit Society (1864 to 1874) (SOM 769). The 1843 rules specified 'a white rod, brass spear and red ribbon' (The National Archives FS 1/615/304, rules), but the pole head pattern was not described. The society met at the Globe Inn. This version is probably a steward's brass, on account of its height.

F 034/3   9.9″   Plymouth City Museum and Art Gallery / 1936.2.34

The Ponsonby-Fane Plymouth notebook indicates Wick, Gloucestershire, for these brasses, but no further location details are given (Plymouth City Museum and Art Gallery: 1936.2.32, 1936.2.34 & 1936.2.35). The three Plymouth specimens (c.10″), and other identical specimens, are stamped with membership numbers, indicating a series used by a particular society.

F 035   10.1″   MERL / Allen / 550852

This specimen is verified for **Milborne Port Perpetual Benefit** Society (1849 to between 1871 and 1875) (SOM 415), which met at the Guildhall. Milborne Port Tradesmen's Society, which met at the Queen's Head Inn, was reported '[to] have lately purchased new spears and flags' (*Yeovil Times*, June 5th, 1849), presumably for its successor, a new club registered as the Milborne Port Perpetual Benefit Society, which commenced that year. The brasses are engraved 'MP BS', standing for Milborne Port Benefit Society or for Milborne (Port) Perpetual Benefit Society. MP is engraved on one side, BS on the other.

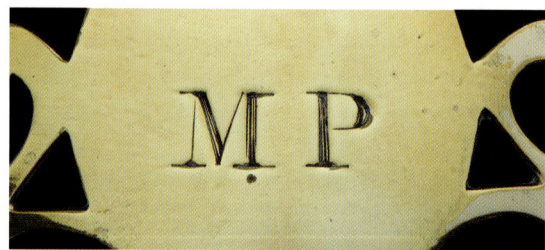

MP (obverse) and BS (reverse) Milborne Port (Perpetual) Benefit Society.

F 036   16″   MERL / Allen / 551090

Allen claimed that this specimen belonged to Milborne Port, but without any supporting evidence. The large size indicates a steward's brass or flagpole top, but there is no inscription of MPBS.

F 037   11.1″   MERL / Allen / 550800

This design is verified for **Witham Friary Friendly Society** (1786 to present) (SOM 302), which met at the Seymour Arms Inn. Michael McGarvie's *Around Frome*, 1997, p.105, pictures the members at the Seymour Arms, c.1910, with one pole head visible (see also www.withamfriary.org.ok/history for another photograph (c1910) of Witham Friary Friendly Society, with one member holding a pole with a brass top (accessed 27/1/2016).

F 038/1   10.8" MERL / Allen / 550854

Bruton Friendly Society members carried rods, but the pattern of the pole head is unknown. From 1817 Bruton Friendly Society (1761 to after 1867) (SOM 289) was officially renamed the Old Bell Friendly Society, due to a transfer from the Bell Inn to the Blue Ball Inn. Allen, along with all other collectors or museums, ascribed this design to Bruton, but no supporting evidence has emerged, and the pattern of the Bruton pole head remains unverified. Nevertheless, the 1793, 1830 and 1832 rules of the society specify that members should 'carry a rod' on Feast Days, purchased by the society (The National Archives FS 1/615/289). This design is often found stamped with the member's roll number: this one is no.67.

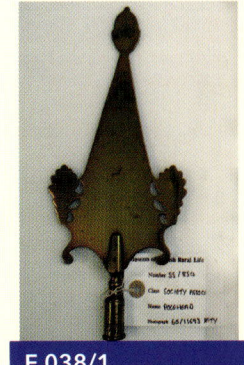

F 038/1

F 038/2   18.5" Blaise Castle House Museum / T9357

Bruton Friendly Society members carried rods, but the pattern of the pole head is unknown (The National Archives FS 1/615/289). From 1817 Bruton Friendly Society (1761 to after 1867) (SOM 289) was officially renamed the Old Bell Friendly Society, due to a transfer from the Bell Inn to the Blue Ball Inn. Blaise Castle House Museum has no provenance for this design, which appears to be a banner top. Allen and others ascribed the members' equivalent to Bruton, but with no supporting evidence. Two other large versions (c.17.6" & c.21.5") were shown in the Wainwright collection catalogue, but their locations are now unknown (Eunice B Overend, ed., *Catalogue of the Wainwright Collection of Friendly Society Brasses* [dispersed], The Phillips Museum, Brokerswood [defunct], Autumn 1971, p.4).

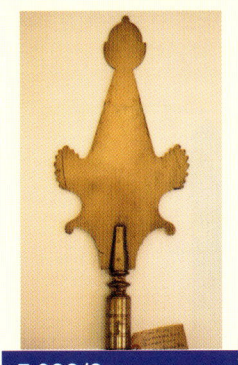

F 038/2

F 039   9.6" MERL / Allen / 550928

Allen ascribed this design to Maiden Bradley, but he offered no evidence.

F 039

F 040   11.3" MERL / Allen / 550804

Allen ascribed this design to Maiden Bradley, but he offered no evidence. Similar stewards' or flag pole top specimens are known at MERL (Jardine 61244192: 11.1"), at Salisbury Museum (1950.112.1: 11.3"), and at Blaise Castle House Museum (T7500: 13.1").

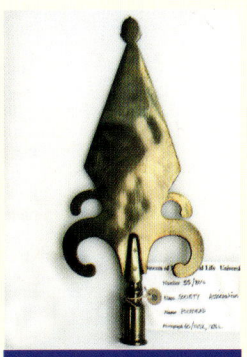

F 040

F 041   9.7" MERL / Allen / 550857

Allen provided no evidence for attributing this design to Crowcombe Friendly Society (1858 to 1913) (SOM 696). Nevertheless, the initial CFS on the pole head seem to indicate Crowcombe. Another early suggestion was Combe Florey, nearby, but the latter did not have a friendly society. Members of Crowcombe Friendly Society, however, were described as 'bearing their club staffs' (*West Somerset Free Press*, May 24th, 1904, also May 30th, 1885).

Crowcombe Friendly Society banner

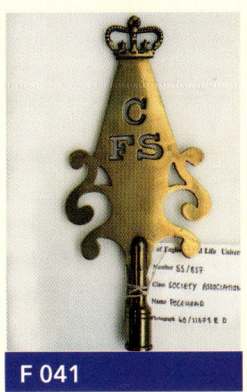

F 041

61

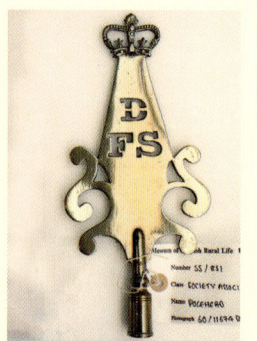

F 042

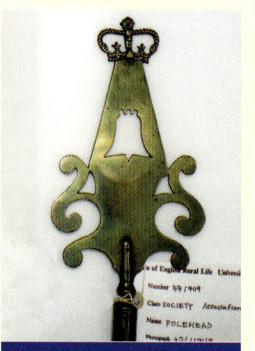

F 043

F 044

F 045/1

F 045/2

F 042   9.75″   MERL / Allen / 550851

This design is verified for **Dowlish Wake Friendly Society** (1837 to 1955) (SOM 074), which met at the School Room. A letter of 1932 to Jardine from the Rev LC Mallet, Chairman of the Dowlish Friendly Society at the time, confirmed the design (MERL Jardine DDX993). The 1913 Rules (SHC, Tite Collection), required members on the feast day to carry a pole mounted with brass and one blue ribbon, while the *Chard and Ilminster News*, June 17th, 1876, reported that each member carried a 'brass-mounted club pole gaily decorated with flowers'.

F 043   9.5″   MERL / Allen / 550909

This design is verified for **Zeals True Blue Friendly Society**, Wiltshire, (1837 to after 1876), which met at the Bell and Crown Inn. This pole head pattern has only ever been identified by early collectors with the Bell and Crown Inn at Zeals. The name of the inn is so unusual that the match with the design seems deliberate, and the ascription justifiable. No other confirmation, however, has come to light.

F 044   6.4″   MERL / Allen / 550864

There is some evidence for **Magor Union Benefit Society**, Monmouthshire, (1838 to 1897) (MON 182), which met at the Wheatsheaf Inn. Allen claimed that Magor was the source, but he provided no evidence. Jardine, however, in a letter dated March 14th, 1933, wrote that he had obtained his example from a man whose great-grandfather came from Magor (MERL Jardine DDX/1787). Nevertheless, this man could have migrated from elsewhere. The design of the wheatsheaf on the brass, however, almost certainly confirms the provenance.

F 045/1   7.2″   MERL / Allen / 550867

Allen quoted Westonzoyland as the origin of this design, but earlier sources all quoted Castle Cary. Nevertheless, there is no definite proof for either. Members of the Westonzoyland Benevolent Friendly Society (1790 to 1840) (SOM 373), meeting at the Greyhound Inn, carried blue poles, but the pole head design is unknown (Club Rules 1814, SHC DD\OS/8). Both Castle Cary clubs had brasses, but the designs are also unconfirmed. The two clubs were the United Britons' Friendly Society (1834 to after 1896) (unregistered), which met at the Britannia Inn, and the Castle Cary Friendly Benefit Society (Canon Meade's Club) (1861 to 1912) (SOM717), which met at the National School Room. According to T Salisbury Donne, writing to Jardine in 1932, both societies had brasses (MERL Jardine DDX/993/1). There is a large variation in the size of these specimens, ranging from under 7″ to well over 7.5″.

Pattern of F 045/1 marked W Penn, Waterloo, 1826: the reference has not been traced.

F 045/2   11″   Private collection

Despite some resemblance to F 045/1, there is no evidence linking this specimen to either Westonzoyland or Castle Cary, and only one example has been recorded. From its large size it would appear to be a steward's brass, but there is no record of a smaller version. The spear shape, the circular piercing, and the protected tip all resemble the smaller member's brass of F 045/1, but the bottom feet are of a different pattern.

F 045/3   13″   Private collection

Despite strong resemblance to F 045/1, there is no evidence linking this specimen to either Westonzoyland or Castle Cary. The spear shape, the circular piercing, and the protected tip all resemble the smaller members' brass of F 045/1. From its size this would appear to be a steward's or flag-pole brass, but the specimen has no known provenance, and only one example has been recorded. The large size of this specimen can be appreciated by comparing the rounded tip with that of the members' brass. It has a diameter of 1.25″, compared with 0.35″.

Members' and stewards' pole head size difference: F 045/1 and F 045/3.

F 045/3

F 045/4   7″   MERL / Shickle / 510911

Fuller (1964) did not include this pattern, characterised by its central diamond piercing, although many examples survive. None have any reliable provenance, but some early sources suggest Castle Cary, along with the similar version with the circular piercing. Castle Cary Friendly Benefit Society (Canon Meade's Club) (1861 to 1912) (SOM 717) or the United Britons' Friendly Society (1834 to after 1896) (unregistered) are possibilities, since according to T Salisbury Donne, writing to Jardine in 1932, both societies had brasses, although their patterns were unconfirmed (MERL Jardine DDX/993/1).

F 045/4

F 045/5   11.3″   Private collection

Fuller (1964) did not include any version of this pattern, characterised by its tip, its central diamond piercing and its square feet. There is no known provenance for this specimen, which from its large size appears to be a steward's brass. Only one example has been recorded, and it is not known if a smaller version exists.

The spear shape, the diamond piercing, and the protected tip all resemble the smaller members' brass of F 045/4, but the bottom feet here are of a different pattern, being square rather than rounded.

F 045/5

F 046   7.1″   MERL / Shickle / 510903

Members of Charlton Horethorne Friendly Society (1853 to after 1871) (SOM 618) had poles, but there is no information about pole heads. The society met at the Red Lion Inn. No evidence has emerged to confirm that this was the design used at Charlton Horethorne. Allen received this attribution from Sir Spencer Ponsonby-Fane, but the latter gave no further information. The club rules in 1853 specified a pole with the proper colours, but did not make reference to a pole head (The National Archives FS 1/623/618).

F 046

F 047   7″   MERL / Allen / 551136

No evidence has emerged to link this design to a particular place. Kelway suggested St Pierre, near Chepstow, Monmouthshire, but gave no supporting details (SHC Taunton Museum, Kelway notebook c.1920s, no 224, p.94). Only two examples have been recorded. Fuller repeats Allen's description as 'origin unknown'. An appropriate friendly society for St Pierre has not been identified.

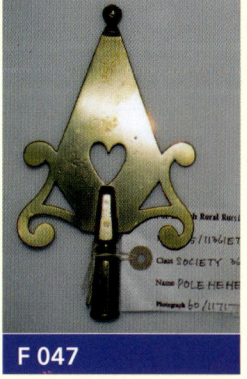

F 047

F 048a

F 049

F 050

F 051/1

F 051/2

F 048 9" MERL / Allen / 550872

This pattern is not confirmed for either North Cadbury or Nailsea. In this version of the design the applied sprigs on each side differ. The obverse side (F 048a) has a 4 leaved sprig bottom left, while the reverse side (F 048b) has only 3 leaves. Several examples of this arrangement have been seen. In the other version (F 049) there are sprigs of 3 leaves on the bottom left of both sides. North Cadbury is thought to have had the 3 leaf variant (F 049), so perhaps Nailsea had the mixed design (F 048a and b) although there is no evidence that Nailsea had either. Fuller made the opposite attribution, but is contradicted by the information in F 049 that follows.

F 048b

F 049 9.25" MERL / Forster / 55233

This design with 3 leaves on the bottom left sprig of each side of the specimen is verified for **North Cadbury**, but not for Nailsea. **North Cadbury Benefit Society** (1869 to 1875) (SOM 835) met at the School Room. In a letter to Jardine in 1933 the Rev Moline referred to two old brasses in the possession of Mr Alfred Pitman, farmer, of Woolston (in North Cadbury parish), one initialled SP (possibly Samuel Pitman) each with groups of three leaves (MERL Jardine DDX/993). The 1866 Kelly's *Directory of Somerset* confirms that the Pitman family were farming at Woolston. There are other examples which also have this configuration of leaves.

F 050 8.7" MERL / Jardine / 61244228

This general design has been linked to Butleigh, Chew Magna and Somerton, but the three patterns are slightly different. F 050 is verified for **Butleigh** (not Somerton as claimed in Fuller [1964]). **Butleigh Friendly Society** (1832 to 1912) (SOM 291) met at their Club House, which was a barn near Mr A Higgins' house (WG June 3rd, 1881), In 1890 the members were reported as 'carrying brass headed poles' (*Wells Journal*, June 5th, 1890). The Butleigh pole head at SHC was last carried in procession by John Field (SHC 2/83/1989/11). Jardine's brass (61244228) is engraved 'J. Knit', identified as J Knight who, according to the 1841 census, lived at Butleigh. Details of the pole head dimensions of the two very similar patterns were reported in a letter (nd) to Jardine from Hugh A Clark of Butleigh House, who wrote; 'an antique dealer says Butleigh is 8.75" by 3.6", Chew Magna is 9.25" by 3.9", and has a more slender top' (MERL Jardine Index). The example retained as a banner top in Butleigh Church is 8.75". Statistical analysis of the heights of 49 specimens of this general pattern shows a clear clustering of values at 8.75", 9" and 9.25", with few intermediate values. The 8.75" specimens are verified for Butleigh and the 9.25" specimens for Chew Magna. Somerton, also linked with this pattern, would appear by default to be the 9" type.

F 051/1 8.75" MERL / Allen / 550810

Two varieties of this pole head have been verified as having been used by **Bishop Sutton and Stowey Friendly Society** (1799 to after 1925: only registered between 1885 and 1893) (SOM 918). The 1885 rules do not indicate pole carrying (SHC A\ CBU/6/2), and newspapers do not mention pole heads, but an undated photograph in a private collection shows the society lined up outside the Red Lion Inn with members' pole heads and stewards' pole heads visible, and two specimens of this type have known local provenance. The shorter variety of the pattern (8.75") (F 051/1), illustrated here, has a more slender top and the taller one (9.25") (F 051/4), has a distinctive diamond-shaped top. Since both have a provenance from Bishop Sutton, they were probably ordered for the society at different times.

F 051/2   8.9   Private collection

There is no evidence to link this specimen to Bishop Sutton. It is a variant of F 051/1, but it has a different socket and a distinctly smaller heart cut-out. From the 1829 date pricked on the face it may be a very early specimen from Bishop Sutton, which is known to have had two other slightly different designs with distinctive sockets and upper parts (F 051/1 and F 051/4).

F 051/3   14.7"   Private collection

This pattern is verified as a steward's brass from **Bishop Sutton and Stowey Friendly Society** (1799 to after 1925) (the society was only registered between 1885 and 1893) (SOM 918). The 1885 rules do not indicate pole carrying (SHC A\CBU/6/2), and no newspapers mention pole heads, but an undated photograph in a private collection shows the society lined up outside the Red Lion Inn with members' pole heads and stewards' pole heads visible. Two distinct varieties of the members' brasses exist: the shorter one (8.75") (F 051/1) has a more slender top, the taller one (9.25") (F 051/4) has a distinctive diamond-shaped top. The much larger stewards' brass, illustrated here, has a slender top like F 051/1.

F 051/3

F 051/4   9.25"   MERL / Allen / 550808

This pattern is verified for **Bishop Sutton and Stowey Friendly Society** (1799 to after 1925) (the society was only registered between 1885 and 1893) (SOM 918). The 1885 rules do not indicate pole carrying (SHC A\CBU/6/2) and no newspapers mention pole heads, but an undated photograph in a private collection shows the society lined up outside the Red Lion Inn with members' pole heads and stewards' pole heads visible. Two distinct varieties of the members' pattern exist: the shorter one (8.75") (F 051/1) has a more slender top, and the taller one (9.25") (F 051/4), illustrated here, has a distinctive diamond-shaped top. Both are verified for Bishop Sutton and were probably made at different times.

F 051/4

F 052   11.5"   MERL / Allen / 550820

Allen suggested Barton St David as the provenance for this design, but offered no evidence, and no other information has emerged of the use of brass pole tops in this village. Other possibilities are Butleigh, Chew Magna or Somerton. The much larger size of this specimen in comparison with the usual members' brasses (F 050, F 053/1, F 053/2 and F053/4) indicates that this is a steward's brass or banner top.

F 052

F 053/1   9.1"   MERL / Allen / 550812

Brass pole heads were used at Somerton, and this pattern appears to be the most likely one used. In the 1833 rules of Somerton Friendly Society (1823 to 1851) brass tops were specified, and the same requirement was stated in the 1852 rules of its successor, Somerton Provident Society (1851 to 1865) (SOM 635) and (1865 to 1912) (SOM 800). Pole carrying was frequently mentioned for this place, such as the entry 'brass spear' in *Western Gazette*, May 29th, 1868. See also the notes for F 050.

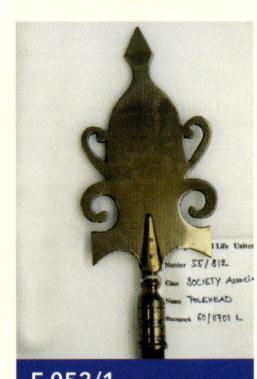

F 053/1

F 053/2   9.25"   MERL / Allen / 550806

Allen did not identify a location for this design, but it was used by **Chew Magna (Patriotic) Society of Yeomen and Tradesmen** (1789 to c.1868) (SOM 040), which met at the Bear and Swan Inn. A letter from Mrs EE Colston, Corner House, Chew Stoke (SHC Taunton Museum archives) includes a tracing of a brass of height 9.25" from Chew Magna, dated 1793. See also the notes for F 050.

F 053/2

F 053/3

F 054

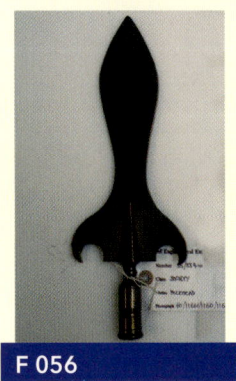

F 055/1

F 053/3   9.3"   Plymouth City Museum and Art Gallery / 1958.154

From its height and general shape this specimen would appear to be a Chew Magna brass, but there are minor variations compared with F 053/2, such as the width, the diamond-shaped top, and the socket pattern. There is no provenance for this design. It may nevertheless be from a batch ordered by the Chew Magna society at a different time from the other variants, and produced by different manufacturer.

F 054   13.4"+ MERL / Shickle / 510940

CW Shickle suggested Butleigh, but AW Allen disagreed. Neither of them provided any evidence (List of the Shickle Collection at MERL, with comments by Allen). This appears to be a banner top, and has lost part of its socket.

F 055/1   8.8"   MERL / Allen / 550862

This design is usually attributed to Midsummer Norton, but, although brass pole heads were used there, the pattern has not been confirmed. Midsomer Norton Tradesmen's Union Society (also known as the Whit Monday Club) (1827 to after 1869) (SOM 199) variously met at Stone's Cross Hotel and the Greyhound Inn. In 1859 the Whit Monday Club members were described as parading 'with glittering spears, decorated with various colours' (*Wells Journal*, June 18th, 1859). The Jardine Collection specimen (MERL 61244019) is marked 'H Ashman', but the name has not been traced to Welton or Midsomer Norton.

F 055/2   13.9"   Blaise Castle House Museum / T7705

This appears to be the stewards' version of F 055/1, which has been attributed to Midsomer Norton, but without confirmation. Midsomer Norton Tradesmen's Union Society (also known as the Whit Monday Club) (1827 to after 1869) (SOM 199) variously met at Stone's Cross Hotel and the Greyhound Inn. In 1859 the Whit Monday Club members were described as parading 'with glittering spears, decorated with various colours' (*Wells Journal*, June 18th, 1859) This large specimen is finished in the same way as the smaller members' brasses (F 055/1): at the base of both top arms there is an engraved line leading into the face of the blade. In this specimen one of the top arms has been replaced. An even larger brass of this pattern, probably a banner top, was in the Wainwright Collection and measured c.15-17", but its location is now unknown (Eunice B Overend, ed., *Catalogue of the Wainwright Collection of Friendly Society* Brasses [dispersed], the Phillips Museum [defunct], Brokerswood, Autumn 1971, p.6}.

F 056   12.3"   MERL / Allen / 550834

The design is verified for **West Pennard Friendly Society of Tradesmen, Farmers and Others** (1799 to 1844) (SOM 455), which met at the New Inn, and for the subsequent **West Pennard Ten Years Benefit and Friendly Society** (1844 to 1878) (SOM 457), which met at West Pennard Inn. In 1839 the members were described as carrying 'ensigns' (*Sherborne, Dorchester and Taunton Journal*, May 9th, 1839), while the 1844 rules specified a 'white rod' (The National Archives FS 1/618/457 rules 1844). Two specimens are used as Churchwardens' staves in West Pennard Church, pricked 'TN' and '1839' on their faces, and additionally pricked with the outline of a cross. Mr Dunkerton, village undertaker, made the staves. Some specimens seen are marked 'EP', suggesting that the members came from East Pennard. There are two types of socket mounting for brasses from this club, the split hexagonal spire type, with the face twice pinned into it, and a simpler hollow, rounded version, like that on the steward's brass illustrated at F 057. It is not clear which version is the older.

F 057   15.7"   Blaise Castle House Museum / T7478

This pattern is almost certainly a steward's version of F 056. The design without the side wings is verified for **West Pennard Friendly Society of Tradesmen, Farmers and Others** (1799 to 1844) (SOM 455), which met at the New Inn, and for the subsequent **West Pennard Ten Years Benefit and Friendly Society** (1844 to 1878) (SOM 457), which met at West Pennard Inn. In 1839 the members were described as carrying 'ensigns' (*Sherborne, Dorchester and Taunton Journal*, May 9th, 1839), while the 1844 rules specified a 'white rod' (The National Archives FS 1/618/457 rules 1844). Two specimens are used as Churchwardens' staves in West Pennard Church, pricked 'TN' and '1839' on their faces, and additionally pricked with the outline of a cross. Mr Dunkerton, village undertaker, made the staves. Some specimens seen are marked 'EP', suggesting that the members came from East Pennard. This larger version with wings has a pattern of socket found only in this society (but it is also seen on some of the members' brasses). An identical stewards' brass, 15.7" in height, is in the SHC collection, OSFS 144.

F 057

F 058/1   8.5"   MERL / Allen / 551032

The design with a short socket attachment, and a socket and blade cast in one piece, is verified for the late revival **East Harptree Friendly Society** (c.1905 to after 1908) (unregistered). The meeting place is not recorded. Ethel W Gunn's article 'Club Spear Heads' describes the recent rebirth of the club at East Harptree (*SDNQ*, Vol IX, Sept 1905, pp 305 to 307). Mr and Mrs Kettlewell had encouraged the revival and presented 36 reproduction spear heads to the club. In a photograph c.1905 (private collection) some 50 members are shown, with around 30 short socket attachment pole heads. The pole head from the original club had a much longer socket attachment than the one illustrated here, and the earlier brasses are about an inch taller than the replacement versions (see F 058/2).

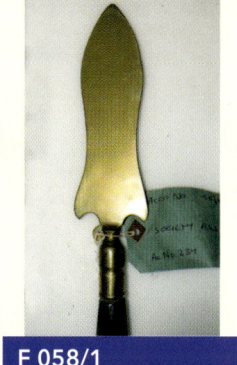

F 058/1

F 058/2   9.6"   St Laurence Church, East Harptree

This design is verified for **East Harptree**, but it is not clear which of two societies used it, namely East Harptree (or Harptry) Friendly Society (SOM 088) (enrolled in 1794) and East Harptree (or Harptry) Friendly Society (SOM 090) (also enrolled in 1794). A specimen in the church is engraved 'WL EH 1804'. These two societies were extant in 1803, and probably in 1804 (Abstract of Answers and Returns 1803), but no documents relating to either of them have survived in the National Archives, despite their official enrolment. The socket attachment is longer than the modern (1905) version, and the overall height at 9.6" is around 1" taller. In 1907 Mrs Kettlewell, who was responsible for the more modern version of the pole head, presented her 'Old Club' specimen to Taunton Museum (SHC OSFS 081). It measures 9.6" and has the long socket (illustrated here).

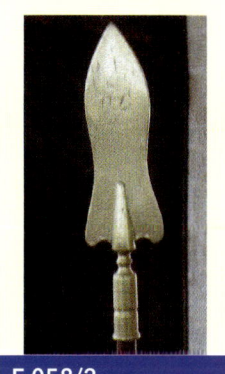

F 058/2

F 058/3   9.8"   MERL / Allen / 551104

This brass is sometimes associated with Twerton (otherwise written as Tiverton), a Bath suburb, but no evidence has emerged in support. It was not identified by Allen. Several specimens exist.

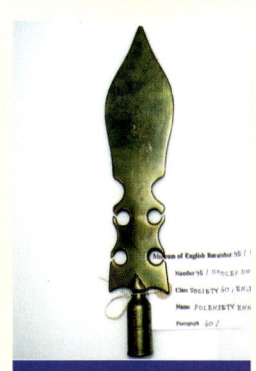

F 058/3

F 059   12.8"   MERL / Allen / 550838

This pattern is verified for **Batcombe**, but it is not clear which of two societies used it. Holburne Museum, Bath, has the HJ Hooper pre-1922 collection of pole heads, together with Hooper's 'Red Book' of photographs of the collection. In the 1920s the museum curator added notes to the 'Red Book', and made reference to an example of the pattern shown here, commenting that it was at that time owned at Box Bush Farm, Batcombe. The farm has long since changed hands and the location of the specimen is now unknown. At Batcombe two societies ran consecutively between 1800 and 1870 (SOM 255 and SOM 742), but their rules do not include any reference to poles, so it is not possible to say which of them had this pattern. Batcombe pole heads are usually stamped with the member's number.

F 059

F 060/1

F 060/2

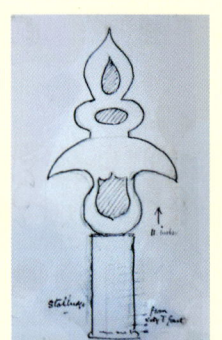

F 060/3

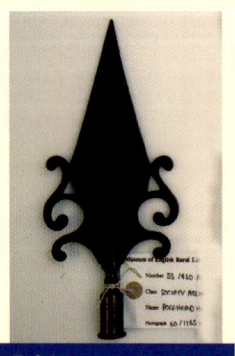

F 061

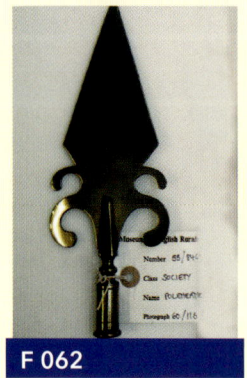

F 062

F 060/1   13.3"   MERL / Allen / 550844

This design is verified for **Stalbridge Union of Foresters** (1846 to 1906) (DOR 050), which met at the Red Lion Inn and at other inns in rotation. The 1846 rules specified 'a pole' and 'proper ensigns' (The National Archives FS 3/49/050). In a letter to Jardine dated July 13th, 1934, the Rev ES Merriman confirmed this design, and wrote that there were some left [in the village] (MERL Jardine Index). Stalbridge Foresters Society and other societies formed the Stalbridge Union Society of Foresters, but kept their own pole heads. The last Secretary of the Stalbridge Union Society of Foresters wrote that in the procession 'the Deer' walked first, then the 'Crowns', then the 'Spades', then the others with a 'sort of Battle Axe' (the design shown here) (MERL Ponsonby-Fane notebook, opp. p.50). These designs are respectively F 258, F 077, F 060/3, F 060/1 (members) and F060/2 (stewards).

F 060/2   13.3"   Private collection

This example belongs to a private collection which acquired its various Stalbridge pole heads on the 1906 break-up of **Stalbridge Union Society of Foresters** (1846 to 1906) (DOR 050). The society met at the Red Lion Inn and at other inns in rotation. The 1846 rules specified 'a pole' and 'proper ensigns' (The National Archives FS 3/49/050). In a letter to Jardine dated July 13th, 1936, the Rev ES Merriman confirmed the members' version of this design and wrote that there were some left [in the village] (MERL Jardine Index). Stalbridge Foresters Society and other societies formed the Stalbridge Union Society of Foresters, but kept their own pole heads. The last Secretary of the Stalbridge Union Society of Foresters wrote that in the procession 'the Deer' walked first, then the 'Crowns', then the 'Spades', then the others with a 'sort of Battle Axe' (MERL Ponsonby-Fane notebook, opp. p.50). These designs are respectively F 258, F 077, F 060/3, F 060/1 (members) and F060/2 (stewards). This pattern was created from a member's brass (F 060/1), for use by a steward.

F 060/3   11"   MERL / Ponsonby-Fane notebook, p50, no 3 D 85/11/1

This design is illustrated and described in the Ponsonby-Fane notebook, and is verified for **Stalbridge Union of Foresters** (DOR 050), which met at the Red Lion Inn and at other inns in rotation. The 1846 rules specified 'a pole' and 'proper ensigns' (The National Archives FS 3/49/050), but at its demise the club had a variety of other pole-heads from the societies which had amalgamated with it. This pattern was described by the last secretary of the club as a spade, and he wrote that in the procession 'the Deer' walked first, then the 'Crowns', then the 'Spades', then the others with a 'sort of Battle Axe' (MERL Ponsonby-Fane notebook, opp. p.50). They are respectively F 258, F 077, F 076, F 060/3, F 060/1 (members) and F060/2 (stewards). A version of F 060/3 exists with the date 1818 cut out.

F 061   10.1"   MERL / Allen / 550850

This design was attributed to South Brewham by Allen, but no evidence has emerged in support of the suggestion. Wainwright attributed it to Longwell Green, also with no evidence (Eunice B Overend, ed., *Catalogue of the Wainwright Collection of Friendly Society Brasses* [dispersed], the Phillips Museum [defunct], Brokerswood, Autumn 1971, p.7).

F 062   8.9"   MERL / Allen / 550846

Members of the North Brewham Friendly Society (1824 to after 1878) (SOM 554) carried rods, but the pattern of the pole head is unknown (The National Archives FS 1/622/544 1824 rules). Allen attributed this design to North Brewham, but offered no supporting evidence. A difficulty in interpretation lies in the fact that the rules indicate that this society met at the Bull Inn in South Bruham (sic).

F 063/1   12.9″ MERL / Allen / 550836

Allen attributed this design to Corsley, but he offered no evidence in support. This is one of the largest ordinary members' brasses for any society. A wooden pole head for Corsley has been verified (F 304/2).

F 063/1

F 063/2   20.4″ Blaise Castle House Museum / T7570

This very large specimen, probably a banner top, is listed in the Le Gros collection at Blaise Castle House Museum as originating from Corsley Heath. It clearly comes from the same society as F 063/1, but there are no supporting details to confirm the attribution. A wooden pole head for Corsley has been verified (F 304/2).

F 064   14″ MERL / Allen / 550840

The design is verified for **Evercreech Friendly Society** (1770 to c.1873) (SOM 091) and (1874 to 1903) (SOM 085), which respectively met at the George Inn and the Bell Inn. Jardine recorded that the pattern was identified by the Rector (MERL Jardine notes, reference to a letter, n.d., but c.1932), who wrote of a larger Steward's specimen of 15.7″, but an example has yet to be seen. A member's brass in a private collection is marked 'John Lambert'. He was an Evercreech resident and was mentioned in the *Sherborne Mercury* on August 7th, 1855. Most examples are numbered and stamped by the manufacturer Blinman & Co., Bristol. A few have a stamp but no number, while a very small number have no stamp at all. The 1770 rules specified a 'pole', and the 1825 and 1842 rules a 'spear' (The National Archives FS 3/328/91). In 1875 the members were reported as carrying 'formidable staves with brass devices' (*Western Gazette*, June 4th, 1875).

Detail of Evercreech pole head.

F 063/2

F 064

F 065   11.7″ MERL / Allen / 550830

This design is verified for **Mells Friendly Society** (1844 to 1950) (SOM 408), which met at the School Room. Allen's specimen is inscribed 'Mells School, 1853 (2) S Cook'. The 1851 census shows Samuel Cook, age 45, as a widower, a journeyman edge tool maker, and living at Mells. There is also a specimen, illustrated by Ethel W Gunn in the *Somerset Year Book* of 1922, p.53, with the initials B L, representing Benjamin Long, who lived at Mells. There was a larger steward's version, location now unknown, in the Wainwright Collection (dispersed) measuring c.13″ - 14″ (Eunice B. Overend, ed., *Catalogue of the Wainwright Collection of Friendly Society Brasses* [dispersed], The Phillips Museum [defunct], Brokerswood, Autumn 1971, no.65/65).

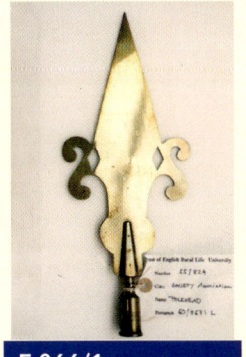

F 065

F 066/1   12.4″ MERL / Allen / 550824

This design is verified for **Keevil Old Friendly Society** (1799 to 1892) (WILTS 113), which met at the Rose and Crown Inn. In 1932 the Rev FM Weller wrote to Jardine stating: 'your design is still seen in some of the cottages ...examples of the old and new club staves are owned by a retired farmer, Mr Worthy Ghey, who was formerly an honorary member' (MERL Jardine Index).

F 066/1

F 066/2

F 066/3

F 067

F 068/1

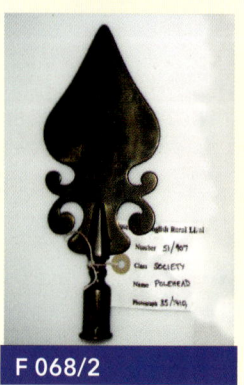

F 068/2

F 066/2   12.7″ SHC / OSFS / 071

This design is verified for **Keevil (New) Friendly Society** (c. 1892 to 1896) (WILTS 468), which met at the Beach Arms. Charles Wainwright's specimen of this brass had belonged to a member (letter to Sir S Ponsonby-Fane, June 25th, 1915: MERL D85/11/1). In a 1932 letter to Jardine the Rev FM Weller wrote: '49 young members of the old club formed a new club with headquarters at the Beach Arms. The pole head comprises a fleur de lys & Maltese Cross' (MERL Jardine Index). The design of the Keevil New Club brass uses the Old Club pattern as a basis, but it is differentiated by a fleur de lys and a Maltese Cross extending either side, just above the socket.

F 066/3   15.9″ SHC / OSFS / 072

This design is verified for **Keevil (New) Friendly Society** (c.1892 to 1896) (WILTS 468), which met at the Beach Arms. Charles Wainwright's specimen of this brass had belonged to a member (letter to Sir S Ponsonby-Fane, June 25th, 1915: MERL D85/11/1). In a 1932 letter to Jardine the Rev FM Weller wrote: '49 young members of the old club formed a new club with headquarters at the Beach Arms. The pole head comprises a fleur de lys & Maltese Cross' (MERL Jardine Index). The design of the Keevil New Club brass uses the Old Club pattern as a basis, but it is differentiated by a fleur de lys and a Maltese Cross extending either side, just above the socket. This larger version is a steward's brass: there is another example at Blaise Castle House Museum (T9349).

F 067   11.1″ MERL / Allen / 550900

Allen attributed this design to Rode (Road), but he provided no evidence. From a topological point of view the design is practically the same as the earlier pole head for Rode, F 068/1, and this may well be deliberate, but no other evidence of provenance has emerged.

F 068/1   9.7″ MERL / Allen / 550832

Rode (Road) and Buckland Dinham have both been suggested as locations for this design, but neither is confirmed, although Rode seems the more likely. The Buckland Denham Society of Several Tradesmen and Others (1779 to date unknown) (SOM 293) and the Rode Friendly Society of Tradesmen and Others (1790 to c 1896) (SOM 479) both met at inns called 'The Bell'. In a letter dated June 12th, 1928, S Lloyd Harvey wrote that William Bray, age 75, of Buckland Dinham, owned an example which belonged to his father, a member of the Bell Inn Club. The location was not stated, but it broke up before he could remember (SHC Taunton Museum archives). No newspaper accounts of either of these Bell Inn societies have been traced. Wainwright, on the other hand, positively identified this as the Road Old Wesleyan club, but his notes are missing (Eunice B Overend, ed., *Catalogue of the Wainwright Collection of Friendly Society Brasses* [dispersed], The Phillips Museum [defunct], Brokerswood, Autumn 1971, no.68/49). The 1794 Rode club rules specified 'staves and spears' (The National Archives FS 1/330/479).

F 068/2   8.4″ MERL / Shickle / 510907

Apart from the Shickle specimen two other examples are recorded, but none has a known provenance.

F 068/3   c. 12.25" Wainwright collection (dispersed): location untraced

The location of the only known example, in the Wainwright collection (dispersed), is now untraced. The pole head is verified for **Paulton Patriotic Friendly Society**, also known as **Paulton Old True Blues** (1806 to before 1882) (SOM 4353), which met at the Red Lion Inn. Wainwright attributed this design to Paulton on the basis of the inscription on the brass (Eunice B. Overend, ed., *Catalogue of the Wainwright Collection of Friendly Society Brasses* [dispersed], The Phillips Museum [defunct], Brokerswood, Autumn 1971, no.0/139). The inscription reads 'Paulton - Patriotic Society - instituted 1806'. It is not known if there were other examples of this brass. An indistinct photograph of the specimen can be seen in the *Somerset Standard*, June 11th, 1971.

F 068/3

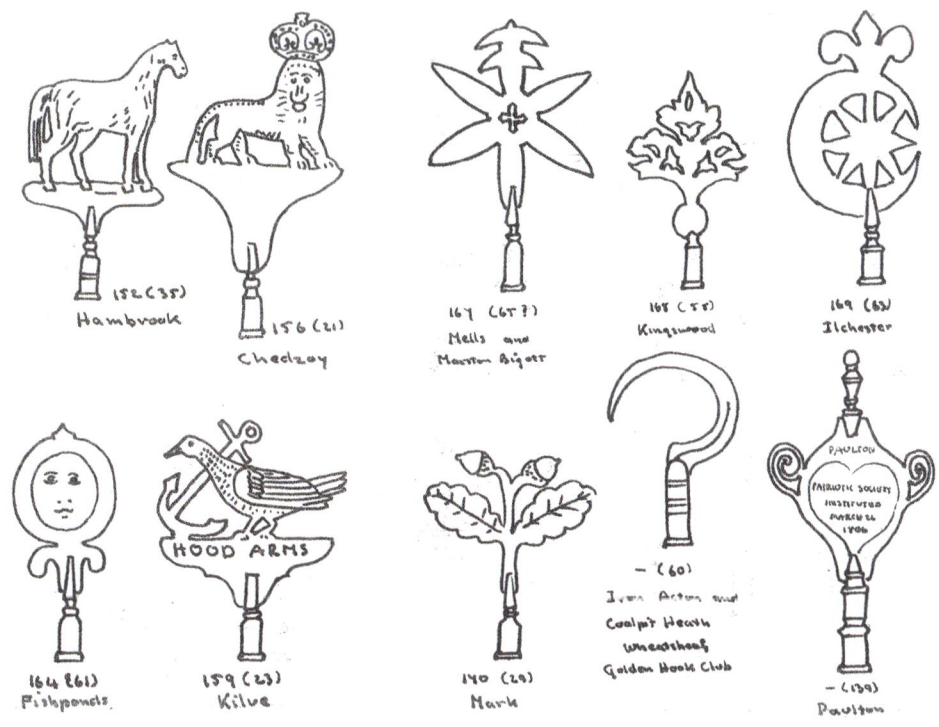

Extract of 1971 Wainwright collection catalogue.

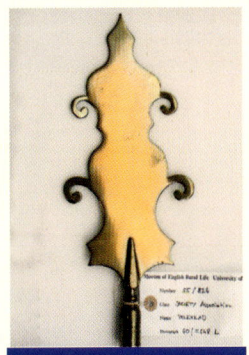

F 069

F 069   12.5"   MERL / Allen / 550826

This design is generally attributed to **Temple Cloud**. One specimen (private collection) has very old engraving on one side 'Temple Cloud', but it is not clear which society used it.

F 070/1   9.5"   MERL / Allen / 550848

No evidence has emerged to link this pattern to Writhlington. Only three examples have been recorded (MERL Allen 550848, MERL Shickle 510942, and private collection).

F 070/1

F 070/2   9.5"   MERL / Shickle / 510942

No evidence has emerged to link this pattern to Writhlington. This is the only known specimen of this design: it appears to be an uncompleted version of F 070/1 in which the lower part has not been cut away.

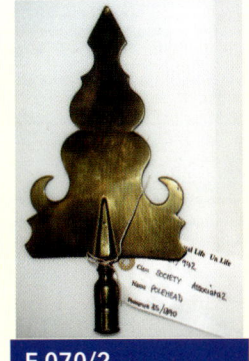

F 070/2

F 071   5.9"   MERL / Allen / 550884

Redhill Union Friendly Society (1843 to 1888) (SOM 330), which met at the Darlington Arms, has been suggested as the provenance of this pole head. The 1843 rules specify 'a blue staff surmounted with a brass crown', which could apply to this specimen, but the description is not sufficiently precise to confirm the pattern (The National Archives FS 3/330/330).

F 071

F 072

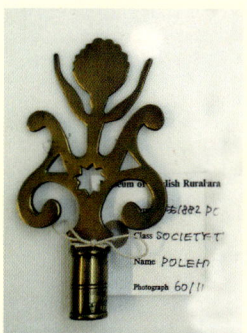

F 073

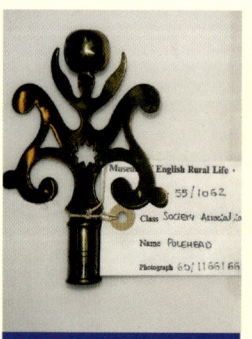

F 074

F 075

F 076

F 072   9.6"   MERL / Shickle / 510954

Redhill Union Friendly Society (1843 to 1888) (SOM 330), which met at the Darlington Arms, has been suggested as the provenance of this pole head. The 1843 rules specify 'a blue staff surmounted with a brass crown', which could apply to this specimen, but the description is not sufficiently precise to confirm the pattern (The National Archives FS 3/330/330). This would appear to be a steward's brass of the same society as F 071. There was another even larger steward's version (location unknown) in the Wainwright Collection (dispersed) measuring c. 10.5 - 11.5", but its current location is unknown (Eunice B. Overend, ed., *Catalogue of the Wainwright Collection of Friendly Society Brasses* [dispersed], The Phillips Museum [defunct], Brokerswood, Autumn 1971, no 71/3).

F 073   7.5"   MERL / Allen / 550869

This design was not attributed to any location by Allen, and no further evidence has been found.

F 074   5.5"   MERL / Allen / 550882

This design was not attributed to any location by Allen, and no further evidence has emerged. The top of this pattern appears to be a flower with a leaf on each side. F 117 is similar, but the flat flower has been replaced by a ball in the round.

F 075   5.1"   MERL / Allen / 551062

This design was not attributed to any location by Allen, and no further evidence has come to light. The top of this pattern is a ball in the round, unlike F 116, which has a flat flower.

F 076   11.6"   MERL / Allen / 550821

No evidence has emerged for Banwell, but instead this is possibly a cut-down version of F 077 from Stalbridge. The crown topped version of this pattern is extremely vulnerable, and an example exists where the crown has become detached from the other portion, suggesting that maybe the lower half, as in F 076 here, has been mistaken for a separate design. For other pole heads carried by the Stalbridge Union Society of Foresters see F 060/, F 060/2, F 060/3, F 077, and F 258.

F 077   24.4"   Private collection; a second example is at SCH / Du Cann Collection / 201891

This design is verified for **Stalbridge Union Society of Foresters** (1846 to 1906) (DOR 050), which met at the Red Lion Inn and at other inns in rotation. The 1846 rules specified 'a pole' and 'proper ensigns', but at its demise the club had a variety of different pole-heads, the result of amalgamations between clubs (The National Archives FS 3/49/50). Sgt-Maj Chas. Stanbrook, the last secretary of the Stalbridge Union Society of Foresters, referred to pole heads of this design as 'crowns' (details are repeated in a letter from Lady Theodora Guest to Sir Spencer Ponsonby-Fane, placed in the Ponsonby Fane Notebook of Club Brasses MERL, p.50). Members carrying pole heads with this design came second in the club processions. For other pole heads used by this society see F 060/1, F 060/2, F 060/3, F 076 and F 258.

F 078   10.1″   MERL / Allen / 550907

This design is often attributed to the Meare Old Club, but the pattern has not been confirmed. The club had a chequered existence: Meare Friendly and Benefit Society lasted from 1843 to 1874 (SOM 402); it restarted (unregistered) in 1874, again in 1890, and yet again in 1914. No evidence has emerged to attribute this design to any of the manifestations of the club, but the Meare Friendly and Benefit Society rules of 1843 required members to carry a 'blue pole with a brass head' (The National Archives FS 1/617B/402). It seems likely that the other pattern (F 024) attributed to Meare is associated with the re-establishment of the club in 1874 (this date is suggested from the appearance of a related design at High Ham in 1875 – see F 078). In 1892 it was reported that brasses were sold to members, but the design is unknown, and the batch may have been a repeat order of the 1874 pattern (*Western Gazette* June 3rd, 1892). If the F 078 design belonged to the earlier club (1843), it was probably discarded on the closure of the society in 1874, whereupon some may have been sold to the High Ham School House Friendly Society, whose attributed design appears to have been derived from the Meare pattern (see F 079).

F 079   10.4″   MERL / Shickle / 510931

In 1875 it was reported that staves were carried by the four stewards of the High Ham School House Friendly Society (1852 to 1931) (unregistered), but the pattern of the pole head has not been confirmed (*Langport Herald* May 22nd, 1875). The members simply had sashes and rosettes (*Langport Herald*, May 22nd, 1867). Only four specimens are known of the pattern said to have been used by the society. Two have the diamond-shaped top scarfed into the main part of the blade. It would appear that they are altered versions of F 078 from the Meare Friendly and Benefit Society (1843 to 1874). It may be that the birds in the Meare specimens (F 078) broke off, since at least two such broken versions exist. The SHC Du Cann specimen, however, is all in one piece (201810). It seems plausible that the High Ham pole heads were of the pattern shown here and could have been bought from the Meare Old Club (F 078) in 1874.

F 080/1   10″   MERL / Allen / 550799

No evidence has emerged to confirm that this pole head was used at Stoke St Michael (Stoke Lane), and the only support for the claim is that the design was said to have been based a fleur de lys pattern in the church. Two clubs existed in this village simultaneously, registered numbers SOM380 and SOM397, and it is not recorded whether either of them used this design. At the feast day in 1894 members of the society known as Stoke St Michael Friendly Society, which met at the Brickdales Inn, were reported as carrying spears with tassels, but the design was not described (*Shepton Mallet Journal*, June 1st, 1894).

F 080/2   7.25″   MERL / Jardine / 6124433

No evidence supports Jardine's attribution of this design to Castle Cary, and it is not even clear whether this is a pole top used by a friendly society: the emblem is unusually small, and the tapered socket is most rare. Other examples are known, such as at Wells and Mendip Museum, Box 196. The pole head may be of ecclesiastical origin.

F 077

F 078

F 079

F 080/1

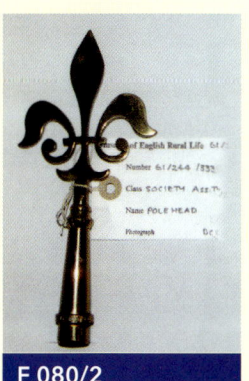

F 080/2

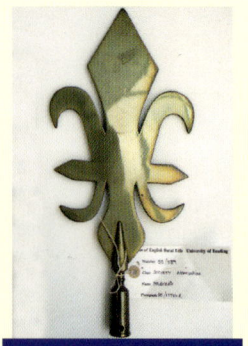

F 081

F 082

F 083

F 084

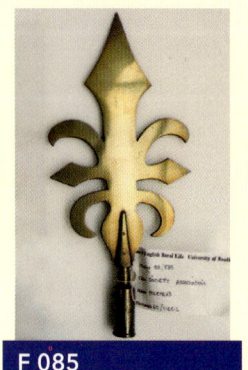

F 085

F 081   14.9″   MERL / Allen / 550839

Analysis of the heights of 20 of this design shows two distinct clusters around 14.2″ and 14.9″. This pattern is verified for two societies: **Chelynch Club** (in the parish of Doulting) (from before 1793 to after 1894) (unregistered), which met at the Chelynch Inn, and **Pilton Friendly Society** (1854 to 1864) (SOM 730a) followed by **Pilton Provident Five Year Society** (1864 to after 1904) (SOM 730b), which met at the School Room. AT Wickes wrote to AW Allen, January 18th, 1937, that one of Charles Wainwright's staff found a Chelynch example at the Chelynch Inn (MERL Classified Index: societies / associations). A letter to the curator of Taunton Museum from AW Allen, March 2nd, 1941, included a full-size outline sketch (c.14.9″) and explained that a pole head of that design was carried by a Pilton Club old member (SHC Taunton Museum archives). The larger version of this design would therefore seem to belong to Pilton. Furthermore, the drawings in the Wainwright catalogue indicate Pilton as the larger variety, and Chelynch the smaller (Eunice B Overend, ed., *Catalogue of the Wainwright Collection of Friendly Society Brasses* [dispersed], The Phillips Museum, Brokerswood [defunct], Autumn 1971, p.9). Some of the members' brasses have the roll number stamped on.

F 082   13.8″   MERL / Shickle / 510946

The design is verified for **Heytesbury Union Society** (1788 to after 1813) (WILTS 733), which met at the Red Lion Inn. This specimen from the Shickle collection is engraved: 'Uinion Society, Comd Jany 12th 1788. WT (sic)' on one side; and on the other 'WT' and 'William Thorn 1764-1807'. The Allen collection has a similar brass, inscribed 'WP' (MERL Allen 550842), and another (private) example is stamped '19' and engraved 'AJC' and '1807', indicating the very early use of brass pole heads. Comparison of this design with F 099/2, a very large steward's brass from the dispersed Wainwright collection (Eunice B Overend, ed., *Catalogue of the Wainwright Collection of Friendly Society Brasses* [dispersed], The Phillips Museum, Brokerswood [defunct], Autumn 1971, p.3) reveals that the outline is topologically similar to the Heytesbury member's brass. The steward's brass F 099/2, however, has in addition a pierced face which includes the lettering G lll R and the date 1788, the date when the Heytesbury society was formed. Its present location is untraced.

F 083   11.3″   MERL / Allen / 550805

Allen offered no suggestions for the provenance of this specimen, while Fuller (1964) indicates Cranmore, but gives no further details. Other specimens of this height exist at MERL (Shickle), MERL (Jardine) and SHC (OSFS 060). The outline of the arms of this pattern in quite distinct from those of F 081, F 082 and F 084.

F 084   13.3″   MERL / Allen / 550843

No evidence confirms the use of this design at Sutton Veny, Wiltshire. In AW Allen's notes is a claim by W.E. Edwards, a collector, that 'the club heads were purchased 1861 or 1862' (MERL Notes accompanying the Allen Collection). No helpful newspaper references have come to light. The brass is of thicker than normal gauge, and has the edges chamfered towards one face.

F 085   13″   MERL / Allen / 550835

Members of Warminster Friendly Society (1829 to 1867), which met at the Cock Inn, carried brasses, but the pattern has not been confirmed. In 1867 the club procession was headed by a brazen cock which was followed by each member carrying 'a brazen-headed javelin' (*Frome Times*, June 19th, 1867). Almost certainly the design illustrated is the correct one for Warminster, but there is no definitive proof.

F 086   13″   MERL / Allen / 550837

This design is verified for **Norton St Phillip**, but it is not clear which society used it. Five societies existed at Norton St Phillip at various times between 1785 to 1842 and beyond, but their official papers have not survived. In a letter to Jardine dated September 29th, 1943 the Vicar of Norton St Phillip, the Rev Prebendary KC Jachin, verified that the brass had been used in the village, and made reference to the specimen in the church (MERL Jardine DDX/993). The vicar also told AT Wicks that he had been at considerable pains to secure it as a relic of the former local club (SHC Taunton Museum archives: notes by AT Wicks). Compton Martin has also been suggested as a provenance, but no supporting evidence has emerged. These specimens were sometimes mutilated, with various pairs of arms broken off.

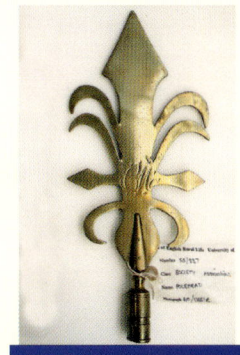

F 086

F 087/1   13.8″   MERL / Allen / 550841

This design is verified for **Binegar Friendly Society of Tradesmen, Farmers and Others** (1807 to 1874) (SOM 127), which met at the George Inn, Gurney Slade. There was also an earlier club in the parish. The Rector, the Rev WM King-Warren, in correspondence with Charles Wainwright, c.1932, stated that his example of the design had been carried by a Mr Targett, a centenarian, whose daughter vouched for him, and added that the club was held at Gurney Slade (MERL Jardine DDX/993). The Binegar brasses are often stamped with the member's roll number. The Allen specimen is no. 40.

F 087/1

F 087/2   17″   Private collection

This design appears to be a steward's brass from Binegar, even though the cut-out pattern at the top is different from the diamond shape of the smaller brass of the members, but there is no supporting evidence.

F 088/1   18.4″   MERL / Shickle / 510960

This design appears to be a steward's brass from Norton St Phillip (or perhaps Compton Martin, but there is no supporting evidence). For a slightly different version see F 088/2.

F 087/2

F 088/2   17.8″   SHC / OSFS / 055A

Three similar specimens of this pattern exist, slightly shorter than F 088/1, and with wavy ornamentation to the top edges of the diamond shape below the crown. No proof of provenance is recorded for any of them.

Detail of F 082, Heytesbury, dated 1807.

F 088/1

F 088/2

F 089/1

F 089/2

F 090

F 091/1

F 091/2

F 089/1   12.8″   MERL / Allen / 550827

This design is verified for **Wincanton Friendly Society** (1773 to 1842) (SOM 137) and (1842 to 1849) (SOM 371), **Wincanton Septennial Friendly Society** (1849 to 1856) (DOR 171), and **Wincanton United Friendly Society** (1856 to 1895) (SOM 623, but unregistered from 1895 to c.1936), which met at the Swan Inn, later at the Trooper Inn, and then at the National School Room. A steward's version of the smaller brass is at F 090. In 1930 DK Sweetman gave Taunton Museum the specimen OSFS 205, which is engraved GS, i.e. George Sweetman (great-grandfather of the donor), and the date on the label reads 1847 (SHC Taunton Museum archives). The grandfather of the donor was the author of *The History of Wincanton*, 1903. The 1834 rules specify 'a rod', the 1849 rules also specify 'a spear', and there is a newspaper reference of 1866 to spears (The National Archives FS 1/615/317 1834 rules; SHC Tite collection of Friendly Society Rules, Wincanton 1849; *Western Gazette*, June 1st, 1866). Specimens vary in height according to the variations in the type of socket that was used, and may be a little shorter than the one shown here.

F 089/2   12.5″   Private collection

This design was illustrated by Emanuel Green in 'Somerset Club Brasses', *J Brit Arch S*, NS, vol XV,1909, opposite p.57, but with no suggestion of origin. It is a probably a cut-down version of the Wincanton brass, but this is uncertain, as more than one example is known.

F 090   21.4″   MERL / Allen / 550921

This design is verified for **Wincanton Friendly Society** (1773 to 1842) (SOM 137) and (1842 to 1849) (SOM 371), **Wincanton Septennial Friendly Society** (1849 to 1856) (DOR 171), and **Wincanton United Friendly Society** (1856 to 1895) (SOM 623 but unregistered from 1895 to c.1936), which met at the Swan Inn, later at the Trooper Inn, and then at the National School Room. This is a steward's version of the smaller brass is at F 089/1. In 1930 DK Sweetman gave Taunton Museum the members' brass (OSFS 205), which is engraved GS, i.e. George Sweetman (great-grandfather of the donor), and the date on the label reads 1847. The grandfather of the donor was the author of *The History of Wincanton*, 1903.

F 091/1   12.5″   MERL / Allen / 550825

This design is verified for **Buckhorn Weston Benefit Friendly Society** (1856 to 1908) (DOR 169), which met at the Stapleton Arms and later at the Mission Room. In a letter to Jardine, December 11th, 1943, the Rev James Hutton, Rector of Buckhorn Weston, wrote: [an] 'old inhabitant still possesses a brass' (MERL Jardine Index). In Dorset Museum, Dorchester, the specimen was donated Miss Agnes Williams of Buckhorn Weston. It had been in the family for several generations: James Cross, her great-great-grandfather had used it in club walks (1956.35.1)

F 091/2   12.7″   Holburne Museum / VE090

It is not clear whether this is simply a cut-down version of the Buckhorn Weston pattern or a design in its own right. Jardine regarded it as a mutilation. The Holburne specimen from the Hooper collection has no further evidence.

F 092/1   12.1"   MERL / Allen / 550823

This design is verified for **Marnhull Friendly Society** (1833 to 1896) (DOR 371), which met at the Crown Inn. In a letter dated September 22nd, 1943 the Rector of Marnhull wrote: 'your design represents the Crown Hotel here, also the wheel is a Catherine wheel which was connected with a charity once at the church' (MERL Jardine Index). The initials MFS on the brass confirm the society.

F 092/1

F 092/2   13.4"   MERL / Shickle / 510956

Shickle provided no evidence for what seems to be a unique specimen, but it probably relates to Marnhull, Dorset. The top flat portion outline is the topological equivalent of the Marnhull Friendly Society brass (F 092/1), but is slightly shorter and considerably narrower. To add to the resemblance, the face is engraved with an eight pointed star below which is a dagger. The initials EHM surrounding the star have not been identified.

F 092/2

F 093   11.7"   MERL / Allen / 550829

This design is verified for **Temple Combe Ten Year Friendly Society** (1857 to 1867) (SOM 669), and was probably used by the preceding **21 Year Society** (1835 to 1856) (SOM 497), both of which met at the Blue Boar Inn. The initials TCFS confirm the design as belonging to Temple Combe Friendly Society. In 1886 the members were reported as 'carrying poles and ribbons' and 'the pole head itself is pierced with the initials of the club, TCFS' (*Western Gazette*, May 25th, 1866).

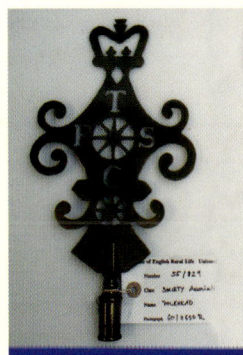

F 093

F 094/1   12"   MERL / Allen / 550833

This design is verified for **Ditcheat**, also for **Frome**, but there is no evidence for Ansford. The 1791 Ditcheat Friendly Society (SOM 070) seems not to have survived beyond c.1815, so the pole head was probably used by the **Ditcheat United Society** (c.1870 to c.1916) (unregistered). In a letter to Jardine dated December 15th, 1943, Tom Vincent, a Ditcheat dairy farmer (according to Kelly's 1935 *Directory of Somerset*), wrote: the 'late Albert Higgins had one. [He was] a member of the club from its start about 65 years ago: it lasted 46 years' (MERL Jardine Index). For Frome the evidence lies in two brasses, each with a member's name and 'Frome' engraved (Holburne Museum, VE005, and a private collection). It is unclear which Frome Friendly Society is relevant, as no other supporting evidence has come to light.

F 094/1

F 094/2   12"   Private collection

There are several examples of this type, identical to the Ditcheat / Frome specimens, except that they are all neatly engraved 'SH' above the cut-out wheel and a further 'S' and 'H' respectively to the left and right of the wheel. They clearly belong to a particular society, but to which one is unknown, since the initials SHSH have not been identified.

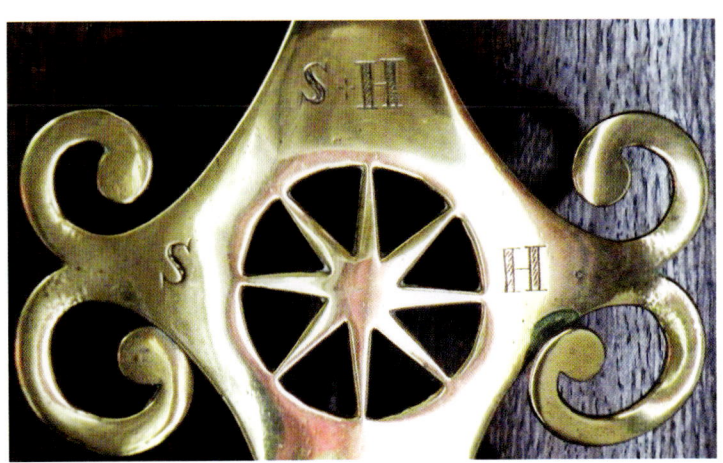

F 094/2

Detail of F 094/2 to show SHSH.

F 094/3

F 095/1

F 095/2

F 096

F 097

F 094/3   12″   Private collection

This design was illustrated by Emanuel Green in 'Somerset Club Brasses', *J Brit Arch S*, NS, vol XV, 1909, opposite p.57, but with no suggestion of origin. It is a probably a cut-down version of the Ditcheat / Frome brass (F 094/1), but more than one example is known.

F 095/1   13.2″   Private collection

This design is verified for **West Stower Friendly Society** (1823 to 1857), which later became **West Stower United Friendly Society** (1857 to c.1891) and finally **West Stower Benefit Society** (c.1891 to 1915) (DOR 123), but it was only registered from 1857 to c.1891). It met at the Ship Inn, West Stour, Dorset, but held its feast day celebrations, by rotation, at West Stour, East Stour and Fifiehead Magdalen. A note in the MERL Jardine Index, n.d., from the widow of Charles Clark, states: 'the club died 28 years ago. She has one of its pole

Detail of F 096/1 with one of two versions of the ship's rigging

heads dated 1879'. There is a large variety of heights of these specimens, mainly due to variations in the design of the sockets, ranging from 12.4″ to 13.4″. The cast-in details of the ship also confirm the identity of the club headquarters. There is more than one variant of the ship's details, since in one version (of which there are several identical examples) the ship's rigging has fewer ropes.

F 095/2   12.4″   SHC / OSFS / 273

This design is verified as a steward's brass of **West Stower Friendly Society** (1823 to 1857), which later became **West Stower United Friendly Society** (1857 to c.1891) and finally **West Stower Benefit Society** (c.1891 to 1915) (DOR 123), but it was only registered from 1857 to c.1891). It met at the Ship Inn, West Stour, Dorset, but held its feast day celebrations, by rotation, at West Stour, East Stour and Fifiehead Magdalen. A note in the MERL Jardine Index, n.d., from the widow of Charles Clark, states: 'the club died 28 years ago. She has one of its pole heads dated 1879'. A further example of this steward's brass is in Dorset Museum, Dorchester (1987.95.2), but it is 13.7″. Both are stamped 'G. Weedon - Bath' (brass founders). Unusually for stewards' brasses, this club adopted a design which was wider, rather than taller, than the members' pattern.

F 096   8.1″   MERL / Allen / 550926

No specific evidence has emerged that the design originated from Combe Hay.

F 097   12.1″   MERL / Allen / 551088

Fuller (1964) lists this design as South Wraxall, and the specimen she illustrated, as with most of the images in her list, came from the Allen collection, although he ascribed the design to Bemerton in Wiltshire, but gave no evidence for the claim. No evidence to support a South Wraxall provenance has emerged.

F 098 12.2" MERL / Allen / 550801

No verification has been found for Monkton Farleigh, Wiltshire, as the location of this design, but on the other hand no other suggestions seem to have been made by early collectors.

F 098

F 099/1 8.7" MERL / Allen / 551076

Burton (Wiltshire) is listed as the origin of this design, but there is no evidence in support. No other locations have been suggested.

F 099/2 c. 27.5" The Wainwright collection (dispersed): location untraced.

The Wainwright collection (dispersed): location now untraced. Evidence based on the outline of the brass and date on it suggest that this is probably a Heytesbury officer's specimen. The top diamond shape resembles the top of the Heytesbury members' pattern, as do the three arms each side The Heytesbury Union Friendly Society was founded in 1788, which is also the date on this brass. A poor quality photograph of this specimen (only the outline is distinguishable) appeared in the *Somerset Standard*, June 11th, 1971, when the Wainwright collection was exhibited in Frome Museum, and a drawing appeared in the catalogue of the later exhibition at the Phillips Museum (defunct) (Eunice B. Overend, ed., *Catalogue of the Wainwright Collection of Friendly Society Brasses* [dispersed], Phillips Museum [defunct], Brokerswood, Autumn 1971, p.3). The actual specimen was also referred to in 1887, and by then it belonged to Dr Frederick Porter Smith of Shepton Mallet (*Shepton Mallet Journal*, December 16th, 1887). Subsequently it was in the Wainwright collection, which was dispersed in 1974 (*Christie's Catalogue*, 14th November 1974, lot 166, with accompanying photograph).

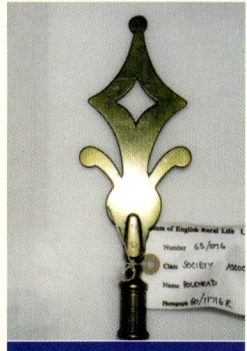

F 099/1

F 099/2

F 099/3 5.9" Blaise Castle House Museum / T9340

This specimen is claimed to be from the Croscombe Friendly Society (unregistered), which existed in 1795 up to a date unknown, and then again from before 1841 to after 1884). Blaise Castle House Museum, however, has no provenance for the specimen shown here. The design appears as number 171 in the catalogue of the Wainwright Collection (dispersed), where it is described as 'Croscombe: a President's emblem, on a short, tasselled staff' (Eunice B. Overend, ed., *Catalogue of the Wainwright Collection of Friendly Society Brasses* [dispersed], Phillips Museum [defunct], Brokerswood, Autumn 1971, p.8). Wainwright (or perhaps Eunice Overend) claimed to have definite proof of the provenance of Croscombe pole heads, but the notes accompanying the collection are lost. The location of the Wainwright example of this particular design is unknown. For the stewards' pole head of the same club see F 218/4.

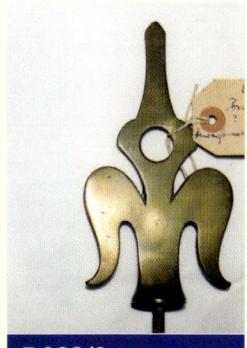

F 099/3

F 100 9.6" MERL / Allen / 550887

No evidence has emerged for any location. Minor inconsistent differences exist between the patterns ascribed variously to Tunley, Carlingcott, Filton and Steeple Ashton, but all are explicable by the inexactitudes of hand-crafting and by the use of sockets of differing lengths. Except for the sockets, F 100 and F 101 appear to have no significant differences, and may belong to the same society. In F 101, above the hollow part of the socket, the split housing for the blade extends further up the face than in F 100, making for a more secure purchase for the two rivets which hold the blade in place.

F 100

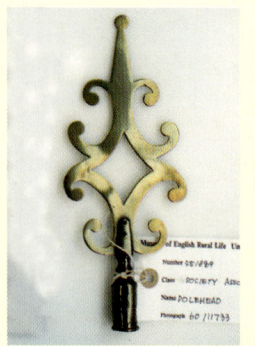

F 101

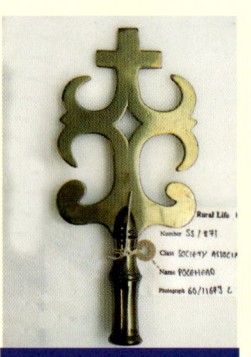

F 102

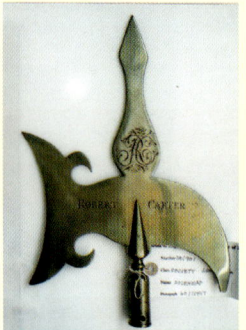

F 103

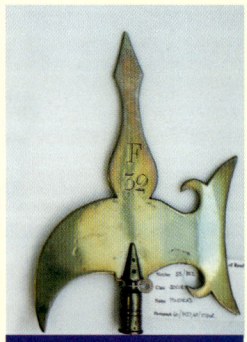

F 104

F 105

F 101   8.9″   MERL / Allen / 550889

No evidence has emerged for any location. Minor inconsistent differences exist between the patterns ascribed variously to Tunley, Carlingcott, Filton and Steeple Ashton, but all are explicable by the inexactitudes of hand-crafting and by the use of sockets of differing lengths. Except for the sockets, F 100 and F 101 appear to have no significant differences, and may belong to the same society. In F 101, above the open part of the socket, the split housing for the blade extends further up the face than in F 100, making for a more secure purchase for the two rivets which hold the blade in place.

F 102   8.2″   MERL / Allen / 550871

This design was claimed to have been used first at Woolavington by the Woolavington and Polden Hill Friendly Society 1854 to 1860 (SOM624), which met at the White Lion Inn, and by its successor (1860 to 1875) (unregistered). On the disbandment of the latter in 1875 the pole heads were then used by **The Benefit and Friendly Society at Catcott, Edgington, Chilton and Neighbourhood,** also known as **West Polden Friendly Society** (1839 to 1913, but re-established in 1875) (SOM 443), which met at the White Hart Inn at Chilton Polden (SHC Taunton Museum archives, Friendly Society notes by AT Wickes dated September 1936, with information from the Vicar of Chilton Polden and Mr Dewar). The pole head can be seen in a 1908 photograph of members of the West Polden Friendly Society (private collection). The 1845 rules of the nearby Moorlinch Friendly Society (1845 to 1868) (SOM 407), which met at the Ring o' Bells Inn, specified that members were to process carrying a blue pole with a brass head, but the design has not been identified, and it is just possible that they were the ones later used by the two previously mentioned clubs (The National Archives FS 1/617B/407 1845 rules).

F 103   12.6″   MERL / Allen / 550901

Allen suggested both Litton and Ston Easton, but there is no clear proof from either location. Due to the long socket the overall height is distinctive: F 104 is much shorter. The blade, however, is the same as F 104, and both types are found with engraved initials and / or names written in full, so it is not obvious whether they come from one location or two. The names found on these brasses cannot always be traced in censuses, but many of the inscribed surnames persist throughout several decades in the contiguous parishes of Litton, Farrington Gurney, Ston Easton and Chewton Mendip. The initials here are RC and the name is Robert Carter, but the individual has not been verified as living at one of these villages.

F 104   11.7″   MERL / Allen / 550802

Allen suggested Farrington Gurney or Chewton Mendip, but there is no clear proof from any location. Due to the short socket (F 103 is much longer) the overall height is distinctive, but the blade is the same as F 103, and both types are found with engraved initials or whole names. Many of these brasses are engraved with the letter 'F', followed by a number in a bold, distinctive script, giving a strong hint that they were used at Farrington Gurney: they are all of the short socket variety. Others have a very small stamped number instead, but it is unclear whether they come from the same numbering system as the bold script or whether they represent the identification system of an entirely different society.

F 105   9.8″   MERL / Allen / 551109

This specimen was unidentified by Allen. No other example has been seen with the particular pattern above the axe blade: it appears that the extreme top may have been snapped off and the remaining upstanding portion suitably filed down to disguise the damage. The resulting height is less than normal. Other specimens have been seen with the top spike completely absent, but these all appear to be mutilations, as does this specimen.

F 106/1   13.5"   SHC / OSFS / 092D

This specimen has no provenance, but it appears to be a flagpole top, a banner top, or an official's brass, from the same society as F 103 or F 104. Only one example is known. Implied in the design, which shows elements of both a common spear and a halberd, is that the same manufacturer was responsible for examples of both patterns.

F 106/1

F 106/2   5.1"   Blaise Castle House Museum / T 9351

Only one example of this pattern has been seen in museum collections: it has no recorded provenance and may not even be of Friendly Society origin. Decorative halberds have been used by other organisations, such as the Orange Orders of Ulster, where they were used on the tops of poles bearing the union flag. This example has suffered some damage: the top portion is bent over, and the lower portion of the left hand extension has been broken off.

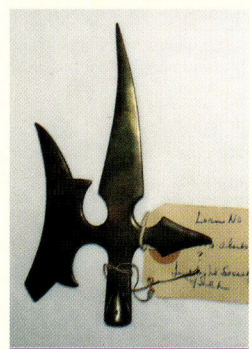

F 106/2

F 107   6.4"   MERL / Allen / 550813

No evidence has emerged to support Allen's suggested provenance of Downend. The heights of various examples vary within c.1/2" depending on the detail of the sockets. The main differences in design between F 107 and F 108 lie in the absence of the decorative nail holes in the horse shoe in F 107 and the contrasted lower edges of the bar. The sockets also show some contrasts.

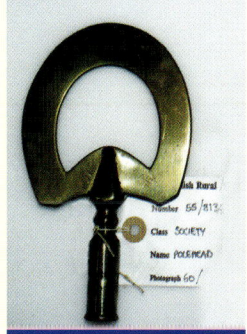

F 107

F 108   6.3"   MERL / Allen / 550880

Siston, Filton and Failand have been suggested as the origin of this design, but no supporting evidence has emerged in favour of any of the three. Although the name 'Horseshoe Inn' is indicative of location, there are several inns of this name in the region. The main differences in design between F 107 and F 108 lie in the absence of the decorative nail holes in the horse shoe in F 107 and the different lower edges of the bar. The sockets also show some contrasts.

F 108

F 109/1   8.3"   MERL / Allen / 551085

Siston, Filton and Failand have been suggested as the origin of this design, but no supporting evidence has emerged in favour of any of the three. Although the name 'Horseshoe Inn' is indicative of location, there are several inns of this name in the region. This version is probably a steward's brass: three at this size have been recorded. Two even larger versions, at c.11" and 16", locations now unknown, were in the Wainwright Collection (dispersed) (Eunice B. Overend, ed., *Catalogue of the Wainwright Collection of Friendly Society Brasses* [dispersed], The Phillips Museum [defunct], Brokerswood, Autumn 1971, numbers 109/96 and 109/116. They were labelled Failand Farmers' Friendly Society, but without any further details).

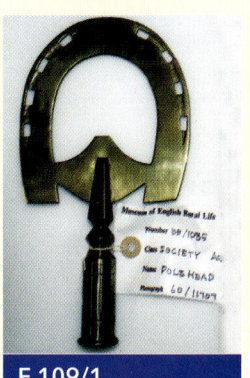

F 109/1

Detail of the distinctive engraved membership number: F 104.

F 109/2

F 110

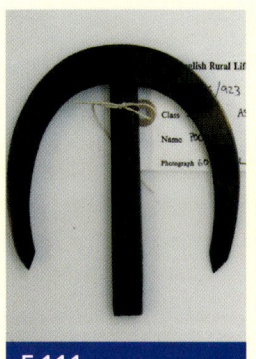

F 111

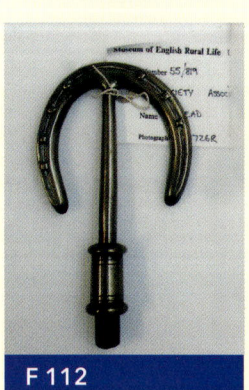

F 112

F 113

F 109/2   4.75"   SCH / OSFS / 251

Only one specimen has been recorded of this design, and it has no proof of provenance. It is similar to the Hanham brasses, but without the crown (F 113 and F 115). It may have been cut down, but there is no evidence of such an alteration, as the top edge is smooth. SCH indicates that this specimen came from the Kelway collection, but it is not illustrated in James Kelway's Notebook of drawings (SHC Taunton Museum archives).

F 110   4.5"   MERL / Allen / 550918

This design is verified for **Bowlish Horse Shoe Club** (before 1860 to 1868) (unregistered), which met at the Horse Shoe Inn. In a letter to Jardine dated September 27th, 1932, Charles R Wainwright wrote: 'my father had an old coachman who was a member [who confirmed the design]' (MERL Jardine Index). There are two variants: this one has a conventional socket, but the other type (F 111) only has a downward projecting plate, which fits into a slot on the top of the wooden pole.

F 111   4.8"   MERL / Allen / 550923

This design is verified for **Bowlish Horse Shoe Club** (before 1860 to 1868) (unregistered), which met at the Horse Shoe Inn. In a letter to Jardine dated September 27th, 1932, Charles R Wainwright wrote: 'my father had an old coachman who was a member [who confirmed the design]' (MERL Jardine Index). There are two variants: the first (F 110) has a conventional socket, but this one (F 111) only has a downward projecting plate, which fits into a slot on the top of the wooden pole.

F 112   6.6"   MERL / Allen / 550819

Between 1863 and 1903 the Filton Junior Benefit Society (GLOS 0817) moved from the Anchor Inn, Filton, to the Horseshoe Inn, then back, and finally again to the Horseshoe Inn. It was reputed to have changed emblems when moving from one to the other. Filton is suggested as the provenance of this brass, and the design would be appropriate, but there is no other confirmation for the provenance.

F 113   8"   MERL / Allen / 550816

The Friendly Society at the Crown and Horseshoe Inn, Hanham (before 1800 to 1819) (GLOS 0087), was dissolved in 1819, and the 'flags and sticks' were sold to members (probably, therefore, pole heads were included) (*Bristol Mirror*, January 18th, 1819). This is the only evidence so far to emerge to link this design (together, perhaps, with F 114 and F 115) to Hanham. The name of the club and the name of the inn are consistent with the design. A subsequent club which met here, the Royal (later Loyal) Victoria Benefit Society (1841 to after 1868), appears to have been an annual non-walking society, and it would not have needed pole heads (*Bristol Mercury*, June 13th, 1868).

F 114   15.6"   Blaise Castle House Museum / T7507

The Friendly Society at the Crown and Horseshoe Inn, Hanham (before 1800 to 1819) (GLOS 0087), was dissolved in 1819, and the 'flags and sticks' were sold to members (probably, therefore, pole heads were included) (*Bristol Mirror,* January 18th, 1819). This is the only evidence so far to emerge to link this design (together, perhaps, with F 113 and F 115) to Hanham. The name of the club and the name of the inn are consistent with the design. A subsequent club which met here, the Royal (later Loyal) Victoria Benefit Society (1841 to after 1868), appears to have been an annual non-walking society, and it would not have needed pole heads (*Bristol Mercury*, June 13th, 1868). This example appears to be a steward's version of F 113, or a banner top.

F 115   8.3"   MERL / Allen / 550815

The Friendly Society at the Crown and Horseshoe Inn, Hanham (before 1800 to 1819) (GLOS 0087), was dissolved in 1819, and the 'flags and sticks' were sold to members (probably, therefore, pole heads were included) (*Bristol Mirror*, January 18th, 1819). This is the only evidence so far to emerge to link this design (together, perhaps, with F 113 and F 114) to Hanham. The name of the club and the name of the inn are consistent with the design. A subsequent club which met here, the Royal (later Loyal) Victoria Benefit Society (1841 to after 1868), appears to have been an annual non-walking society, and it would not have needed pole heads (*Bristol Mercury*, June 13th, 1868). Fuller (1964) suggests that this may be a variant of F 113, but there is no evidence for any provenance.

F 114

F 116   7.3"   MERL / Allen / 550875

No specific evidence has emerged to associate this design with Corston, except the initials 'CS' (possibly for Corston Friendly Society). Clutton has also been suggested, but again without proof.

F 115

F 117/1   9"   MERL / Allen / 550913

This design has been attributed to a society meeting at the Portcullis Inn, Great Badminton, Gloucestershire, but there is no supporting evidence, which allows the possibility that this design came from elsewhere. The Langport town arms comprise a portcullis, and this motif was adopted at Langport both by the Oddfellows (Portcullis Lodge: 1848 to 1849) and the Foresters (Court Portcullis: 1876 to 1927). The 1827 Langport Friendly Society rules specified a red pole with a brass knob and white ribbon, but the design has so far not been identified (SHC Q/RSf 6, 1827 rules, Langport Friendly Society). The pole head labelled Langport by Fuller (F 294) is clearly wrong: the brass is a marriage of two unrelated parts, since the top is a brass sheath from a knitting belt, and has nothing to do with friendly societies.

F 116

F 117/2   c. 14.4" Wainwright collection (dispersed): location untraced.

This larger version of F 117/1 is a steward's brass and was in the Wainwright Collection (dispersed) (Eunice B. Overend, ed., *Catalogue of the Wainwright Collection of Friendly Society Brasses* [dispersed], Phillips Museum [defunct], Brokerswood, Autumn 1971, no 117/133). It was listed as originating at Badminton. but there is no supporting evidence, which allows the possibility that this design came from elsewhere. The Langport town arms comprise a portcullis, and this motif was adopted at Langport both by the Oddfellows (Portcullis Lodge: 1848 to 1849) and the Foresters (Court Portcullis: 1876 to 1927). The 1827 Langport Friendly Society rules specified a red pole with a brass knob and white ribbon, but the design has so far not been identified, raising the possibility that it might be the one shown here and at F 117/1 (SHC Q/RSf 6, 1827 rules, Langport Friendly Society). The pole head labelled Langport by Fuller in 1964 (F 294) is clearly wrong: the brass is a marriage of two unrelated parts, since the top is a brass sheath from a knitting belt, and has nothing to do with friendly societies.

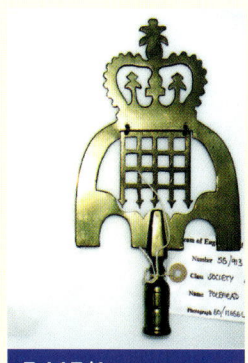

F 117/1

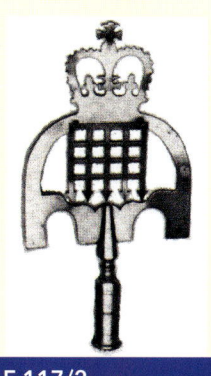

F 117/2

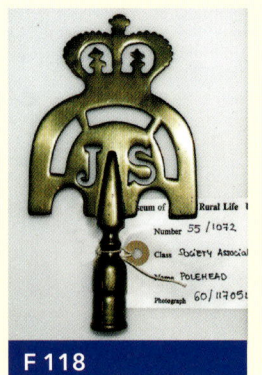

F 118

F 119

F 120/1

F 120/2b

F 121

F 118   6.3"   MERL / Allen / 551072

This design is verified for **Keynsham Jubilee Friendly Society** (1809 to after 1844) (SOM 168), which met at the Fox and Hounds Inn. The 50th anniversary of the accession of King George III was celebrated not in 1810, but, as was the custom, in 1809, the date when the society was established (*Bristol Mirror*, October 27th, 1810: 'the society was founded last year'). The 1844 rules specify that members should have a staff. The author A.E.S. ('More Somerset Brasses', *Somerset Year Book*, 1936, vol XXXV, p 100) wrote that a brass of this design was carried c.1850 by William John Read of Keynsham, the grandfather of the current owner, Charles H Webb of Keynsham; the same information was repeated in a letter from AE Stephens, April 1936, to the curator of Taunton Museum (SHC Taunton Museum archives).

F 119   6.6"   MERL / Allen / 550865

This design is attributed to the Old Friendly Society at Westbury on Trym (GLOS 0005) (1772 to 1897), but there is no evidence to support the claim, save that the club was known to have carried staves (*Bristol Mercury*, May 31st, 1861). The design does not relate to their meeting place.

F 120/1   9.8"   Blaise Castle House Museum / T7502

This design is attributed to the Old Friendly Society at Westbury on Trym (1772 to 1897) (GLOS 0005), but there is no evidence to support the claim, save that the club was known to have carried staves (*Bristol Mercury*, May 31st, 1861). The design does not relate to their meeting place. Unlike the members' brass, this larger stewards' version has the crown sitting on a cushion. Two examples of similar size and outline exist, one unpainted as here (F 120/1), the other painted in proper colours (F120/2).

F 120/2   9.8"   SHC / Du Cann collection / 201823

This design is attributed to the Old Friendly Society at Westbury on Trym (GLOS 0005) (1772 to 1897), but there is no evidence to support the claim, save that the club was known to have carried staves (*Bristol Mercury*, May 31st, 1861). The design does not relate to their meeting place. Unlike the members' brass, this larger stewards' version has the crown sitting on a cushion. In the Ponsonby-Fane notebook at MERL, p.65, illustrated here (F 120/2b), the surfaces are shown with detailed painting in reds, greens and golds. Two examples of similar size and outline exist, one unpainted (F 120/1), the other, as here, painted in proper colours, albeit with considerable fading (F 120/2a).

F 120/2a

F 121   7.3"   MERL / Allen / 550814

This pattern is ascribed to the Huntspill Friendly Society (1854 to after 1898) (SOM 619), which met at the Crossway Inn, but the suggestion has not been confirmed. Although the design with its crown and oak leaves seems to suggest the name of an inn, there is no matching building. The 1855 club rules specify a blue pole and a brass head (The National Archives FS 1/623/619).

F 122   8.2″   MERL / Shickle / 510957

This design is verified for **Ston Easton**, but it is uncertain which society used it. The pole head probably belonged to the Old Down Club at the Old Down Inn, Ston Easton (1809 to 1867 or later) (SOM 393). The example of this design in the MERL Shickle collection is inscribed 'C.J.Gait', and below the name, 'S.E.'. Charles J Gait lived in Ston Easton ('S.E.') in 1881, having been born there in 1851. The Old Down Club of Ston Easton broke in 1866, but was re-established by 1867 (*Shepton Mallet Journal*, June 21ˢᵗ, 1867).

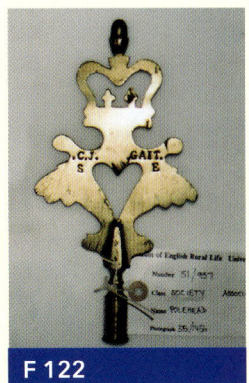

F 122

F 123/1   8.5″   MERL / Allen / 550807

This design is verified for **Chilcompton Benefit Society** (1837 to 1877) (SOM 054), which met at the Britannia Inn. It was identified by the Rev Ethelbert Horne in a letter to Sir Spencer Ponsonby-Fane, June 9ᵗʰ, 1915 (MERL D/85/11/3), and in SHC Taunton Museum archives are notes dated 1915 from the Rev Ethelbert Horne, stating that he knew the son of the member who had this design (SHC DD/SAS/C/795). Chilcompton Benefit Society accounts show several payments for poles, tassels and brass spears between 1838 and 1840, apparently bought at Bristol (SHC DD/SAS/C/795).

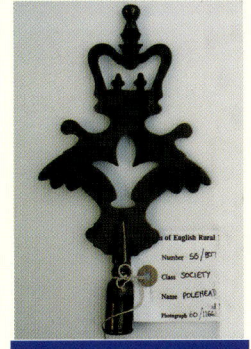

F 123/1

F 123/2   12.1″   Radstock Museum / E07

This design is verified for **Chilcompton Benefit Society** (1837 to 1877) (SOM 054), which met at the Britannia Inn. It was identified by Rev Ethelbert Horne in a letter to Sir Spencer Ponsonby-Fane, June 9ᵗʰ, 1915 (MERL D/85/11/3), and in SHC Taunton Museum archives are notes dated 1915, also from the Rev Horne, stating that he knew the son of the member who had this design (SHC DD/SAS/C/795). Chilcompton Benefit Society accounts show several payments for poles, tassels and brass spears between 1838 and 1840, apparently bought at Bristol. (SHC DD/SAS/C/795). This specimen is a larger version of F 123/1. The accounts indicate that a sum of £7 was paid for large tassels and 3 brass spears for flag poles, and there were payments for large poles for stewards in 1838.

F 123/2

F 124   7.8″   MERL / Allen / 550809

This design is verified for the **Friendly Society held at the Rose and Crown Inn, Nether Stowey** (1775 to 1839, then 1839 to 1856 and 1856 to 1912) (SOM 419 and SOM 427). The Rev EH Smith, Rector of Enmore, in *Happy Memories of West Somerset*, Bridgwater, 1945, pp 146 – 148, describes the brass of the 'First of May Rose and Crown society', indicating that the design was based on the inn sign where they met. The 1839 rules specify a pole (The National Archives FS 3/330/427). The *West Somerset Free Press*, May 8ᵗʰ, 1909, referred to 'members with their brass-tipped wands of office'. Two large stewards' brasses of the same pattern as the members' were owned by the society (SHC A/DWK/1/21).

F 124

F 125   6.9″   MERL / Allen / 550876

This design is verified for **Bridge Yate**, Gloucestershire, but it is unclear which society used it. In the MERL Jardine Index is the comment 'your sketch was recognised here'. The source of statement is not given, but is among notes which focus on correspondence with clergy from the relevant parishes, mainly in 1932 and 1933 (MERL DDX/1787). It is not clear which group carried this brass: there were several societies at different dates at the White Hart Inn and the Griffin Inn in the village. Many of these brasses are stamped with a number on the left lower side of the crown.

F 125

F 126

F 127

F 128

F 129

F 130

F 126   9″   MERL / Allen / 550910

The small version of this design (F125) is verified for **Bridge Yate**, Gloucestershire, but it is unclear which society used it. Almost certainly the specimen here is the appropriate steward's brass, but there is no proof of provenance for it other than its similarity to the members' brass. An identical specimen in the Shickle Collection (MERL 510973) is attributed to Hele and Bradninch (Devon), but without any supporting evidence.

F 127   7.9″   Holburne Museum / VE042

The provenance of this specimen is not known. Its pattern is the same as F 125, save for the border of the crown, which is dog-toothed instead of smooth. Only one specimen of this type has been seen.

F 128   6.5″   Holburne Museum / VE072

Soundwell is generally supposed to be the location for this design, but no evidence has emerged in support. Many of these specimens have the top of the finial above the crown broken off. Some are stamped with a member's number.

F 129   9.9″   Holburne Museum / VE024

Soundwell is generally supposed to be the location for this design, but no evidence has emerged in support. This specimen may have been a steward's brass or from a banner top. The cresting above the crown is not seen on other designs.

F 130   9.6″   MERL / Allen / 551084

Soundwell is generally supposed to be the location for this design, but no evidence has emerged in support. This specimen is large enough to suggest that it might have been a stewards' brass or a banner top, but one of the known examples of this type is marked with the initials NM, perhaps indicating that it was in fact a member's brass.

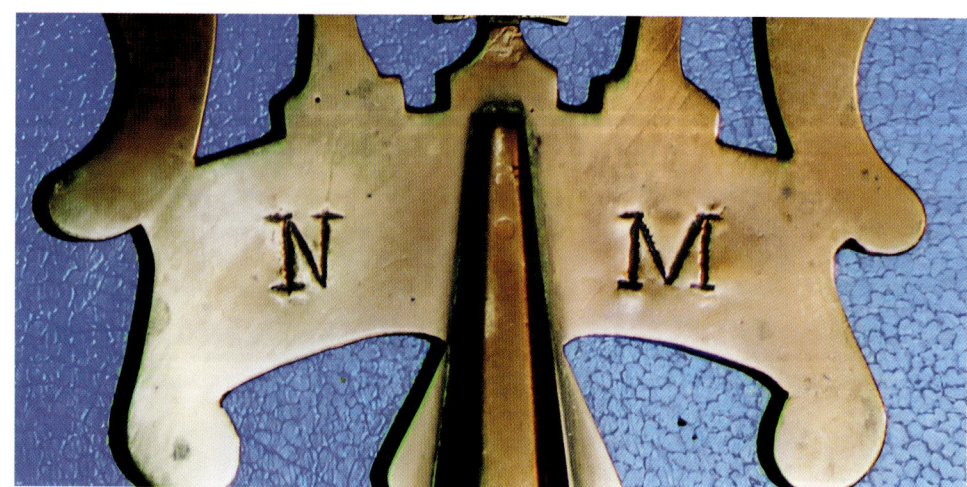

Member's iniitials on F 130 showing that it is nor a steward's pole head.

F 131　　10.4″　SHC / OSFS / 263

There is no evidence of any provenance, but the design suggests a rose and crown motif associated with the name of an inn, and it is probably a steward's brass.

F 132/1　　12.7″　Blaise Castle House Museum / T9348

There is no evidence of any provenance for this design. It is probably a steward's brass. Several specimens are known, and one is dated 1761, which is probably the year of establishment of the club, rather than the age of the brass.

F 132/2　　11.6″　MERL / Shickle / 510981

There is no evidence of any provenance for this design. It is probably a steward's brass. The specimen is engraved, which is unusual, and is dated 1748, which is probably the year of establishment of the club, rather than the age of the brass. A small cross may originally have projected from the orb at the top of the crown.

The 1748 date on F 132/2 is probably the year of formation of the club.

F 133/1　　7.7″　MERL / Allen / 550892

This design is invariably attributed to the Crown and Dolphin Inn at Wick (Gloucestershire). There seems to have been no registered society at Wick which warrants this design, and no evidence has been found to support the existence of an inn there named the Crown and Dolphin.

F 133/2　　11.9″　Private collection

This design is invariably attributed to the Crown and Dolphin Inn at Wick (Gloucestershire). There seems to have been no registered society at Wick which warrants this design, and no evidence has been found for an inn there named the Crown and Dolphin. This larger example of F133/1 is a steward's brass.

F 131

F 132/1

F 132/2

F 133/1

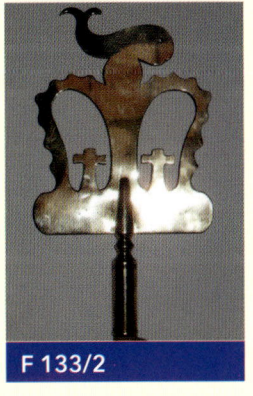
F 133/2

F 134

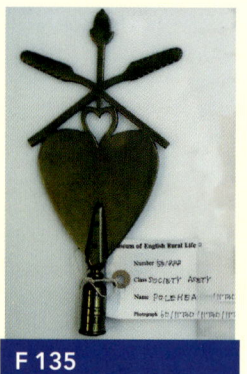

F 135

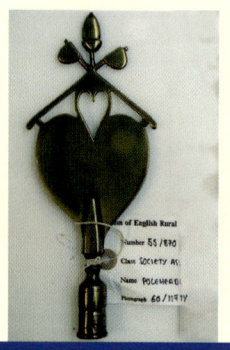

F 136

F 137

F 138

F 134　　8″　　MERL / Allen / 551171

This design is verified for **Kelston Friendly Society of Tradesmen, Farmers etc.** (1791 to 1862) (SOM 159), which met at the Crown Inn. The match of initials, probably standing for 'Kelston Society', supports the suggested provenance of this pattern, as does the crown incorporated in the pattern. The requirement for a 'brass ornament' first appears in the amended rules of 1820 (The National Archives FS 1 /609B/159).

F 135　　9.5″　　MERL / Allen / 550888

No evidence has emerged to link this design with Street, but notes accompanying various collections mention 'Heart (or Hearts) of Oak, Street' which almost certainly is a mistaken reference to the Hearts of Oak Benefit Society (an independent club, not part of the Hearts of Oak affiliated order), which met at the Hearts of Oak Inn, Benedict Street, Glastonbury (not Street) (*Wells Journal*, September 21st, 1867). The design of the brass includes two hearts and an oak apple, but the significance of what appear to be two ears of wheat is not obvious.

F 136　　8.3″　　MERL / Allen / 550870

This design is verified for **Wedmore New Friendly Society** (1818 to before 1856) (SOM312) and **Wedmore Friendly and Benefit Society** (1856 to date unrecorded) (SOM 671), which met at a private house. The three known dated brasses relate to **Wedmore New Friendly Society**. The cudgels (above the heart) were 'single sticks', for which Wedmore men had a strong reputation

Wedmore pole head of James Ganfield

('Nunney sports day', *Dorset County Chronicle*, September 24th, 1829). The Jardine Index mentions that 'Dr Bracey (of Wedmore) has a local club head dated 1843' (MERL Jardine Index DDX /993). The SHC Kelway collection example is inscribed '1828 James Ganfield, Wedmore' (SHC OSFS / 190). In the 1841 census James Ganfield, aged 20, is shown as head of a household of two in Wedmore: he was probably the son of the late owner of the brass, and he had the same name as his father. The Shickle example is dated 1827, and has the initials RH, but these are untraced (MERL 511026).

F 137　　9.1″　　MERL / Allen / 550874

This design is reputed to belong to Long Ashton, but the link is unconfirmed. Members of the Long Ashton Friendly Society carried poles, but the design was not specified (The National Archives FS 1/610/170, 1823 rules). The society existed between 1780 and 1864, and met at the Coach and Horses Inn and later at the Angel Inn (1780 to 1823) (SOM 169), (1823 to 1833) (SOM 170) and (1833 to 1864) (SOM 171). Two similar designs exist: this one, F 137, has a crown top, but F 139 does not.

F 138　　6.3″　　MERL / Allen / 551123

No evidence of provenance has emerged for this design. Several examples are recorded. The features of the pattern suggest the 'Hand and Heart Friendly Society' of East Chinnock, but there is no evidence as such, and other societies of the same name are recorded. The motif is principally used by the Oddfellows.

F 139   8.75″   Holburne Museum / VE114

No evidence of provenance has emerged. Two similar designs exist: one has a crown top (F 137), but this one (F 139) does not. It is marked 'AFS', which may well signify the 'Angel Friendly Society' (properly called the Long Ashton Friendly Society), which at one time met at the Angel Inn. No other evidence appears to link this design to Long Ashton. All known specimens of this design include the membership number engraved below the AFS initials.

F 139

F 140/1   7.5″   MERL / Allen / 550911

Early collectors, including Kelway, ascribed this design to Nibley or to Staplehill, but there is no supporting evidence for either. Two variants exist: this one with straight sides (c.7.5″ tall), and the other with curved sides (c.7.75″ tall: F 140/3). It is not clear if this implies two separate societies at one or more places or else simply differences in the manufacture.

F 140/2   10″   MERL / Shickle / 511031

This large specimen was probably a steward's pole head or a flag pole top from the society with the F 140/1 design (straight sided). Early collectors, including Kelway, ascribed the equivalent members' design to Nibley or to Staplehill, but there is no supporting evidence for either. Two variants exist: this one with straight sides (c.7.5″ tall), and the other with curved sides (c.7.75″ tall: F 140/3). It is not clear if this implies two separate societies at one or more places or else simply differences in the manufacture. Another large specimen, c. 12.5″, was in the Wainwright Collection: the location is unrecorded (Eunice B Overend, ed., *Catalogue of the Wainwright Collection of Friendly Society Brasses* [dispersed], the Phillips Museum [defunct], Brokerswood, Autumn 1971, p.18).

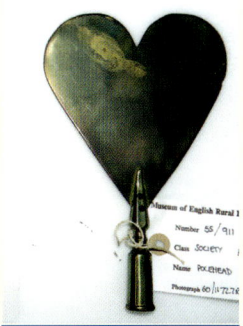

F 140/1

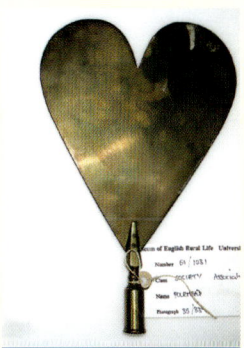

F 140/2

F 140/3   7.75″   Blaise Castle House Museum / T7508

Early collectors ascribed this design to Nibley or Staplehill, but without supporting evidence. Two slight variants exist: F 140/1, with straight sides (c.7.5″ tall), and this one, with curved sides (c.7.75″ tall). It is not clear if this implies two separate societies at one or more places or else simply differences in the manufacture.

F 141   8.8″   MERL / Allen / 551040

This design is usually said to have been used at the Ship Inn, Alveston, but no proof has emerged for Alveston or for any other location. There is a Ship Inn at Alveston, where two separate societies met (the 'May' and the 'Old June' clubs), and the 1850 rules of the Alveston May club specify the use of staffs, but the design of the pole top is not recorded (The National Archives FS 1/165/364). It is not known if members of the Old June club carried poles.

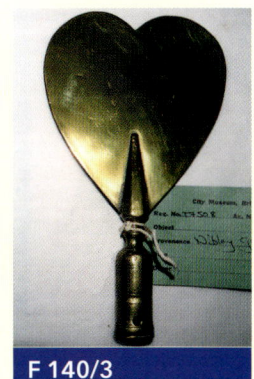

F 140/3

F 141

F 142

F 143/1

F 143/2

F 144

F 145

F 142   8.8″   MERL / Allen / 551099

There is no evidence in support of the claim that this design came from Swinford. The only friendly society there for which there is a record is the Friendly Society of All Trades, which met at the Swan Inn (1795 to after 1803) (GLOS 0079).

F 143/1   12.3″   MERL / Allen / 551107

This large specimen was probably a steward's brass from the same society as in F 142. There is no evidence in support of the claim that this design came from Swinford. The only friendly society there for which there is a record is the Friendly Society of All Trades, which met at the Swan Inn (1795 to after 1803) (GLOS 0079).

F 143/2   12.8″   SHC / OSFS / 282

The large size overall and the width of the socket suggest that this specimen was used as a banner top in the same society as in F 142. On this particular example the space below the ship is engraved 'England expects that every man will do his duty'. There is no evidence in support of the claim that this design came from Swinford. The only friendly society there for which there is a record is the Friendly Society of All Trades, which met at the Swan Inn (1795 to after 1803) (GLOS 0079).

Patriotic inscription on F 143/2.

F 144   8.7″   MERL / Allen / 550898

This design is verified for **Combwich Friendly Society** (1839 to 1901) (unregistered), which met at the Anchor Inn. In a letter (n.d., c.1930s) to Jardine the Rev EW Hamper wrote: 'Your sketch is a Combwich Club brass, headquarters at the Anchor Inn, which ceased in 1901' (MERL Jardine Index DDX/993). Two examples became churchwardens' staves at Otterhampton Church, where the Brickmakers' Club (also known as the Anchor Friendly Society and the Cumbwitch (sic) Friendly Society) celebrated their feast-day service. Red poles were used. The Jardine Collection example (MERL 61244023) carries the date 1840.

F 145   13″   Blaise Castle House Museum / T7717

This larger version of F 144 (two are recorded) is a steward's brass from the same club as in F 144. The design is verified for **Combwich Friendly Society** (1839 to 1901) (unregistered), which met at the Anchor Inn. In a letter (n.d., c. 1930s) to Jardine the Rev EW Hamper wrote 'Your sketch is a Combwich Club brass, headquarters at the Anchor Inn, which ceased in 1901' (MERL Jardine Index DDX/993). Two examples on poles became churchwardens' staves at Otterhampton Church, where the Brickmakers' Club (also known as the Anchor Friendly Society and the Cumbwitch (sic) Friendly Society) celebrated their feast-day service. Red poles were used. The Jardine Collection member's brass (MERL 61244023) carries the date 1840.

F 146/1   7.9"   MERL / Allen / 550895

Although this design is invariably linked with the George Inn, Bitton, there is no supporting evidence, and the name of the inn is not distinctive enough to guarantee the location. The initials BS could apply to the Bitton Britons' FS, but it is unknown whether that society met at the George Inn. The George Inn was last recorded in 1821 (*Bristol Mirror*, November 3rd, 1821). Both sides of the brass are usually engraved with an eye, and sometimes with further facial details. Many of the brasses are stamped with the member's roll number.

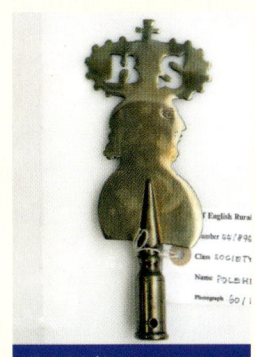

F 146/1

F 146/2   8.9"   V & A Museum / M181.1930: given by Sir Barry Jackson. (Photograph © Victoria and Albert Museum)

This substantially larger specimen appears to be a steward's version of the member's brass in F 146/1. Although this design is invariably linked with the George Inn, Bitton, there is no supporting evidence, and the name of the inn is not distinctive enough to guarantee the location. The initials BS could apply to the Bitton Britons' FS, but it is unknown whether that society met at the George Inn. The George Inn was last recorded in 1821 (*Bristol Mirror*, November 3rd, 1821).

F 146/2

F 147   7.5"   MERL / Allen / 550891

The Friendly Society of Sundry Trades and Callings at Willsbridge (1797 to after 1816) (GLOS 0195), which met at the Queen's Head Inn, is invariably stated as the producer of this design. Apart from the outline of the Queen's head on the brass no supporting evidence has emerged, and the name of the inn itself is not distinctive enough to confirm that the design was used at Willsbridge.

F 147

F 148/1   9.8"   MERL / Allen / 551064

Redlands Union Friendly Society (or Benefit Society) (1781 to 1879) (GLOS 0708) met at the Black Boy Inn, but by 1862 had moved to the Coach and Horses Inn, Durdham Down. The society is invariably associated with this design, which includes details of the faces and clothing of the two men. *The Bristol Daily Post*, May 14th, 1861, in describing members at their anniversary, observed that 'blue rosettes adorned their best beavers', and on May 13th, 1862, made reference to the members' 'snow white ducks, Sunday black coats,[and] red waistcoats', while the *Bristol Mercury* of May 13th, 1865, noted that the members had 'scarves and rosettes', and were 'carrying their staves and banners'. These details of dress in the newspaper accounts conform to the features engraved on the brasses and seem to be reasonable proof of provenance.

F 148/1

F 148/2   11.3"   SHC / OSFS / 258A

Redlands Union Friendly Society (or Benefit Society) (1781 to 1879) (GLOS 0708) met at the Black Boy Inn but by 1862 had moved to the Coach and Horses Inn, Durdham Down. The society is invariably associated with this design, which includes details of the faces and clothing of the two men. *The Bristol Daily Post*, May 14th, 1861, in describing members at their anniversary, observed that 'blue rosettes adorned their best beavers', and on May 13th, 1862, made reference to the members' 'snow white ducks, Sunday black coats,[and] red waistcoats', while the *Bristol Mercury* of May 13th, 1865, noted that the members had 'scarves and rosettes', and were 'carrying their staves and banners'. These details of dress in the newspaper accounts conform to the features engraved on the brasses and seem to be reasonable proof of provenance. This taller version is a steward's brass. Another large example was in the Ponsonby-Fane collection (dispersed) and was illustrated in the Connoisseur of 1913 (Ponsonby-Fane, Sir Spencer, 'Somerset Friendly Society Pole Heads', *The Connoisseur*, XXXVII, 1913, p.69).

F 148/2

F 148/3

F 149

F 150

F 151

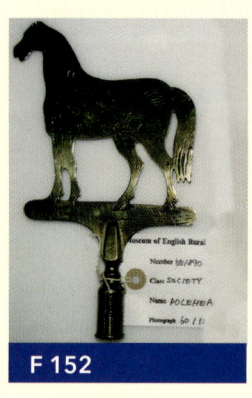

F 152

F 148/3   12″   Private collection

Redlands Union Friendly Society (or Benefit Society) (1781 to 1879) (GLOS 0708) met at the Black Boy Inn, but by 1862 it had moved to the Coach and Horses Inn, Durdham Down. The society is invariably associated with this design, which includes details of the faces and clothing of the two men. *The Bristol Daily Post*, May 14th, 1861, observed that 'blue rosettes adorned their best beavers', and on May 13th, 1862, made reference to the members' 'snow white ducks, Sunday black coats,[and] red waistcoats', while the *Bristol Mercury* of May 13th, 1865, noted that the members had 'scarves and rosettes' and were 'carrying their staves and banners'. These details of dress in the newspaper accounts conform to the features engraved on the brasses, and seem to be reasonable proof of provenance. This taller version is a steward's brass, and is the largest recorded. It has some differences in detail compared with F 148/2 due to individual hand crafting. Another large version was in the Ponsonby-Fane collection (dispersed) and was illustrated in the Connoisseur of 1913 (Ponsonby-Fane, Sir Spencer, 'Somerset Friendly Society Pole Heads', The *Connoisseur*, XXXVII, 1913, p. 69): it is probably the same specimen that was later included in the Du Cann collection (11.5″) (SHC / Du Cann collection / 201865).

F 149   8.6″   MERL / Allen / 550893

This design is usually attributed to a society that met at the Salutation Inn, Mangotsfield, but while the name of the Inn coincides with the features of the pole head, the name 'Salutation' was used by inns other than at Mangotsfield, and no supporting evidence has emerged. A slightly smaller specimen (8.15″) is in the SHC / Du Cann collection / 201842.

F 150   10.8″   Private collection

This design is usually attributed to a society that met at the Salutation Inn, Mangotsfield, but while the name of the Inn coincides with the features of the pole head, the name 'Salutation' was used by inns other than at Mangotsfield, and no supporting evidence has emerged. This taller version is a steward's brass.

F 151   13.4″   MERL / Shickle / 511028

This design is verified for **Hambrook Friendly Society** (1783 to c.1827) (GLOS 0118), (1827 to 1849) (GLOS 0343), and (1849 to after 1850) (unregistered), which met at the White Horse and from 1849 at the Crown Inn. In a letter to Jardine of 1932, EM Ball wrote: 'Mrs Flux, Walton Farm, Hambrook, lived at the White Horse and says that the head (sketched) is the White Horse Club. Mr Heaven, [of] Frenchay, has a club head' (MERL Jardine Index DDX/993). This much larger version than F152 and F 153/1, with its wide socket, is probably a flag pole top. The brasses are stamped 'Hale & Co Bristol'. It is not clear which of the three successive clubs used the design.

F 152   8″   MERL / Allen / 550890

This design is verified for **Hambrook Friendly Society** (1783 to c.1827) (GLOS 0118), (1827 to 1849) (GLOS 0343), and (1849 to after 1850) (unregistered), which met at the White Horse and from 1849 at the Crown Inn. In a letter to Jardine of 1932, EM Ball wrote: 'Mrs Flux, Walton Farm, Hambrook, lived at the White Horse and says that the head (sketched) is the White Horse Club. Mr Heaven, [of] Frenchay, has a club head' (MERL Jardine Index DDX/993). The brasses are stamped 'Hale & Co Bristol'. It is not clear which of the three successive clubs used the design.

F 153/1   10.7"   MERL / Allen / 551086

F 153/1

This design is verified for **Hambrook Friendly Society** (1783 to c. 1827) (GLOS 0118), (1827 to 1849) (GLOS 0343), and (1849 to after 1850) (unregistered), which met at the White Horse and from 1849 at the Crown Inn. In a letter to Jardine of 1932, EM Ball wrote: 'Mrs Flux, Walton Farm, Hambrook, lived at the White Horse and says that the head (sketched) is the White Horse Club. Mr Heaven, [of] Frenchay, has a club head' (MERL Jardine Index DDX/993). It is not clear which of the three successive clubs used the design. This version, larger than the members' brass at F 152, was probably carried by stewards. There is one of a similar size at SHC OSFS 245. The brasses are stamped 'Hale & Co Bristol'. It is not clear which of the three successive clubs used the design.

F 153/2   9"   SHC / OSFS / 719

F 153/2

There is no evidence of provenance for this design. Only one specimen has been recorded: it belongs to the Caley collection now in The Museum of Somerset at Taunton. The design suggests a club which met at an inn called the Jockey or the Race Horse, but there is no certainty that it was used by a friendly society. The Race Horse Inn at Taunton was used by friendly societies, but no evidence of pole-carrying at this venue has emerged.

F 154/1   9.6"   MERL / Allen / 550885

F 154/1

This design is verified for **Theale and Panborough Friendly Society** (1856 to c.1883) (unregistered), which met at the Panborough Inn. In a letter to Jardine (1930s) the Rev HJ Thomas, vicar of Theale wrote: 'There are two or three of these lions in the village' (MERL Jardine DDX/993/1). There was only the one Panborough club, and its adoption of the lion symbol is unexplained. There are two types of socket for this pattern, with slightly different overall heights, and various batches of the cast brass lions have slightly different chasing.

F 154/2   9.5"   SHC / Du Cann Collection / 201819

F 154/2

This design is verified for **Theale and Panborough Friendly Society** (1856 to c.1883) (unregistered), which met at the Panborough Inn. In a letter to Jardine (1930s) the Rev HJ Thomas, vicar of Theale wrote: 'There are two or three of these lions in the village' (MERL Jardine DDX/993/1). There was only the one Panborough club, and its adoption of the lion symbol is unexplained. There are two types of socket for this pattern, with slightly different overall heights, and various batches of the cast brass lions have slightly different chasing. This specimen, however, is the only one known, and is a variant on the usual two patterns. Before it was added to the Du Cann collection (now at SHC) it was originally owned by S Ponsonby-Fane (MERL Ponsonby-Fane notebook, p.64). The design is unique, since the lower part is not original: it has been joined to the upper part half way down the thin lower supports on each side. Why the marriage was made is unknown.

F 155   14.8"   Blaise Castle House Museum / T 7490

F 155

This design is verified as a flagpole brass for **Theale and Panborough Friendly Society** (1856 to c. 1883) (unregistered), which met at the Panborough Inn. In a letter to Jardine (1930s) the Rev HJ Thomas, vicar of Theale, wrote: 'Two large lions were carried on staves on each side of the flag' (MERL Jardine DDX/993/1). There was only the one Panborough club, and its adoption of the lion symbol is unexplained.

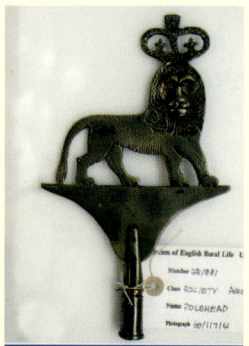

F 156

F 157/1

157/2

F 158

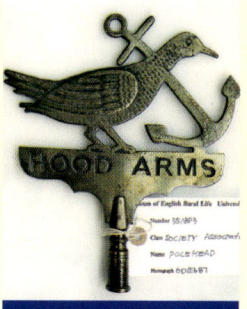

F 159

F 156   9″   MERL / Allen / 550881

No evidence has emerged that this design was used by Chedzoy Friendly Society (1862 to 1879) (unregistered) or the Chedzoy Friendly and Benefit Society (1879 - duration unknown) (unregistered), which met at the Crown Inn. The adoption of the lion symbol is unexplained. The Jardine notes (MERL DDX993) suggest that there was an Old Lion Inn at the village, but the statement is unverified.

F 157/1   7.8″   MERL / Allen / 550886

The design is verified for **Holcombe**, and for the Green brewery family, but there is no evidence of an association with Pucklechurch. The two clubs at Holcombe were the Holcombe Friendly Society (1821 to 1879) (SOM139) and the Holcombe Brewery Club (for Arthur Green's Brewery employees) (1860 to c.1888, the date when the brewery changed hands) (unregistered). It is not known which of the two clubs used the design, but it may be the case that they were one and the same, but known by a variety of names. One example (private collection) is engraved 'James Ashman Green Esq - Holcombe Club' (he was the owner of Holcombe brewery). Emanuel Green FSA (probably a son of the brewer) was a collector of friendly society rule books, which are now in Bristol Central Library. His 1909 article on friendly society brasses shows this pattern, also a larger steward's version (F 157/2) (*Journal of the British Archaeological Association*. New series, vol XV, 1909, illustration opposite p. 57). These brasses are sometimes stamped with the member's roll number. The Holburne Museum example is labelled Holcombe, as is one at SHC., where notes by AT Wicks claim that the pattern was chosen because the squire (i.e. James Ashman Green) kept deer in his park (SHC Taunton Museum archives). Green's heraldic achievement also depicted a deer.

157/2   11″   Photograph from the collection of Emanuel Green (1909): current whereabouts of specimen unknown.

The design is verified for **Holcombe**, and for the Green brewery family, but there is no evidence of an association with Pucklechurch. The two clubs at Holcombe were the Holcombe Friendly Society (1821 to 1879) (SOM139) and the Holcombe Brewery Club (for Arthur Green's Brewery employees) (1860 to c.1888, the date the brewery changed hands) (unregistered). It is not known which of the two clubs used the design, but it may be the case that they were one and the same, but known by a variety of names. One example (private collection) is engraved 'James Ashman Green Esq - Holcombe Club' (he was the owner of Holcombe brewery). Emanuel Green FSA (probably a son of the brewer) was a collector of friendly society rule books, which are now in Bristol Central Library. His 1909 article on friendly society brasses shows the members' pattern (F 157/1), also this larger steward's version, with the top antler broken. The complete specimen would probably measure 11.5″ (*Journal of the British Archaeological Association*, New Series, vol XV, 1909, illustration opposite p. 57). Notes by AT Wicks claim that the pattern was chosen because the squire (i.e. James Ashman Green) kept deer in his park (SHC Taunton Museum archives). Green's heraldic achievement also depicted a deer.

F 158   9.2″   SHC / OSFS / 723

No provenance has been proved for this design. Three examples are known. The pattern may be from the White Hart Inn of Pucklechurch.

F 159   8.1″   MERL / Allen / 550883

This design is verified for **Putsham Friendly Society at the Hood Arms** (1838 to 1921) (SOM 437). The Hood Arms, Kilve (in the parish of Putsham), still uses this symbol as an inn sign, and it has specimens of the pole head (type F 160), but they have been bought in. This version is cast in low relief and the lettering is readable on both sides. The society at one time met at the Half Moon Inn (pre-1838) (The National Archives FS 15/593 1838 rules). Apart from the design and the inscription on the brasses, there is further confirmation of the pattern in an 1882 account of a feast day procession (*West Somerset Free Press*, May 20th, 1882).

F 160   8.4″   MERL / Shickle / 511020

This design is verified for **Putsham Friendly Society at the Hood Arms** (1838 to 1921) (SOM 437). The Hood Arms, Kilve (in the parish of Putsham), still uses this symbol as an inn sign, and it has specimens of the pole head (type F 160), but they have been bought in. This version is produced from flat sheet brass, so the cut out lettering is correct on one side only. The society at one time met at the Half Moon Inn (pre-1838) (The National Archives FS 15/593, 1838 rules). Examples of another slightly different version of the flat brass type exist with a stub-topped socket (SHC OSFS / 099A and in a private collection).

F 160

F 161   5.8″   MERL / Allen / 550896

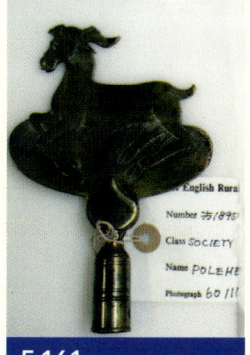

No provenance has been suggested for this design, and only three examples are known. The Allen specimen has engraved detailing, as has the one in the SHC collection, but an unengraved example exists in a private collection. The goat shown on this brass may indicate the name of the inn where the society met.

F 161

F 162   9.4″   MERL / Allen / 551141

No conclusive evidence of a provenance for this design has emerged, but the inscription '1838' appears to refer to when the relevant society was established, and the Swan pattern is indicative of the name of an inn as a meeting place. The most likely society is the Bradford Union Friendly Society (unregistered), which met at the Swan Inn, Bradford on Tone. It is known to have had poles with brass tops (*Western Gazette*, May 25th, 1866) and it celebrated what appears to be its first anniversary in 1839, at the Swan Inn, Bradford-on-Tone, with a new flag (*Taunton Courier*, May 22nd, 1839), thus confirming the date of its establishment as 1838.

F 162

F 163   5″   MERL / Allen / 550897

The only example of this design in the public domain is this one. It is probably the pole head of the Bristol apprentices sponsored by The Grateful Society (a Bristol benevolent institution). No link between this pole head and any friendly society has been found and, given its curious design, it seems likely that if it had been used by such an organisation it would have provoked comment. Instead, two press articles refer to the fact that gilt dolphins were carried in procession by Bristol apprentices sponsored by the Grateful Society. In 1823 it was noted: 'boys apprenticed by the society [were] carrying rods surmounted by dolphins' (*Bristol Mercury*, November 17th, 1823), and in 1859: 'lads, usually 80, [were] carrying banners and wands surmounted by gilt dolphins' (*Bristol Times*, November 13th, 1859).

F 163

F 164/1   7.6″   MERL / Allen / 550894

This design is verified as having been used by **The Royal Victoria Union Friendly Society** (1836 to 1876) (GLOS 0340), which met at the Full Moon Inn, Fishponds. The *Bristol Mirror* of June 10th, 1843, carried the announcement: 'Royal Victoria Union Friendly Society - Members are to meet the Stewards at the Full Moon Inn, Fishponds, on Monday, carrying a blue staff, bearing a representation of the Moon'. All specimens have the design of the man in the moon on each side. After the collapse of the Royal Victorian Union in 1876 the pole head was used briefly by its successor, a branch of the Bristol, West of England, and South Wales Labourers Union (a trade union) (*Bristol Mercury*, June 18th, 1878).

F 164/1

F 164/2

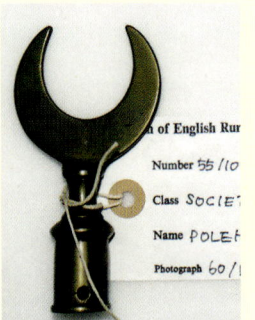

F 164/3

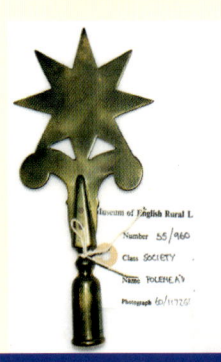

F 165/1

F 165/2

F 165/3

F 164/2   10.4″   Blaise Castle House Museum / T7549

This design is verified for **The Royal Victoria Union Friendly Society** (1836 to 1876) (GLOS 0340), which met at the Full Moon Inn, Fishponds. The *Bristol Mirror* of June 10th, 1843, carried the announcement: 'Royal Victoria Union Friendly Society - Members are to meet the Stewards at the Full Moon Inn, Fishponds, on Monday, carrying a blue staff, bearing a representation of the Moon'. All specimens have the design of the man in the moon on each side. After the collapse of the Royal Victorian Union in 1876 the pole head was used briefly by its successor, a branch of the Bristol, West of England, and South Wales Labourers Union (a trade union) (*Bristol Mercury*, June 18th, 1878). This larger specimen is a steward's brass.

F 164/3   4″   MERL / Allen / 551096

Three examples are known (two in a private collection), but none has a provenance.

F 165/1   7.1″   MERL / Allen / 550960

The Star Inn at Fishponds has been suggested as the provenance of this design, but no supporting evidence has emerged apart from the star-like shape of the pole head. There are many inns called 'The Star'.

F 165/2   6.1″   MERL / Allen / 550927

This design was not identified by Allen, and was not included in Fuller's 1964 list. Several examples exist, but no provenance has been suggested. The symbol may represent a star, and it may refer to the name of an inn.

F 165/3   7,5″   Holburne Museum / VE046B

The Hooper Collection notes have no verified provenance for this design, which may have originated in a branch of one of the affiliated orders or perhaps a Masonic lodge. One other example of this pattern has been recorded with the same casting of the body, but with a different socket (SHC OSFS 293).

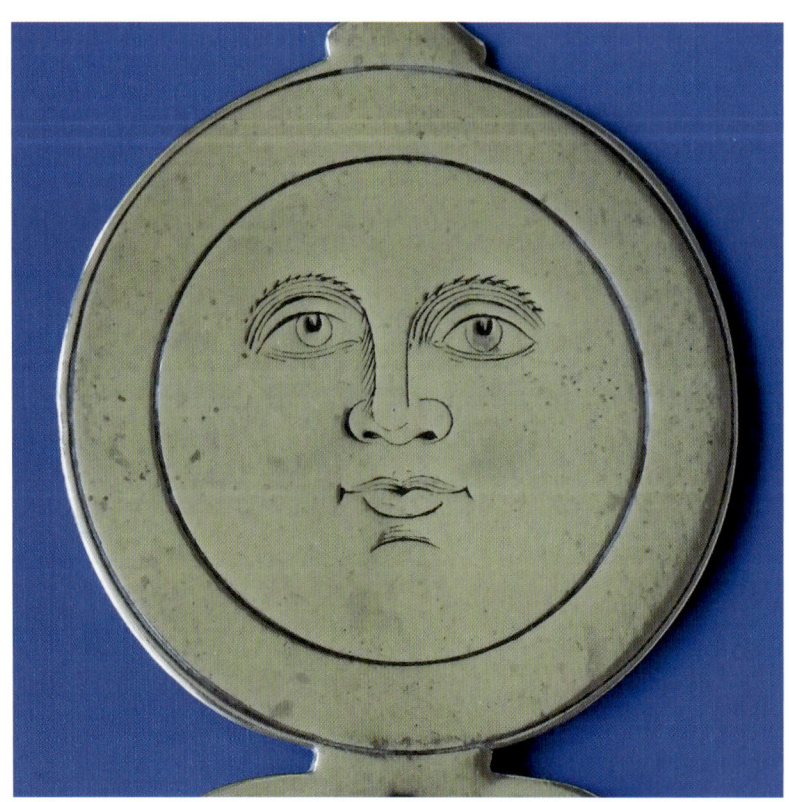

Detail of the engraving of the Full Moon Inn pole head: each example is slightly different.

F 166   6.6"   MERL / Allen / 551139

Studley, Wiltshire, has been suggested as the provenance of this design, but there is no supporting evidence. The symbol represents the sun, and may refer to the name of an inn.

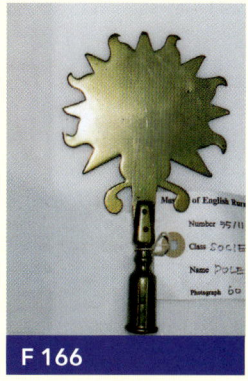

F 166

F 167   8.8"   MERL / Allen / 550906

The most convincing evidence for identifying this design comes from a banner dated 1823, which shows the pattern of this pole head in one corner (SHC 5454/1 and 2). The banner was created for **Downside Friendly Society** (1822 to c.1850) (SOM 198), which met at the George Inn, Nettlebridge, in the parish of Midsomer Norton. On the demise of the club the banner was sold c.1850 to **Stratton on the Foss Friendly Society** (1823 to after 1900) (SOM 550) (Shepton Mallet Journal March 29th, 1929). Later still it was presented to Taunton Museum by I Perry and the Rev Ethelbert Horne (Prior of Downside), who had dealings with the Stratton Friendly Society. The pole heads therefore would seem to have accompanied the banner, and to have originated with the George Inn club at Nettlebridge and ended up with the Stratton club. An alternative provenance was suggested by AW Allen, who claimed to have identified this design as originating at the Old English Establishment at Marston Biggott. in the 1830s the club moved to Nunney, where it was known as the Nunney Old English Establishment (its registration ended 1886) (SOM 190). Nevertheless, Allen left no evidence for the pole head identification, nor for why the latter society was known as the spear club. Marston Biggott certainly had 'an ornamental staff' (The National Archives FS 1/611/190 rules, 1830), and Nunney had brass pole heads (*Somerset Standard*, June 18th, 1971), but it seems that their design is not known. The Allen suggestion is less plausible than the alternative.

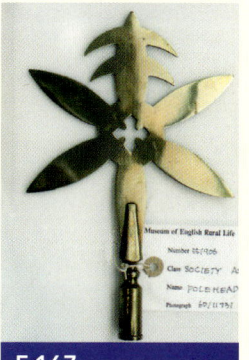

F 167

F 168/1   7.4"   MERL / Allen / 551087

This design was only ever associated by early collectors with the Flower Pot Inn, Kingswood, which was the headquarters of **The Flower Pot Benefit Society** (1824 to after 1838) (GLOS 0372). The pattern of the brass is so unusual and distinctive that the suggestion seems to be correct. No other Flower Pot Inn is known in the region.

F 168/1

F 168/2   6.8"   SHC / OSFS / 715

This design has been attributed to the society meeting at the Salutation Inn, Henbury, but apart from the symbolism of the clasped hands there is no evidence to support the claim. Other inns of this name are known.

F 168/3   4.75"   MERL / Shickle / 510966

Larkhall Union Hope Fraternity, Bath, which met at the Larkhall Inn (1825 to 1836) (SOM 361) and (1836 to 1883) (SOM 872), has been suggested as the provenance of this pattern, the evidence resting on the design not of this specimen, but of F 168/4. On the basis of the feature of the shaking hands, the three pole heads F 168/3, F 168/4 (which shows the letter 'S'), and F 168/5 appear to belong to the same society. The identification rests on a statement that the clerk, wardens and stewards carried their own wands with the official letter denoting his office (*Bath Chronicle*, September 24th, 1938). Another specimen of F 168/3 is in the MERL Jardine Collection (61244183).

F 168/2

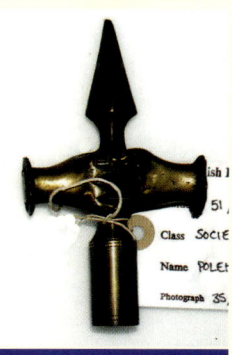

F 168/3

F 168/4

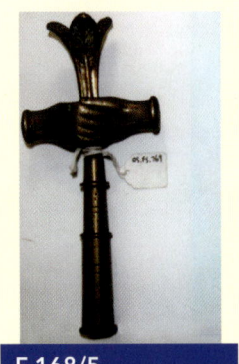

F 168/5

F 169/1

F 169/2

F 169/3

F 168/4   6.8"   MERL /Shickle / 510967

Larkhall Union Hope Fraternity, Bath, which met at the Larkhall Inn (1825 to 1836) (SOM 361) and (1836 to 1883) (SOM 872), is suggested for the provenance of this pattern, the evidence resting on the design not of this specimen, but of F 168/4. On the basis of the feature of the shaking hands, the three pole heads F 168/3, F 168/4 (which shows the letter 'S'), and F 168/5 appear to belong to the same society. The identification rests on a statement that the clerk, wardens and stewards carried their own wands with the official letter denoting his office (*Bath Chronicle*, September 24th, 1938). The 'S' here appears to indicate that this is a steward's version of F 168/3 and F 168/5. Two other specimens are recorded (MERL Allen 551108 and MERL Jardine 61244174). This design was not included in Fuller's 1964 list.

F 168/5   7.1"   SHC / OSFS / 769

Larkhall Union Hope Fraternity, Bath, which met at the Larkhall Inn (1825 to 1836) (SOM 361) and (1836 to 1883) (SOM 872), is suggested for the provenance of this pattern, the evidence resting on the design not of this specimen, but of F 168/4. On the basis of the feature of the shaking hands, the three pole heads F 168/3, F 168/4 (which shows the letter 'S'), and F 168/5 appear to belong to the same society. The identification rests on a statement that the clerk, wardens and stewards carried their own wands with the official letter denoting his office (*Bath Chronicle*, September 24th, 1938). This design was not included in Fuller's 1964 list.

F 169/1   9"   MERL / Allen / 550904

This design is verified for **Ilchester Benevolent Society**, also known as **Ilchester True Blues** and **Ilchester Old True Blues** (1798 to 1808) (SOM 144), (1808 to 1814) (SOM 146) and (1814 to c.1875) (SOM 149), which met at the Bull Inn and later at the Town Hall. Rule books of various dates specify a blue pole and gilt head (The National Archives FS 1/609a/149 rules, 1814). The design is associated with Ilchester, since the etoile is also used as the heraldic arms of the town. J Stevens Cox, *SDNQ*, XXV, March 1948, p 81, describes this as type 3, noting that 200 of them were bought in 1867 for £18/11/-. In this version there are no slots on either side of the point at the top finial.

F 169/2   9"   MERL / Jardine / 61244099

This design is verified for **Ilchester Benevolent Society**, also known as **Ilchester True Blues** and **Ilchester Old True Blues** (1798 to 1808) (SOM 144), (1808 to 1814) (SOM 146) and (1814 to c.1875) (SOM 149), which met at the Bull Inn and later at the Town Hall. Rule books of various dates specify a blue pole and gilt head (National Archives FS 1/609a/149, rules 1814). The design is associated with Ilchester, since the etoile is also used as the heraldic arms of the town. J Stevens Cox, *SDNQ*, XXV, March 1948, p 81, describes this as type 2, dating before 1867 and introduced before type 3. In this version there is a slot on either side of the point at the top finial.

F 169/3   c. 9"   The location of an example of this design is unknown.

It is verified for **Ilchester Benevolent Society**, also known as **Ilchester True Blues** and **Ilchester Old True Blues** (1798 to 1808) (SOM 144), (1808 to 1814) (SOM 146) and (1814 to c.1875) (SOM 149), which met at the Bull Inn and later at the Town Hall. Rule books of various dates specify a blue pole and gilt head (National Archives FS 1/609a/149, rules 1814). The design is associated with Ilchester, since the etoile is also used as the heraldic arms of the town. J. Stevens Cox, *SDNQ*, XXV, March 1948, p 81, describes this pattern as type 1, introduced around 1800. Cox produced outlines of the patterns, but he did not mention where his examples were kept.

F 169/4   9.4"   MERL / Shickle / 511040

It is highly probable that this is an Ilchester pole head, but the specimen has no provenance, and it is unclear whether it was used by a friendly society. No other examples have been traced.

F 169/4

F 169/5   c. 7.5" Private collection

It is possible that this is an Ilchester pole head, but perhaps not one from a friendly society: it may have belonged to an Ilchester civic organisation, as the town insignia include the heraldic etoile.

F 169 /6   5"   Dorset Museum, Dorchester / R.1995.248

No evidence has emerged to associate this specimen with Chideock, Dorset. The pole head was presented to Dorset Museum, Dorchester, by a relative of a family in Wareham, and it was said that it came from Chideock, but no extra details of the provenance were given. No other specimen has been encountered.

F 169/5

F 170/1   7.4"   MERL / Allen / 550816

This design is verified for **Mark Friendly Society** (1795 to 1865) (SOM 186) and (1865 to 1870) (SOM 791), which met at the Pack Horse Inn from 1795, and then at Mark Inn by 1865. The society secretary's pole head (F 170/2), with a painted tin model of a book, bearing the painted inscription 'Mark Friendly Society', is surmounted by the same brass emblem as this one, and confirms that the two-acorn design belongs to Mark (see F 170/2).

F 170/2   8.7"   Wells and Mendip Museum / 673

This design is verified for **Mark Friendly Society** (1795 to 1865) (SOM 186) and (1865 to 1870) (SOM 791), which met at the Pack Horse Inn from 1795, and then at Mark Inn by 1865. This emblem is the society secretary's pole head, bearing a painted tin model of a book, with the painted inscription 'Mark Friendly Society', surmounted by the members' brass emblem. It confirms that the two-acorn design belongs to Mark (see F 170/1 for the members' design).

F 169 /6

F 170/1

The Ilchester crescent and etoile on Ilchester street furniture.

F 170/2

F 170/3

F 170/4

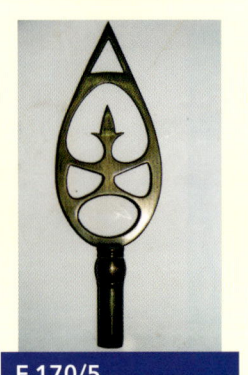

F 170/5

F 171/1

F 171/2

F 170/3   8.9"   Dorset Museum, Dorchester / 1953.20.17

This design is verified for **Beaminster Friendly Society** (1762 to 1827) (not registered), (1827 to 1862) (DOR 111), and (1862 to 1892) (DOR 135), which met at the town hall. The three banner tops illustrated (F 173/3, 4 and 5) were part of the Richard Hine collection. He wrote an account of the Beaminster Friendly Society in 'Friendly Societies and their emblems', *Dorset Natural History and Antiquarian Field Club*, Vol XLIX, 1928, pp 114 to 124.

F 170/4   8.5"   Dorset Museum, Dorchester / 1953.20.18

This design is verified for **Beaminster Friendly Society** (1762 to 1827) (not registered), (1827 to 1862) (DOR 111), and (1862 to 1892) (DOR 135), which met at the town hall. The three banner tops illustrated (F 170/3, 4 and 5) were part of the Richard Hine collection. He wrote an account of the Beaminster Friendly Society in 'Friendly Societies and their emblems', *Dorset Natural History and Antiquarian Field Club*, Vol XLIX, 1928, pp 114 to 124.

F 170/5   12.5"   Dorset Museum, Dorchester / 1953.20.16

This design is verified for **Beaminster Friendly Society** (1762 to 1827) (not registered), (1827 to 1862) (DOR 111), and (1862 to 1892) (DOR 135), which met at the town hall. The three banner tops illustrated (F 170/3, 4 & 5) were part of the Richard Hine collection. He wrote an account of the Beaminster Friendly Society in 'Friendly Societies and their emblems', *Dorset Natural History and Antiquarian Field Club*, Vol XLIX, 1928, pp 114 to 124. The socket makes this specimen taller than the others (F 170/3 and F 170/4).

F 171/1   4.5"   MERL / Allen / 551071

This design has been attributed to Broadway, Worcestershire, but there is no supporting evidence. It closely resembles the Merriott pole head (F 172/1), but the edge at the top of the shaft is milled, as are the edges at the top of the urn and the upper knop, while the cup of the acorn is cross-hatched. Another example of this brass is in the Snowshill Manor collection, N.T.

F 171/2   4.3"   MERL / Allen / 551162

There is no provenance for this design. It closely resembles the Merriott pole head (F 172/1), but the proportions are quite different.

The Town Hall, headquarters of the Beaminster Friendly Society (F 170/3, 4 and 5).

F 171/3   5″   MERL / Allen / 551115

There is no provenance for this design. It closely resembles the Merriott pole head (F 172/1), but the knop below the acorn is more highly pronounced. Another example is at SHC OSFS 785.

F 171/3

F 172/1   4.5″   MERL / Allen / 550968

This design has been verified for **The King's Head Friendly Society, Merriott** (1863 to after 1891) (unregistered), which met at the King's Head Inn. In a letter to Jardine dated September 27th, 1932, the vicar of Merriott, the Rev SE Percival, confirmed this pattern as well as the stewards' brass, which he described as 'a bird with outstretched wings' (MERL Jardine Index DDX / 993). The King's Head Friendly Society carried poles decorated with blue ribbons (*Pulman's Weekly News*, May 26th, 1891). For the stewards' brass, see F 235. The two identical specimens of this design in the MERL Jardine Collection, 61244139 and 61244140, are both still on their original 77″ poles, where the top 9″ section is painted white and the remaining 68″ green, and they are the only recorded examples of green-painted members' poles. Jardine did not provide a provenance for this pair.

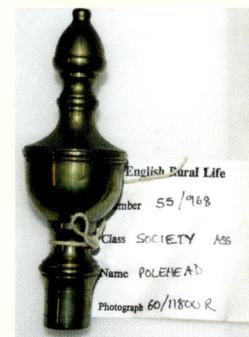

F 172/1

F 172/2   5.6″   MERL / Allen / 550969

Allen gave no provenance for this specimen and no other evidence has emerged.

F 172/3   6.5″   MERL / Allen / 551129

Chipping Campden, Gloucestershire, and Quinton, Warwickshire, have been suggested, but without further evidence (MERL Ponsonby-Fane notebook p.49), and Allen himself gave no provenance for this specimen. The stepped pattern beneath the shallow urn is unusual. Another example is at SHC (OSFS 231A), attributed to the Britannia Club, Chipping Camden, but again without supporting details. F 175 is also claimed to be from Chipping Camden, but without proof.

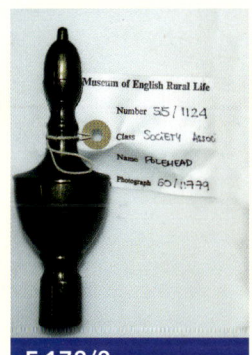

F 172/2

F 172/4   6.8″   SHC / OSFS / 788

Only one example of this design has been found, and no provenance has been recorded.

F 172/3

The headquarters of the King's Head Friendly Society at Merriott (F 172/1).

F 172/4

F 172/5

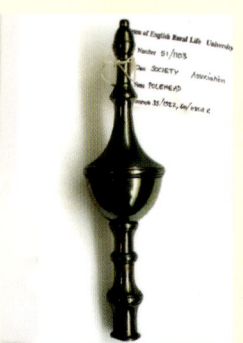

F 172/6

F 173

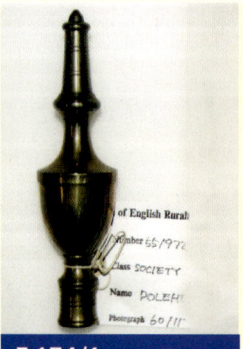

F 174/1

F 172/5   7.8"   MERL / Shickle / 511117

The specimen is inscribed 'Golden Lion Friendly Society - established 1833' and was claimed by Shickle to be from Merriott, but there is no evidence that supports the establishment of a friendly society there in 1833, nor are there records of a Golden Lion Inn. Places which had a Golden Lion Inn include Bristol, Bridgwater, Freshford, Taunton and Wrington. The brass is also stamped by the manufacturers with the detail 'Wasborough Hale & Co Bristol'.

Detail of the Golden Lion Friendly Society pole head.

F 172/6   9.4"   MERL / Shickle / 511107

Shickle gave no provenance for this specimen or for a second identical example (MERL 511102), and no further evidence has emerged. The pair are unusually tall for this type of design.

F 173   5.3"   MERL / Allen / 550971

No evidence was given by Allen in support of a provenance at Ashby St Ledgers, Northampton, and no other evidence has emerged. The upper part of the acorn is unusually tall. Three specimens are known.

F 174/1   5.6"   MERL / Allen / 550972

No verification can be made for Shepton Beauchamp, Bradford Abbas or South Petherton. At Shepton Beauchamp the wooden pole tops were replaced by brass specimens in the mid-nineteenth century, but the original design is unknown (SHC Museum Day Book no 2, Sept 17, 1909: information from Rev J Hamlet). A Shepton Beauchamp club-day photograph in the Duke of York Inn, Shepton Beauchamp, shows pole heads, but not this one. The Bradford Abbas suggestion seems not to be correct: a photograph of the club in 1926 shows two pole heads on staves, but not of this design (Eric Garrett, *Bradford Abbas - The History of A Dorset Village*, Yeovil, 1989, p 223). No evidence to support the South Petherton suggestion has emerged.

F 174/2   6.6"   Blaise Castle House Museum / T9381

The specimen is unidentified. Several others exist, such as in the Shickle Collection (MERL 511129) and in the Allen Collection (MERL 550932). The pattern was not listed by Fuller (1964).

F 174/2

F 174/3   4.9″   MERL / Allen / 551091

The specimen is unidentified. Shickle suggests Blockley, Worcestershire, or Shalford on Avon (an untraced location, possibly a misreading of Stratford) (MERL 51121), but without evidence for either. The SHC example (OSFS 787) is tentatively ascribed to Stratford-on-Avon, but with no supporting details. The design was not included in Fuller's 1964 list.

F 174/3

F 174/4   3.9″   MERL / Shickle / 511147

Shickle did not record a provenance, but a larger version of this design is shown indistinctly on two stewards' pole heads in a photograph of **Stoford Friendly Society** anniversary c.1910'.

F 174/4

F 174/5   4.7″   Private collection

There is no recorded provenance for this pattern: only one has been seen.

F 174/6   6.25″   MERL / Jardine / 61244243

There is no evidence for Blockley, as suggested by SHC (OSFS 230A), once an exclave of Worcestershire and lying 3 miles NW of Moreton-in-Marsh, Gloucestershire. Jardine did not record a provenance for this design. A third example, in a private collection, also has no known provenance.

F 174/5

F 175   5.8″   MERL / Allen / 551077

Allen left no supporting evidence for his claim that this design was used by Chipping Campden's Old Tradesmen's Club, and no other evidence has emerged. A second specimen at SHC (OSFS 231) is similarly described, but again with no supporting details. F 172/3 is also claimed to be from Chipping Camden, but without any verification.

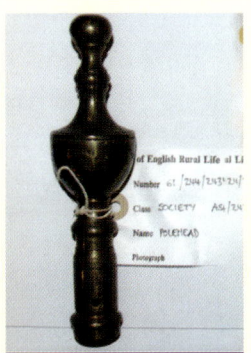
F 174/6

Urn design often used as iron railings finial: here located at Stoke Abbott, Dorset.

F 175

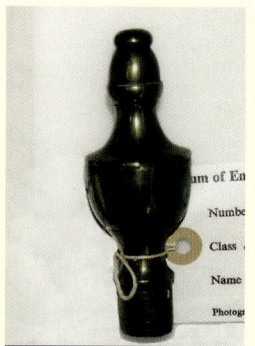

F 176/1

F 176/2

F 177

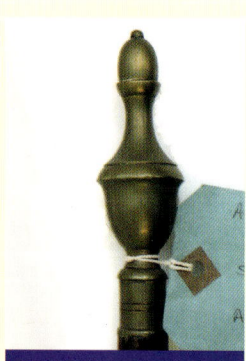

F 178/1

F 178/2

F 176/1   4.3″   MERL / Allen / 550979

No supporting evidence was given by Allen for attributing this design to Broadway, Worcestershire, nor to the Himley Sick Club, Staffordshire, by Shickle. Apart from this 4.3″ example, two other similar specimens are known: Allen (MERL 551063) (4.1″) and Shickle (MERL 511122) (3.9″). They differ in their proportions and are by no means identical.

F 176/2   5.25″   MERL / Allen / 551102

This design was not included in Fuller's 1964 list. No other examples have been seen, and there is no recorded provenance.

F 177   4.3″   MERL / Allen / 551112

It is unclear why Fuller (1964) included this specimen, as it seems to be an ornamental finial possibly from an andiron, and unrelated to a Friendly Society. It was not identified by Allen. The socket is unusually short for convenient use on a pole. A second example is in the Shickle Collection (MERL 511139).

F 178/1   4.3″   MERL / Allen / 550929

Allen left no specific evidence to support his claim that this design was used by a club which met at the Neville Arms, Cockhill, near Alcester, Warwickshire. The pattern is not recorded elsewhere. The ogive-sided urn is unusual.

F 178/2   7.5″   MERL / Shickle / 511109

Shickle suggested Timsbury as the provenance of this design, but without any supporting details, and no other evidence has emerged.

Brass urn pattern used on andirons: similar design to friendly society pole heads.

F 178/3   5.75″   MERL / Allen / 551078

No provenance was recorded for this design, and no evidence has since emerged. As with F 178/1, the urn is ogive-sided. Other examples are at MERL Shickle 511100 and in a private collection.

F 178/3

F 178/4   6.5″   MERL / Allen / 551116

No provenance was recorded for this design, and no evidence has since emerged. As with F 178/1, the urn is ogive-sided.

F 178/5   4.2″   MERL / Allen / 551121

No provenance was recorded for this design, and no evidence has since emerged. As with F 178/1, the urn is ogive-sided. There is another example at SHC OSFS 789.

F 178/4

F 178/6   5.75″   SHC / OSFS / 754

Only one specimen of this pattern has been recorded, but the centre drawing on page 57 of the MERL Ponsonby-Fane notebook is very similar (MERL D 85/11/1). This item was presented to Taunton Museum in 1906, but without any information as to its relationship to a friendly society.

F 178/7   6.5″   Private collection

The provenance is unrecorded. Only one specimen of this pattern has been seen.

F 178/5

F 178/6

Detail of bird casting found on friendly society pole heads and other items.

F 178/7

F 179

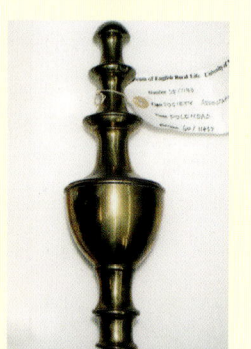

F 180/1

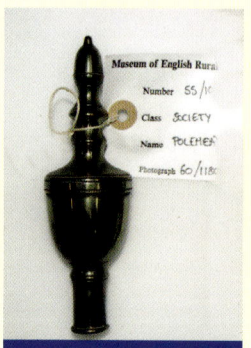

F 180/2

F 180/3

F 181

F 179　　　9.6"　　MERL / Allen / 550936

This design is verified for **Priddy Male Friendly Society** (from after 1815 and extant in 2015) (unregistered), with headquarters at the Victoria Inn (see Albert Thompson, *The Book of Priddy*, Tiverton, 2000, p.132, where the brass is illustrated in the lower photograph). Priddy brasses often carry the member's roll number: this one is no 30.

F 180/1　　11.2"　　MERL / Allen / 551133

This design is verified for **Priddy Male Friendly Society** (from after 1815 and extant in 2015) (unregistered), with headquarters at the Victoria Inn (see Albert Thompson, *The Book of Priddy*, Tiverton, 2000, p.132, where the brass is illustrated in the lower photograph). The larger brass here is a stewards' pole head.

F 180/2　　5.5"　　MERL / Allen / 551066

The Shickle list suggests Ashby St Ledgers, Northamptonshire (MERL 511135), but does not support the claim, and no other evidence for provenance has emerged. The distinctive features of this pattern are the two protruding rings on the stem and the milling at the top of the urn. Three other examples are known.

F 180/3　　7.7"　　SHC / OSFS / 782

No provenance has been recorded for this pattern, and no other examples have been found. There may be a missing element from the top of this specimen, as the topmost surface has a hole.

F 181　　　8.6"　　MERL / Allen / 550934

This design is verified for Felton (near Winford) for **Winford Friendly Society** (1794 to c.1826) (SOM 461), **Felton and Winford Friendly Society** (1826 to 1877) (SOM 713), and **Felton and Winford Friendly Society** (1877 to 1891) (SOM 900), which met at the George Inn (1794), the George and Dragon Inn (1826 and again c.1877), and the Prince of Waterloo Inn (c.1842). The identification was made by the Rev AJH Hobbs, author of *A History of the Parish of Winford, Somerset*, 1954 (Honiton), p.29, where he wrote: 'four brasses, shaped like urns, with baluster stems and about 9" high were carried... one [is] at Taunton Museum'.

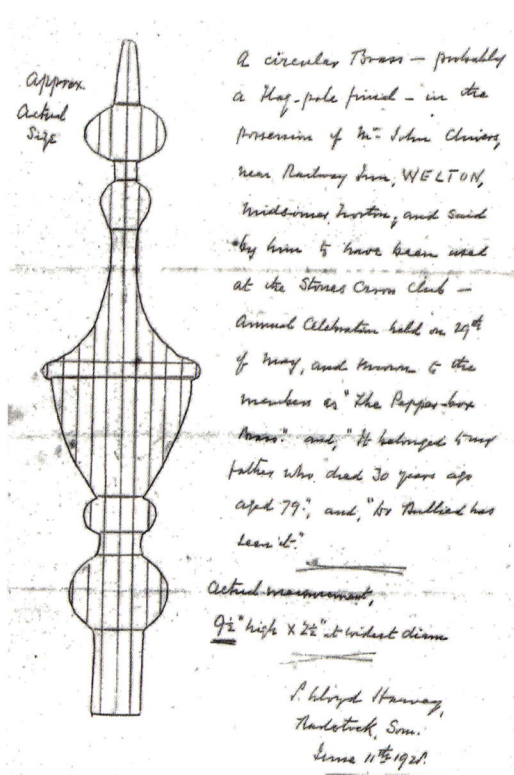

F 183: the Welton 'pepper-pot'.

106

F 182/1   5.9″   MERL / Allen / 550976

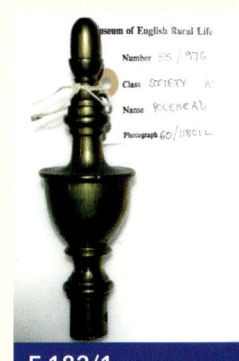

F 182/1

This design is verified for **The Friendly Society at West and Middle Chinnock and Chiselborough** (1848 to 1939) (SOM 565), which met at West Chinnock school. Another example is in the Shickle Collection (MERL 511133), and was originally attributed to Crowcombe or Paulton (without evidence), but the suggested location was later changed to West and Middle Chinnock. A third example in SHC (OSFS 044A) also names the club, but with no further evidence. Three club day photographs in a private collection show the members' pole heads and in one of the photographs the larger stewards' pole heads can be made out. Account details of the West and Middle Chinnock and Chiselborough Friendly Society accounts include references to painting club poles in 1899 and 1923, including one new steward's pole in 1899, but there is no mention of pole heads (SHC D/P/chin.w23/4).

F 182/2   5.8″   SHC / OSFS / 783

F 182/2

This design was probably used by the Bradford Abbas Union Friendly Society (1831 to 1848) (DOR 540), the Bradford Abbas Friendly Society (1848 to 1858) (DOR 127), and the Bradford Abbas Sick Benefit Society (1858 to 1964) (unregistered), which met at the Rose and Crown Inn. No provenance is stated for this SHC specimen, but in the SHC Kelway notebook, no 125, p.196, it is attributed to Bradford Abbas (Dorset). It strongly resembles the two pole heads shown in a 1926 club photograph, although the scale is difficult to confirm (Eric Garrett, *Bradford Abbas - The History of a Dorset Village*, Yeovil, 1989. p.223).

F 183   8.9″   MERL / Allen / 550937

F 183

This design is similar to a larger version which is verified for **Welton** (Midsomer Norton), but no evidence has emerged for its use at Timsbury. Two societies met at Stone's Cross Inn at Welton, and they overlapped in their dates. The pattern shown here probably refers to the 29th of May club rather than the Whit Tuesday club. The larger example has a height of 9.5″ and was described in a letter from S Lloyd Harvey dated June 6th, 1928, to the curator of Taunton Museum. A tracing was included of a pole head, which was said to be a flag pole top from the 29th of May Stone's Cross Club, Welton, and members called the design 'the pepper-box brass'. The actual specimen (location now unknown) belonged to the father of John Chivers, who lived at Welton. The father died in 1898 aged 79.

F 184/1   7″   MERL / Allen / 551132

F 184/1

No evidence has emerged to link this specimen with Shipston on Stour. Two other examples are known. The brass was unidentified by Allen, but Ponsonby-Fane offered the Shipston on Stour suggestion (Plymouth City Museum and Art Gallery, Ponsonby-Fane notebook, p.151).

F 184/2   5.5″   MERL / Allen / 551065

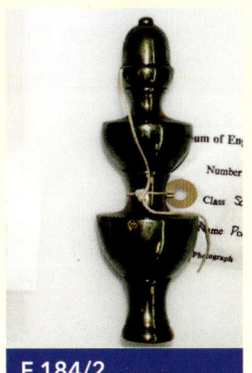

F 184/2

No evidence has emerged to link this design with Clapton in Gordano. A further example (slightly shorter) is in MERL (Jardine 6124496). No provenance was suggested by Allen, and although Jardine indicated Clapton in Gordano, he did not offer any details.

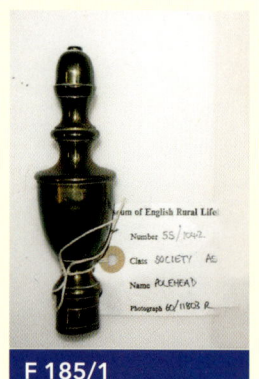

F 185/1

F 185/2

F 185/3

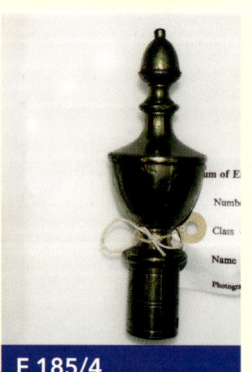

F 185/4

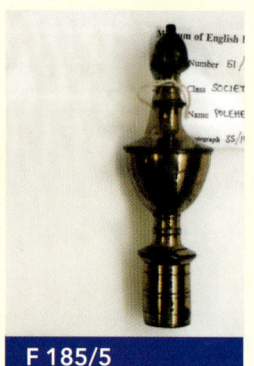

F 185/5

F 185/1   5.6"   MERL / Allen / 551042

The provenance of this design is unknown. Allen suggested West and Middle Chinnock and Chiselborough Friendly Society, but without recording any evidence, while the SHC example is listed as Ashby St Ledgers, again without supporting details (SHC OSFS 224B).

F 185/2   4.5"   MERL / Shickle / 511142

Shickle suggested Main Hill Park as the place where this design was used, but the location is untraced, and there is no other reference.

F 185/3   5.3"   SHC / OSFS / 249B

This design was attributed to the Sick Club at Himley (Dudley, Staffordshire) by the donor, Robert Leigh of Dudley, but no supplementary confirmation has emerged.

F 185/4   5.7"   MERL / Allen / 551117

Allen did not record a provenance for this design, and no further information has emerged.

F 185/5   6.1"   MERL / Shickle / 511137

Shickle did not record a provenance for this design, which is similar to F 185/2, except that it is taller and the column between the base of the urn and the top of the socket is extended. No further information has emerged.

Brass urn pattern used on longcase clock finials.

F 185/6   7.4"   MERL / Allen / 550933

An un-numbered example at SHC (OSFS 224A) is attributed to Ashby St Ledgers, Northamptonshire, but without supporting evidence. The Allen specimen shown here is engraved with the number 155: another numbered example, at Torquay Museum (V 480), is marked No 2; a third, at Plymouth City Museum and Art Gallery (The Box) (1936.2.40) is marked No 118; a fourth, in a private collection, is marked No 176; and a fifth at Snowshill Manor (National Trust) is marked No 175. No further information has emerged.

Members' roll numbers engraved on examples of F 185/6.

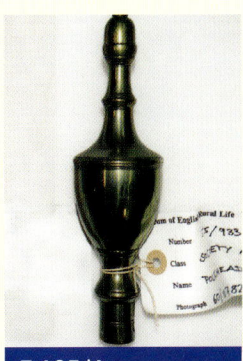
F 185/6

F 185/7   7.75"   MERL / Allen / 550938

Allen gave no suggestion for the provenance of this design. Three other examples are known, all in private collections, but none has any known provenance. The socket on this type is very much longer than usual.

F 185/8   10.5"   Private collection

No evidence of provenance has emerged for this design. As with F 185/7, the socket on this type is very much longer than usual. The pattern is the same as F 185/7, except for the presence of a bird topping the urn, perhaps indicating a steward's pole head.

F 185/7

F 185/8

F 185/9   4.75"   MERL / Allen / 550969

Allen recorded no details for this specimen, and no other evidence has emerged. The design the top finial is characterised by spiral ridges. An identical unidentified specimen is in SHC (OSFS 294).

F 186   6.8"   MERL / Allen / 551031

Allen attributed this design to the Tintinhull Seven Year Male Friendly Society (1820s to 1856) (SOM 503) and (1856 to 1912) (SOM 632), which met at the School Room, and to Limington Friendly Society (1847 to 1913) (SOM 562), where it was said to be used by the stewards, but he produced no evidence for either of these suggestions. J Stevens Cox attributed the same design to the Ilchester Young Men's Friendly Society, and to the Tintinhull club (*SDNQ*, Vol. XXV, March 1948, pp 81 and 82). The Stevens Cox attribution to Ilchester and Tintinhull bears most weight since his verification of other Ilchester brasses is backed up by evidence. For this design, however, he gave no detail, and no other verification has been found.

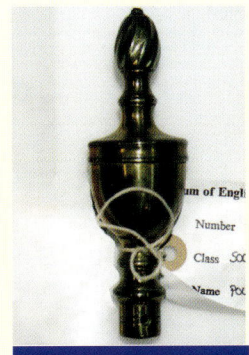
F 185/9

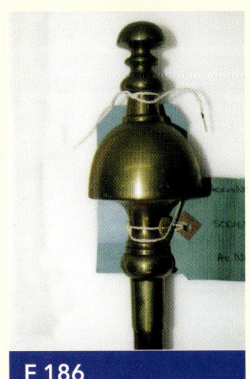
F 186

F 187

F 188

F 189/1

F 189/2

F 189/3

F 187   6.4"   MERL / Allen / 550946

This design is attributed to **Ebrington Friendly Society** (1856 to 1920) (GLOS 663), which met at the Ebrington Arms and later at the school Room. A specimen engraved with the name 'David Wood' links the design with the village. (Private collection).

F 188   8.3"   Wells and Mendip Museum / 729

This pattern is usually associated with the Yeovil Guardians Friendly Society, which met at the Mermaid Inn, but no evidence has emerged to verify the suggestion. The officers of the Yeovil Old True Blues Benefit Society (1782 to 1889) (SOM 783), which met at the Pall Inn, were, however, recorded as carrying 'gilt tipped wands', but the design is not confirmed (*Western Gazette*, June 14th, 1867).

F 189/1   6.8"   MERL / Allen / 550940

Mickleton, Gloucestershire, was the only location suggested for this design by early collectors, but no evidence has emerged to support the claim. A specimen engraved 'R Harrison 1877' has offered no leads. (Private collection).

Detail of user of pole head F 189/1: R Harrison 1877.

F 189/2   6.2"   MERL / Shickle / 511115

This appears to be the only example of this design, and Shickle did not offer a provenance. It does not seem to be a modified version of any similar 'bed-post' pole head.

F 189/3   c. 4"   Private collection, current location unknown

No evidence for provenance has emerged for this design. The top is engraved 'Faithfully Friendly Society 1777', but the location of the society is unknown. A number of 'Faithful Friend' societies, however, were located in Wales. The 1777 date probably refers to the founding of the society, and is not necessarily the age of the specimen.

F 190/1   4.6″   MERL / Allen / 551083

This specimen was sold to AW Allen by AH Isher of Cheltenham as a Toddenham Head (sic) for 25/- , but the Toddenham or Todenham provenance has not been confirmed by any other source (MERL Classified Index 'Friendly Societies', letter, June 11th, 1938). Ponsonby-Fane recorded that his example was 'got at Warwick' (MERL Ponsonby-Fane Notebook, p.34).

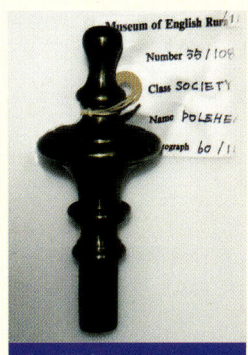
F 190/1

F 190/2   5.3″   Private collection

This specimen is reputed to come from Chadlington, Oxfordshire, but no evidence has emerged to support the claim. No other specimen has been recorded.

F 191/1   6.8″   MERL / Allen / 550983

This design has been verified for both **Martock Male Benefit Society** (1800 to 1912) (SOM 191), which met at the George Inn, and **Crewkerne Royal Old True Blues Friendly Society** (1895 to c. 1896) (SOM 061), which at various times met at the Royal Oak Inn and the White Hart Inn. In an undated letter to Jardine, the Rev GW Saunders wrote: 'I have a specimen identical to this as Martock Men's Club [of the] George Inn' (MERL Jardine DDX-1787), and the members were reported as carrying 'blue poles with brass tops' (*Western Gazette*, May 25th, 1866). A specimen in Martock Church is 6.3″ and proportionately narrow, as are several others. Evidence for use at Crewkerne was provided by Ponsonby-Fane, who wrote that his example was 'bought from the man who carried it' (MERL Ponsonby-Fane notebook, p.47, no 1). The members were recorded as carrying poles (*Pulman's Weekly News*, June 14th, 1881). The Crewkerne brass is probably the taller of the two.

F 190/2

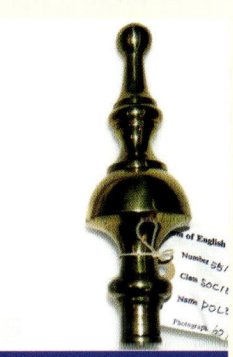
F 191/1

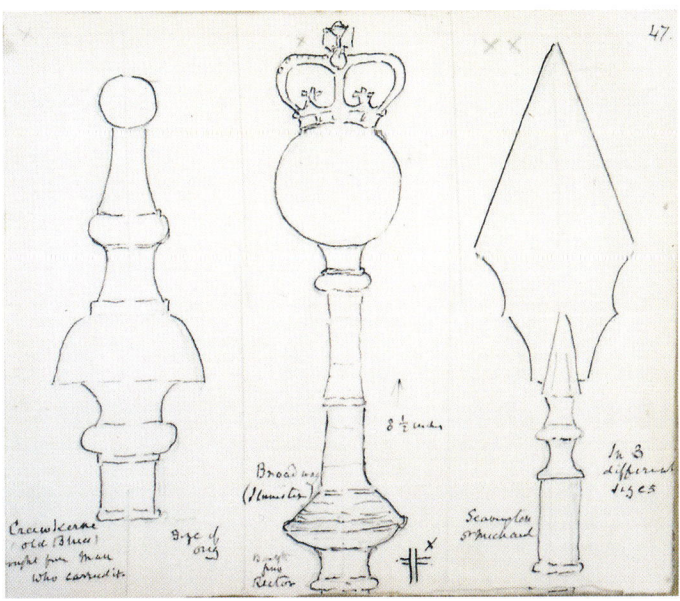

Evidence for location of F 191/1 at Crewkerne: 'bought from the man who used it'.

F 191/2   5″   MERL / Allen / 551101

This pole head was not included in Fuller's 1964 list. Allen gave it no provenance, and no other details have emerged. No other specimen has been recorded: the design is unusual in having a concave under side to the knop. It is similar to F 191/3, but differs in detail.

F 191/2

F 191/3   5″   SHC / Du Cann Collection / 201878

This pole head was not included in Fuller's 1964 list. No other specimen has been recorded, and no details of provenance have emerged. The design is unusual in having a concave under side to the knop. It is similar to F 191/2, but differs in detail.

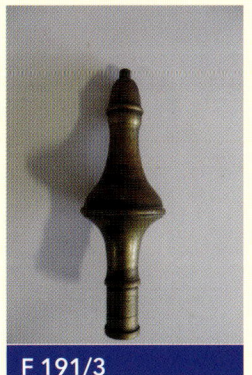
F 191/3

F 191/4

F 191/5

F 191/6

F 192

F 193

F 191/4   5″   MERL / Allen / 551111

Allen did not suggest a provenance for this specimen, but Jardine attributed the design to Bilston, Staffordshire, without providing any supporting evidence (MERL Jardine 61244105). The specimen at SHC was donated by Sir Spencer Ponsonby-Fane, and it was attributed by him to 'Congleton, near Alcester, Warwickshire' (SHC OSFS 231B). Congleton is in Cheshire, so the attribution may be in error for Coughton, near Alcester, Warwickshire, but there is no further evidence for either location. The design was not included in Fuller's 1964 list, and it is unusual in having a concave under side to the knop.

F 191/5   4.7″   MERL / Allen / 551164

The only suggestions as to the provenance are 'Charlcote, Warwickshire' (MERL, Ponsonby-Fane notebook, p.73), and 'from Stratford-on-Avon' (SHC, Kelway notebook, p.203), but no further evidence has emerged. This pole head is not in Fuller's 1964 list. The design is unusual in having a concave under side to the knop. Another specimen is at SHC OSFS 295, but it has no known provenance.

F 191/6   4.3″   SHC / OSFS / 791

The design was not in Fuller's 1964 list. Only two examples have been found and no provenance has been recorded for either. The flat under side of the central portion is unusual. The two specimens differ only in minor detail attributable to hand finishing.

F 192   6″   MERL / Allen / 550981

This design has been attributed (without evidence) to Wrington Friendly Society (1792 to 1822) (SOM 327) and (1822 to 1912) (SOM 328), which met at the Golden Lion Inn. The Allen collection has a second near-identical example, with no reported provenance, while an identical specimen at SHC (OSFS 216) is also listed under the heading of Wrington, but again there is no supporting evidence. These last two specimens both have a rimmed knop, showing that the body was made with a top and a bottom, but the rim does not protrude. Poles were certainly carried by the society, according to the rules of various dates. The 1792 rules mention the carrying of a 'staff' (The National Archives FS 1/616/327), as do the rules of 1823 and 1841 (The National Archives FS 3/329/328). The design shown here, F 192, resembles that of F 195/1, which, however, is claimed to be from Whitchurch. This general design has been variously attributed to Bristol St George, Cheddar, Marksbury, Whitchurch, and Wrington.

F 193   10″   MERL / Allen / 550935

This brass is similar to F192 but is larger, and was probably used by a steward. The design has been attributed (without evidence) to Wrington Friendly Society (1792 to 1822) (SOM 327) and (1822 to 1912) (SOM 328), which met at the Golden Lion Inn. Poles were certainly carried by the society, according to the rules of various dates. The 1792 rules mention the carrying of a 'staff' (The National Archives FS 1/616/327), as do the rules of 1823 and 1841 (The National Archives FS 3/329/328). A very similar specimen at SHC (OSFS 215) measures 9.9″, but is of slightly larger proportions than F 193, albeit with a shorter socket. It has also been labelled 'Wrington'. F 193 and F 194/1 appear to have a similar pattern. This general design has been variously attributed to Bristol St George, Cheddar, Marksbury, Whitchurch, and Wrington.

F 194/1   5.9"   MERL / Allen / 550973

Wrington Friendly Society carried staffs, but the design of the pole head is not confirmed. Wrington Friendly Society (SOM 327) (1792 to 1822) and (SOM 328) (1822 to 1912) met at the Golden Lion Inn. Its 1792, 1823, and 1841 rules all specified the use of a 'staff' (The National Archives FS 1/616/327 and The National Archives FS 3/329/328). F 193 and F 194 appear to have a similar pattern. Bristol St George, Cheddar, Marksbury, Whitchurch, and Wrington have all been suggested provenances for this general design.

F 194/1

F 194/2   5.75"   MERL / Allen / 551001

Allen offered no suggestion for the provenance of this design, and no subsequent evidence has emerged. This specimen is of a similar pattern to F 193, F 194/1 and F 194/3, with the protrusion around the stem towards the top, but it is of different proportions.

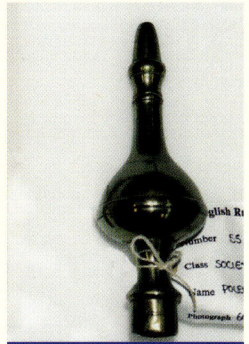
F 194/2

F 194/3   7.5"   Blaise Castle House Museum / T9651

No provenance has been suggested for this specimen. The pattern of this brass is very similar to F 193, F 194/1, and F 194/2, but the socket is much extended. The green colour is due to verdigris on the brass.

Surface discolouration by formation of verdigris.

F 194/3

F 194/4   5.3"   SHC / OSFS / 114

This design has been labelled Marksbury, but without evidence. This specimen closely resembles F 194/1, but it is shorter, mostly due to the socket length.

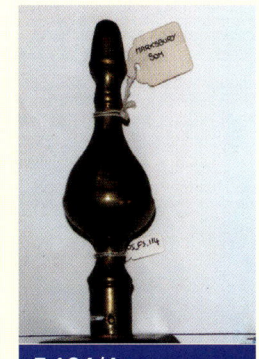
F 194/4

F 195/1   5.9"   MERL / Allen / 550993

Allen attributed this design to Whitchurch, but no evidence in support of the claim has emerged. Bristol St George, Cheddar, Marksbury, Whitchurch, and Wrington have all been suggested as provenances for this general design. The Rev EP Nicholls recalled a 90 year old inhabitant, c.1932, who said, however, that Whitchurch had a flat brass similar to Bishop Sutton (MERL, Jardine notes, DDX / 993).

F 195/1

F 195/2

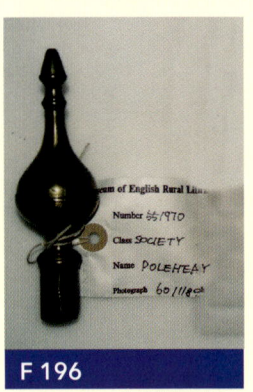

F 196

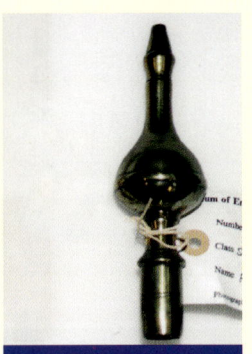

F 197/1

F 197/2

F 197/3

F 195/2   8.9″   Blaise Castle House Museum / T9397

This specimen is attributed to Whitchurch, but there is no supporting evidence. It is larger than many other similar patterns, suggesting that it was a steward's brass.

F 196   5.1″   MERL / Allen / 550970

Allen attributed this specimen to Marksbury, but with no supporting evidence. Bristol St George, Cheddar, Marksbury, Whitchurch, and Wrington have all been suggested as provenances for this general design.

F 197/1   6″   MERL / Allen / 551093

This specimen is attributed to Cheddar, but with no supporting evidence. Bristol St George, Cheddar, Marksbury, Whitchurch, and Wrington have all been suggested as provenances for this general design.

F 197/2   6.1″   Blaise Castle House Museum / TA4569

No evidence has emerged for this design, which is one of a near-identical pair. The other measures 5.9″ (TA 9345). Both have more realistically modelled acorns at the top than is normal with this general type. A third example is in the MERL Allen Collection (550975) measuring 6″.

F 197/3   5.1″   MERL / Allen / 551033

No provenance has been suggested for this design. The pattern is distinguished by a protruding ring towards the top of the stem beneath the acorn. More than one example has been seen, but none has a recorded provenance.

The Le Gros collection: F 195/2 third from right, top shelf (now in Blaise Castle House Museum, Bristol)

F 197/4 5″ MERL / Shickle / 511136

The pattern, slightly different from F 197/3 in its socket, is also distinguished by a protruding ring towards the top of the stem beneath the acorn. This is the only example that has been seen, and there is no accompanying provenance.

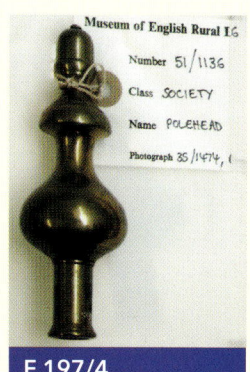

F 197/4

F 197/5 6.35″ SHC / Du Cann Collection / 201874

Only one example of this pattern has been seen, and it has no suggested provenance. It is probably not a friendly society pole head as the socket does not seem suited to fit on a pole.

F 197/6 4.5″ MERL / Allen / 551041

Only one example of this pattern has been seen. It was not identified by Allen, and no evidence has been found for a provenance..

F 197/5

F 197/7 6.6″ Blaise Castle House Museum / T7533

Whitchurch or Cheddar have been suggested as the provenance for this design, but without supporting evidence. Several other examples exist, including one in the Allen Collection and one in the Du Cann Collection. The pattern is not listed by Fuller (1964).

F 197/8 9.4″ Holburne Museum / VE094

This specimen was described by the original collector, HJ Hooper, as a steward's brass from St George, Bristol, but he did not offer any supporting evidence.

F 197/6

F 197/7

The Hooper collection: F 197/8 second from right, top shelf (now in Holburne Museum, Bath).

F 197/8

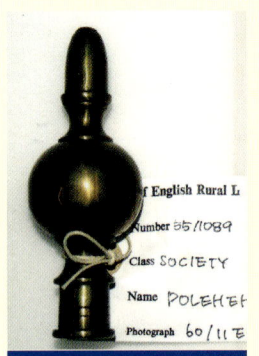

F 197/9

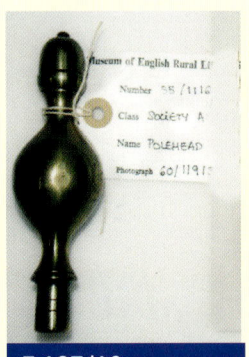

F 197/10

F 197/11

F 198/1

F 198/2

F 197/9   4.25″   MERL / Allen / 551089

This pattern was not included in Fuller's 1964 list, and no recorded provenance has emerged for this type. The design is unusual in the shortness of the stem between the ball and the acorn. Another specimen exists in a private collection.

F 197/10   5.5″   MERL / Allen / 551116

This pattern was not included in Fuller's 1964 list. The Ponsonby-Fane MERL notebook records this design as coming from 'Sollyhull' (sic), but there is no supporting evidence, and no other details have emerged (MERL, Ponsonby-Fane Notebook, p. 76). The surface of the brass is unusual in the lack of detailing between the acorn and the socket.

F 197/11   4.4″   MERL / Allen / 551120

This pattern was not included in Fuller's 1964 list, and no further details have emerged. As with F 197/10, the surface of the brass is unusual in the lack of detailing between the acorn and the socket.

F 198/1   7.0″   MERL / Allen / 550985

Allen left no conclusive provenance for this specimen, but simply listed it as Stoke sub Hamdon. The verified specimen from this village is at F 198/2, but although of a similar pattern it is rather smaller (6.6″ compared with 7.0″).

F 198/2   6.6″   SHC / OSFS / 169A

This design is verified for **The Royal George Seven Year Friendly Society, Stoke sub Hamdon**, (also known as Stoke under Ham) (1829 to 1893) (SOM 448), which met at the Fleur de Lis Inn in 1829 and at the Duke of Cornwall Inn by 1891. This specimen was given by Dr R H Walter (the club doctor to this and other nearby societies). At 6.6″ tall, it is marginally less than other similar specimens, due to the top of the acorn being flattened. Dr Walter described it as a steward's brass from the society, but it is not known if a steward's brass was differentiated from that of an ordinary member. The design was also used at **West Coker** (evidence from club photographs); **North Coker** (MERL Ponsonby-Fane notebook p.5, given by Mrs Troyte Bullock, of North Coker House); **Sherborne** (see F 205, Sherborne Museum); **Thornford** (where it was carried by relative of owner). It was also used at **Leigh** and at **Chetnole** (F 199).

West Coker Mens Friendly Society c.1900.

F 198/3   7.0"   MERL / Allen / 550986

No provenance has been established for this design. This specimen and F 198/1 are similar in height, but the rim around the ball differs in width between the two, and the sockets differ in their configurations.

F 198/4   6.1"   Private collection

This design is similar to F 198/1 and F 198/3, but it is distinctly smaller. No others of this design have been noted, and no provenance has been recorded.

F 199   7.3"   MERL / Allen / 550988

This design is verified for Leigh, Dorset. The Allen specimen shown here and two at SHC (183/1989/23 and 183/1989/24) have dark red fringes. **Leigh Friendly Society** started in 1870 following the end of the nearby **Chetnole Friendly Society**, but it is not known when the brass pole heads were introduced. Leigh pole heads are recorded as having a silk fringe (*Southern Times*, June 10th, 1871, and *Western Gazette*, June 6th, 1873) but no other society with this pattern has been so recorded, except for a specimen at SHC on a pole, tentatively described as from Stoke sub Hamdon: OSFS 169/B). The design was used at **West Coker** (evidence from club photographs); **North Coker** (MERL Ponsonby-Fane notebook, p.5, given by Mrs Troyte Bullock, of North Coker House); **Sherborne** (see F 205, Sherborne Museum); **Thornford** (where it was carried by relative of owner); and **Stoke under Ham** (where the Club Doctor gave one to Taunton Museum – see F 198/2). There is a range of heights for this type.

Leigh pole head with fringe.

Although the pattern is well illustrated in photographs, showing use by clubs at Stoford and West Coker, the actual dimensions of the pole tops are impossible to gauge in most cases. Some have a distinctive wide band encircling the ball (specimen in private collection).

F 200/1   5.8"   MERL / Allen / 551125

Allen did not include a provenance for this specimen. Fuller (1964) suggested Warwickshire, but without giving reasons, and no other details have emerged. In this pattern there is a ridge in the stem, just above the ball (see also F 200/2).

F 200/2   5.8"   MERL / Shickle / 511127

Shickle gave no suggestion as to the provenance of this specimen, and no further details have emerged. As in F 200/1, this pattern has a ridge in the stem, just above the ball. Despite bearing a strong resemblance to F 200/1, the two pole heads are notably different in their finer detail.

F 198/3

F 198/4

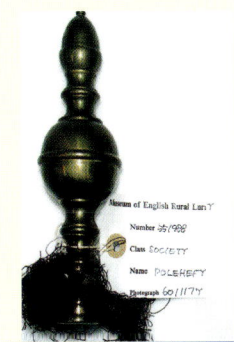

F 199

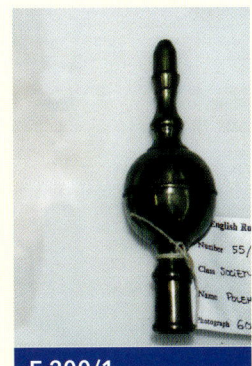

F 200/1

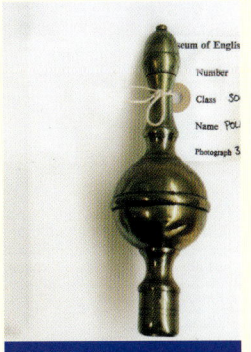

F 200/2

F 200/3

F 200/4

F 200/5

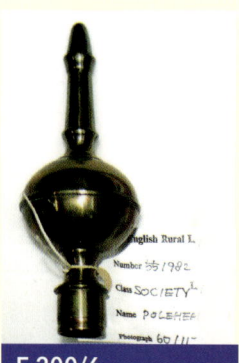

F 200/6

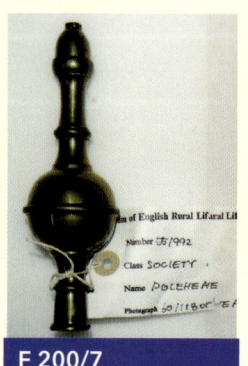

F 200/7

F 200/3   5.1″   Private collection

This is one of three near-identical specimens, which appear to come from the same society, but for which there are no details of provenance. The diameter of the ball is relatively small compared with many others of this general pattern. Although there was an example of this pattern in the MERL Allen collection (551033), it was not included in Fuller's 1964 list.

F 200/4   6.1″   SHC / OSFS / 230

No evidence has emerged that this design was used at Blackheath, Staffordshire. Superficially, this specimen closely resembles F 200/1, 2 and 3, but the detailing of the acorn, the rim of the ball, and the finish of the socket are all quite distinct.

F 200/5   5.5″   MERL / Shickle / 511145

Shickle gave no evidence for Nuttall (an unidentified location) as the provenance of this specimen. In this pattern there is a ridge in the stem, just above the ball. A similar specimen is at MERL (Jardine 61244241) and another in a private collection.

F 200/6   5.8″   MERL / Allen / 550932

Allen did not include a provenance for this specimen, and Fuller omitted it from her 1964 list. Its distinctive feature is a ridge at the base of the stem, just above the ball. A similar but shorter example of this pattern is F 200/5, where it is tentatively ascribed to Nuttall, an unidentified place. Another specimen, height 6.0″, is in a private collection. The ball in both cases is slightly flattened.

F 200/7   6.25″   MERL / Allen / 550992

This specimen was not identified by Allen, and no further evidence has emerged. Although similar to F 200/1 to F 200/6 in pattern, the proportions of all seven of this type are very dissimilar. Another example of this pole head exists in a private collection.

Ball and spire longcase clock finials resemble friendly society pole heads but are usually of lighter construction and lack a pole socket.

F 200/8   5.5"   MERL / Allen / 551067

Allen did not include a provenance for this specimen, and Fuller omitted it from her 1964 list. The sweeping modelling of the stem beneath the acorn is unusual. There is a small milled band on the wide seam of the ball, and further milling on the rim of the acorn cup. No other examples have been seen.

F 200/8

F 201/1   6"   MERL / Allen / 551126

This specimen was not identified by Allen, but Fuller (1964) claimed that it came from Blackheath, Staffordshire, without, however, providing any evidence, and no further details have emerged. Several examples have been traced, and several variants of this design exist. The top and bottom halves of the ball are made individually, and are separated by a plate, square when viewed from above, the whole being kept in place by a threaded rod attached to the socket and to the stem.

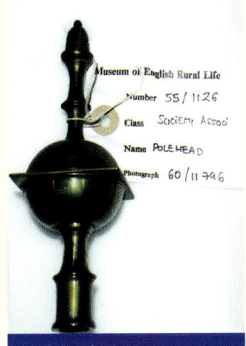

F 201/1

Detail of construction of this type of pole head.

F 201/2

F 201/2   6.5"   Private collection

No evidence has emerged for any provenance, although the design is similar to F 201/1, which was tentatively designated as coming from Blackheath. Besides being rather taller than F 201/1, this specimen has a concave-sided socket, and the rims are milled. The specimen was found at Rubery, which is c. 9 miles from Blackheath, but there is no further evidence of its origin. Several variants of this design exist. The top and bottom halves of the ball are made individually, and are separated by a plate, square when viewed from above, the whole being kept in place by a threaded rod attached to the socket and to the stem.

F 201/3   6.6"   SHC / OSFS / 778

The design is attributed to Woodend, Worcestershire, without supporting evidence, and no further details have emerged. In this specimen the ball is rather elongated. Several variants of this design exist. The top and bottom halves of the ball are made individually, and are separated by a plate, square when viewed from above, the whole being kept in place by a threaded rod attached to the socket and to the stem.

F 201/3

F 201/4   5.7"   Private collection

No provenance has been confirmed for this particular specimen although Chipping Norton has been suggested for F 201/5, which is similar in design. The unusual feature is the spiral top on the end of the stem. The membership number 70 is stamped on the socket, suggesting its use as a friendly society pole top. Two similar examples, unnumbered and slightly taller, exist in different private collections.

F 201/4

F 201/5

F 201/5   6.0″   Private collection

There is no supporting evidence that this design was associated with Chipping Norton, Oxfordshire. This is a slightly larger version of F 201/4, again with a spiral top, but the proportions of the various constituent parts are also different.

F 201/6

F 201/6   4.75″   Dorset Museum, Dorchester / 1953.20.11

This design is verified for **Litton Cheney Old Friendly Society** (1844 to 1884) (DOR 121A) and (1884 to 1949) (DOR 121B), which met at the Rectory School Room. The 1844 Litton Cheney Friendly Society rules required members on the anniversary to be present, 'each with his club stick'. The last use of the club sticks was in 1948 (*Western Gazette*, August 6th, 1948). In at least three photographic post cards dating from 1921 the poles can be seen, and the shapes of the pole heads match this design. Larger specimens exist (F 201/7), and were probably used by stewards. The socket of this specimen resembles that of the Puddletown (Dorset) pole head (F 218). Several specimens have been seen, differing slightly in height. The specimen in the Allen collection measures c.4,7″ (MERL 551164). The design was omitted from Fuller (1964).

F 201/7

F 201/7   6.1″   MERL / Allen / 551130

This design was given no provenance by Allen, but is verified for **Litton Cheney Old Friendly Society** (1844 to 1884) (DOR 121A) and (1884 to 1949) (DOR 121B), which met at the Rectory School Room. The 1844 Litton Cheney Friendly Society rules required members on the anniversary to be present, 'each with his club stick'. The last use of the club sticks was in 1948 (*Western Gazette*, August 6th, 1948). In at least three photographic post cards dating from 1921 the poles can be seen, and the shapes of the pole heads match the design in F 201/6. This specimen is larger than the members' version, and was probably used by a steward. The design was omitted from Fuller (1964). Another example is in a private collection.

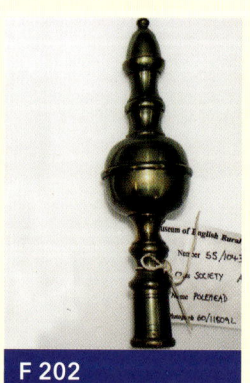

F 202

F 202   7.1″   MERL / Allen / 551043

Although the outline pattern is verified for West Coker, the actual height of the West Coker version is uncertain. A similar observation applies to the pole heads of North Coker, Stoford, Leigh, and Chetnole. The feast days of the West Coker Perpetual Friendly Society (1845 to 1881) (SOM 439) and the West Coker Hand and Heart Yearly Friendly Society (1881 to after 1889) were recorded in several photographic post cards, where the pole heads can clearly be seen: they are of the pattern shown here, but their precise dimensions cannot be ascertained. There are various views of the men's and the women's parades (SHC: DD\NNE\C/1375/6). The pattern was used at **West Coker** and **Stoford** (evidence from club photographs); **North Coker** (MERL Ponsonby-Fane notebook p.5, no1: the specimen came from Mrs Troyte Bullock of North Coker House); **Sherborne** (F205) (Sherborne Museum collection); **Thornford** (carried by relative of owner); **Stoke under Ham** (Club Doctor gave one to Taunton Museum); and at **Leigh** and **Chetnole** (see F 199).

F 203/1

F 203/1   7.5″   MERL / Jardine / 61244185

Fuller (1964) suggested a possible Crewkerne origin, while Jardine suggested the Plymouth Marine Reds, an unidentified body. These flag pole tops were not, however, specific to any one club. As with other flag pole or banner tops of this general type, the specimen here has an eyelet on the stem beneath the ball. They were used by a variety of friendly societies, trade unions, and other organisations.

F 203/2   7.5"   Private collection

There are many varieties of this flag pole- or banner-top, with slightly different heights, and with a variety of finials: halberds, crossed halberds, miniature orbs, acorns on stems, and a kangaroo (RAOB) have been seen, but none has a provenance. They were used by a variety of friendly societies, trade unions and other organisations.

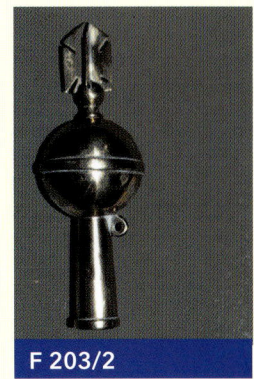

F 203/2

F 204   6.3"   MERL / Allen / 551153

No proof of provenance has emerged to link this design tor Stourport. Only one specimen has been recorded of this design: it was originally in the Ponsonby-Fane collection (MERL Ponsonby-Fane notebook, p.61 no 1). It has a waisted socket, therefore it would be difficult to fit onto a pole, and this suggests that it is an ornamental finial, possibly from an andiron, and with no friendly society association.

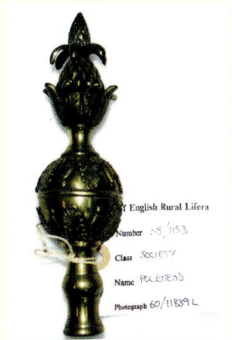

F 204

F 205   7.2"   MERL / Allen / 551068

This design is verified for **Sherborne Union Friendly Society** (the Old Tuesday Club) (before 1796 to 1847) (The National Archives FS 1/113/misc, p.2), which met at the Swan Inn, and by **The Union Friendly Society of Sherborne** (1847 to 1901) (DOR 137) which by 1893 met at the Coffee Tavern, Long Street. The Allen Collection Sherborne pole head is of precisely the same pattern and dimensions as the specimen on a pole painted with the member's name in Sherborne Museum, which was used by the Whit Tuesday Club. Other specimens on poles are also reputed to come from this club, all bearing names (private collections). By the 1796 rules, black rods were to be carried at funerals, the tops covered with a black fringe or horsehair (The National Archives FS 1/113/misc, p.2).

F 205

F 206   5"   MERL / Allen / 551092

Allen suggested that this design was used at Bradford on Tone by the Bradford Union Friendly Society (before 1839 to after 1866) (unregistered), which met at the Swan Inn in 1839 and at the White Horse Inn by 1866, but he offered no supporting evidence. Nevertheless, In 1866 Bradford on Tone FS members were recorded as carrying poles with brass tops (*Western Gazette*, May 25th, 1866), but there is no confirmation that the pattern was the one shown here. The light construction of the supposed Bradford on Tone and Norton Fitzwarren designs suggests that they might have been finials from longcase clock hoods, but a society might have bought them as a cheaper top than a bespoke thicker gauge version. In any case the orb part matches the construction of the verified Bishops Hull type (F 207). Alternatively it is possible that the Bradford design was F 162.

F 206

F 207   6.6"   MERL / Allen / 551011

This design is verified for **Bishops Hull Friendly Society** (1824 to after 1892) (unregistered), which met at the New Inn. Each member had a blue staff, and the club started in 1824 (*Taunton Courier*, June 14th, 1876). An unusually detailed contemporary press report gave details of the pole head: 'Beside the usual brass head and streamers of blue ribbon was a gilt crown and the date of formation of the society, 1824' (*Western Gazette*, June 9th, 1865). The two SHC specimens were donated by J Mayes and J Stevens, both residents of Bishops Hull (SHC OSFS 88 and OSFS 89).

F 207

F 208/1

F 208/2

F 209

F 210

F 211

F 208/1   5.8″   MERL / Allen / 550999

Norton United Benefit Society (1842 to after 1901) (unregistered) met at the Ring o' Bells Inn, Norton Fitzwarren, and members carried blue poles with brass tops, but there is no confirmation that the design of the pole head is the one recorded here (*Western Gazette*, June 2nd, 1865, and *Somerset County Gazette*, June 2nd, 1883). The light construction of the supposed Norton Fitzwarren and Bradford on Tone designs suggests that they might have been finials from longcase clock hoods, but a society might have bought them as a cheaper top than a bespoke thicker gauge version. In any case, the orb part matches the equivalent feature of the verified Bishops Hull type (F 207).

F 208/2   6.6″   MERL / Allen / 550990

This design is verified for **Misterton Male Friendly Society** (1881 to1913) (SOM 992), which met at the Schoolroom. Staves were carried by members on anniversary processions (*Pulman's Weekly News*, June 11th, 1901). In the MERL Shickle Collection (9511129) the pattern is ascribed to Misterton, and in the Ponsonby-Fane notebook is a drawing of this brass, described as 'Misterton, given me by Mr Locke, Rector' [of Misterton] (MERL Ponsonby-Fane notebook, p.44). It is unclear why Fuller (1964) omitted this type, which appears in many collections.

F 209   6.3″   MERL / Allen / 551045

This design is verified as the one used by **The Loyal Brothers Friendly Society** (1802 to 1889) (SOM 384a), (1889 to 1912) (SOM 384b and from 1912 part of the Somerset National Insurance Group), which met at the New Inn and later at the National School, **Shepton Beauchamp**. Members carried 'brass-topped poles' in their anniversary processions (*Western Gazette*, June 13th, 1873). Allen is the only early collector to link this design to Shepton Beauchamp. The pole for Allen's brass has the painted initials JWR, and John Rowsell was a tailor here in the 1860s (1861 Census and *Kelly's Directory of Somerset*, 1866). An undated photograph at the Duke of York Inn at Shepton Beauchamp, c.1910 (copied in 2020), shows the club with pole heads, poles and streamers. Although there are several designs of pole head on display (some possibly carried by visitors), by far the majority are of this pattern as suggested by Allen.

F 210   7.2″   MERL / Allen / 550987

This design is verified for **Barrington Friendly Society** (1807 to 1912) (SOM 254), which met at the Royal Oak Inn and from 1912 at the School Room. It became the Barrington Friendly and Insurance Society from 1912 to 1915 (SOM 254) and the Barrington Five Year Burial Society until 1945 (unregistered). In 1907 several photographic postcards were produced of the Barrington Friendly Society Centenary. Many members (and children) were pictured with club poles, and the pattern of the brass can be seen (SHC A/AEP/11/4/5). The stewards' pattern is at F 294/2. The Rev J Hamlet gave details of the society in his 'History of Barrington Friendly Society' (SHC D/P/barr 23/2). He was the mainstay of the club in its later years, and presented the steward's brass shown at F 294/2 to Taunton Museum (SHC 9727).

F 211   =   MERL / Allen / 551052

The original Allen specimen is missing from the MERL collection, but it was photographed and recorded in Fuller's 1964 list before it was loaned in 1988 and subsequently not returned. Allen was the only person to suggest North Curry as the provenance, but he provided no evidence. The design was, however, used at nearby **Curry Rivel** (F 213). A quite different design was also known at North Curry: the presidents of the North Curry Friendly Society used a silvered version of the Bishop's Lydeard's pole head (see F264/2).

F 212   6.5"   MERL / Allen / 551049

This design is verified for **Pawlett Friendly Society** (1794 to a date between 1844 and 1861) (SOM 454) and its continuation, **Pawlett United Brethren Society** (by 1861 to after 1863), which met at the Shoulder of Mutton Inn, and then **Pawlett Seven Year Friendly Society** (unregistered) (by 1890 to after 1910). In a letter to Jardine, dated March 15th, 1932, the Rev B Turton, Rector, referring to the Pawlett pole head, wrote: 'your sketch is exact. I have one. The club died about forty to fifty years ago' (MERL Jardine Index). The Taunton Courier reported on the club's fiftieth anniversary in 1844 (*Taunton Courier*, June 26th, 1844), while a letter from the secretary to the Registrar of Friendly Societies (n.d., but after 1876) referred to the unregistered society (The National Archives FS 4/44/212).

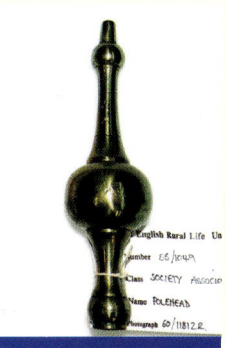

F 212

F 213   6.8"   MERL / Allen / 550984

This design is verified for **Curry Rivel Friendly Society**, also known as the **Old Male Friendly Society** (1790 to 1892) (SOM 012) and (1892 to c. 1940) (unregistered), which met at the Bell Inn. Long after the demise of the society some of the club poles with their pole heads attached were sold from the Bell Inn and passed into private collections. The Ponsonby-Fane pole head illustrated in his notebook was 'secured from Vicar' (MERL, Ponsonby-Fane Notebook, p.46, no 3). Blue poles with brass tops and red ribbons were carried by 1867 right through to at least 1936 (*Western Flying Post*, June 18th, 1867, and *Taunton Courier*, June 3rd, 1936).

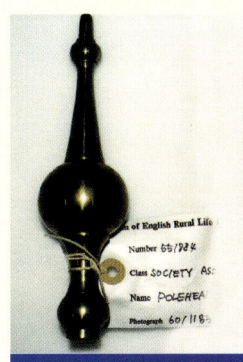

F 213

F 214/1   5.5"   MERL / Allen / 550977

The design is verified for **Stocklinch and Puckington United Friendly Society** (1838 to 1901, but not officially dissolved until 1903) (SOM 492) and earlier by **Stocklinch Magdalen Friendly Society** also known as the **Ilford Bridges Friendly Society**, which ended in 1838 (SOM 492), and which met at the Ilford Bridges Inn. The SHC specimen was purchased by Taunton Museum through the Rev EH Bates (Rector of Puckington) in 1908 (SHC OSFS 165B and Taunton Museum archives, 1908 Daybook). The 1838 Ilford Bridges Friendly Society rules and the 1844 Stocklinch and Puckington United Friendly Society rules both required use of 'a brass knob' (The National Archives FS 3/330/492).

F 214/1

F 214/2   4.4"   Blaise Castle House Museum / T9652

The provenance for this design was given by Allen as Paxton in Warwickshire, but the location is untraced and there are no supporting details. This specimen is on a 71" dark blue pole, with the top 11" white, and further examples (not on poles) are in the MERL Allen Collection 551069 (slightly taller at 4.8"), and the MERL Jardine Collection 61244239. All three cite the provenance as Paxton, but without giving any evidence.

F 214/2

F 214/3   4.6"   MERL / Shickle / 511128

This pattern is similar to F 214/2, but of different proportions. No provenance was given by Shickle, and no further details have emerged.

F 214/3

F 214/4

F 214/5

F 214/6

F 215/1

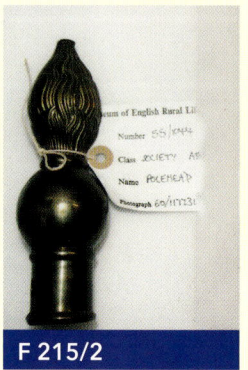

F 215/2

F 214/4   4.8"   SHC / OSFS / 775

No evidence has emerged for this design. The pattern is similar to F 214/2, but of different proportions, and it has a protrusion at the top.

F 214/5   3.9"   MERL / Allen / 551113

No evidence has emerged for this design. The pattern is similar to F 214/2, but of different proportions, and it has a plain socket.

F 214/6   5.5"   Blaise Castle House Museum / T9549

No evidence has emerged for this design. The pole head is on a 71" dark blue pole, of which the top 12" are red. No provenance accompanied this specimen. Another example is in the Allen Collection (MERL 551007).

F 215/1   7"   MERL / Shickle / 511090

Churchill was suggested as the provenance by Ponsonby-Fane, but there was no supporting evidence (MERL Ponsonby-Fane Notebook, p.87, no 3). No other location has been suggested. The cast patterned top is very unusual.

F 215/2   5.75"   MERL / Allen / 551044

In a MERL list of the Shickle collection, amended by an unknown hand, specimen number 511102 is described as coming from Merry, Gloucestershire, but the location is untraceable. In the MERL Ponsonby-Fane notebook the example is described as '[brass-] plated tin' (MERL Ponsonby-Fane Notebook, p.99, no 2). No provenance has been ascertained.

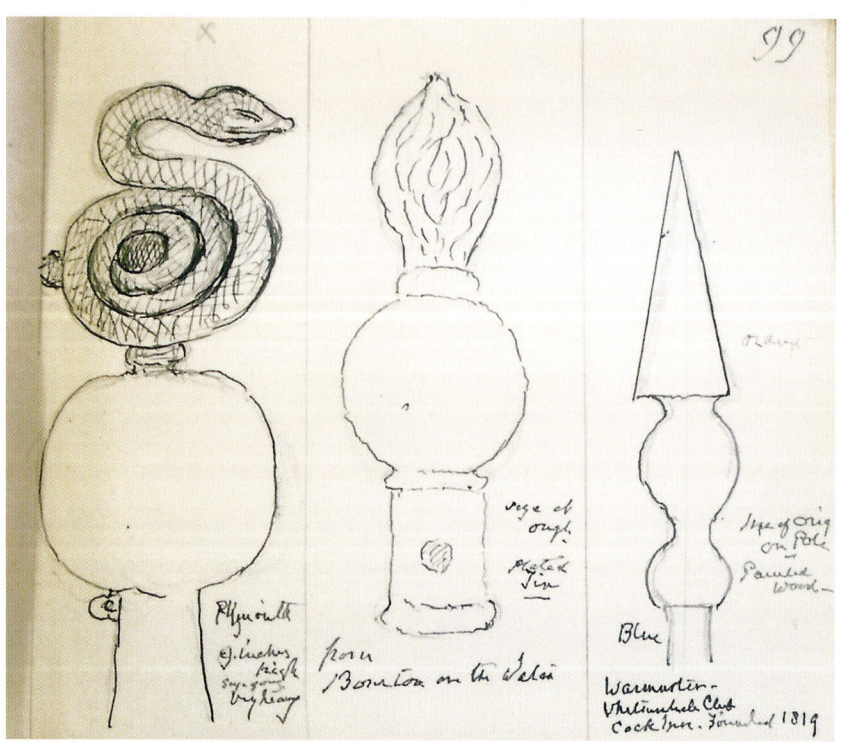

The Ponsonby-Fane record of F 215/2.

F 216   8"   MERL / Allen / 550963

This design is verified for **Crewkerne Friendly Society** (from before 1850 to 1862) (unregistered), which met at the White Hart Inn. The society was also known as the **Whites** and as the **Spikes**. A letter to the *Western Gazette*, September 16th, 1932, from JW Walden, drew attention to the nickname 'Spikes' Club': the reference is to the unique shape of this pole head.

F 217/1   6"   MERL / Allen / 551127

This design is verified for **Willoughby (Warwickshire) Tradesmen's Club**. Fuller incorrectly puts Willoughby in Staffordshire, while Allen gave no provenance for this design. The specimen in the Dr T Hopkins Collection at Taunton was 'bought from the last club secretary, the club, however, now [1909] extinct' (SHC OSFS 286A; Taunton Museum archives, exercise book with the heading 'Friendly Society items from the registers'). Four specimens have been recorded.

F 217/2   5"   MERL / Jardine / 6124495

Jardine provided no evidence for his suggested provenance of East Haddon, Northamptonshire. A second example, at SHC (OSFS 230/3), is labelled Braunston, Northamptonshire, but the original accession data did not give a provenance. There is no supporting evidence for Braunston.

F 218/1   7.9"   MERL / Allen / 550961

Allen does not offer a suggestion for this specimen. Fuller (1964) suggests Puddletown and Moreton (both in Dorset), based on Kelway's suggestion (SHC Taunton Museum archives, Kelway notebook, p 29, no 21), but no evidence has been found to support either attribution. Nevertheless, the socket here resembles that of the pole heads of Litton Cheney, which is also in Dorset (F 201/6 and F210/7)).

F 218/2   6.2"   SHC / OSFS / 772

There is no suggested provenance for either F 218/2 or F 218/3. The topmost portion of each resembles the upper part of F 218/2, while the section just above the ball, although different in each, has elements of F 219.

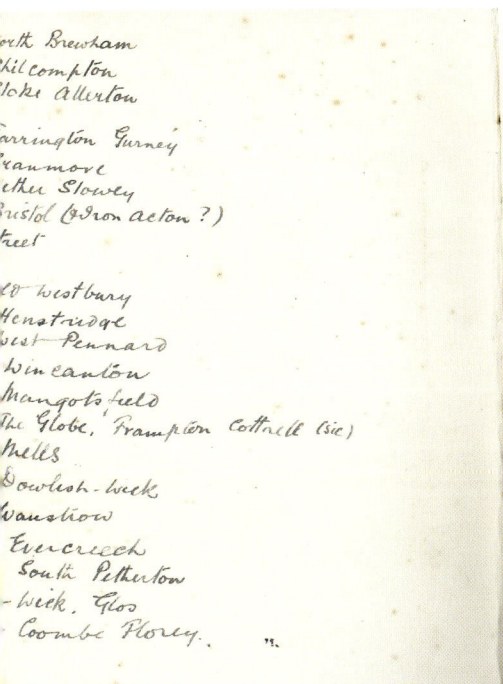

1914 catalogue of the Hopkins collection (Taunton Museum).

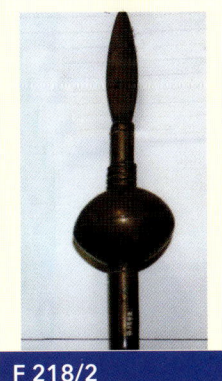

F 218/3

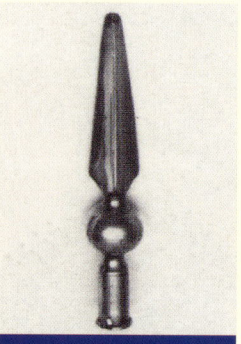

218/4

F 219

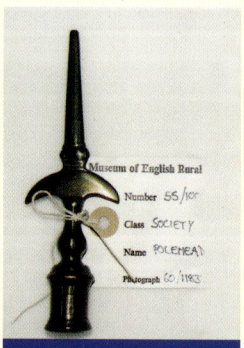

F 220

F 221/1

F 218/3   6.3″   SHC / OSFS / 773

There is no suggested provenance for either F 218/2 or F 218/3. The topmost portion of each resembles the upper part of F 218/2, while the section just above the ball, although different in each, has elements of F 219.

F 218/4   c. 12″   The Wainwright collection (dispersed): location untraced

The Wainwright exhibition catalogue described this specimen as a steward's brass. It attributed the design to Croscombe, near Shepton Mallet and claimed that there was proof, but that the details were lost (Eunice B. Overend, ed., Catalogue of the Wainwright Collection of Friendly Society Brasses [dispersed], The Phillips Museum [defunct], Brokerswood, Autumn 1971, no -/172). Croscombe Friendly Society (1795 to date unknown, then unregistered from before 1841 to after 1884) appears to have left no records of pole carrying. The staff attributed to the President is shown at F 099/3.

F 219   4.8″?   MERL / Allen / 550998

Allen identified this pole head as belonging to **Nether Stowey 29th May Male Friendly Society**, but Fuller (1964) followed an error that had appeared in the later Taunton Museum pole head identification lists (SHC Taunton Museum archives). These mistakenly attributed the design to the Female Society, which, however, never carried poles. Early versions of the lists compiled by the curator, H St George Gray, had nevertheless correctly identified the design as belonging to **Nether Stowey 29th May Male Friendly Society** (1856 to 1913) (SOM 627), which met at the George Inn. A specimen in a private collection is appropriately stamped on one side 'CH May 29' and on the other 'OS 1856' (5″). The society split from the earlier Rose and Crown Friendly Society (see F 124) in 1856, and adopted the Stogursey club rules. The Nether Stowey 29th May Male Friendly Society pole head is illustrated in *Happy Memories of West Somerset*, EH Smith, Bridgwater, c.1942, p.146. W Broadmead's example at the SHC was obtained when the club still met (OSFS 173B). It was recorded that members 'carried staves' (*West Somerset Free Press*, June 9th, 1906). In the accounts and other records of the Women's Club, however, there are no references to poles (SHC DD/TYL/2 and 3).

F 220   5.5″   MERL / Allen / 551000

Allen identified this pole head as a variant of F 219, which belonged to **Nether Stowey 29th May Male Friendly Society**. For the former misattribution to the Nether Stowey Female Society see F219.

F 221/1   15.3″ SHC / OSFS / 173

Fuller (1964) followed an error that had appeared in the later Taunton Museum identification lists (SHC Taunton Museum archives). These mistakenly attributed F 219 and F 220 to the Nether Stowey Female Society, which, however, never carried poles. Early versions of the lists compiled by the curator, H St George Gray, had nevertheless correctly identified the design. It forms the upper part of F 221/3 which was used by **Nether Stowey 29th May Male Friendly Society** (1856 to 1913) (SOM 627), and which met at the George Inn. A specimen in a private collection is appropriately stamped on one side 'CH May 29' and on the other 'OS 1856' (5″). The Nether Stowey 29th May Male Friendly Society pole head is illustrated in *Happy Memories of West Somerset*, EH Smith, Bridgwater, c.1942, p.146. W Broadmead's example at the SHC was obtained when the club still met (OSFS 173B). It was recorded that members 'carried staves' (*West Somerset Free Press*, June 9th, 1906). In the accounts and other records of the Women's Club, however, there are no references to poles (SHC DD/TYL/2 and 3). The design here, with a members' brass topping the tin model book (F 221/1), is the Secretary's pole head of **Nether Stowey 29th May**

Male Friendly Society, presented to Taunton Museum by TG Grandfield, the last secretary of the club (details in the SHC notebook 'Friendly Society items from the registers'). The small silk tassel shown in the photograph was at one time replicated on the right side as well, and was a feature also found on the members' pole heads of the Nether Stowey Rose and Crown Male Friendly Society (F 124).

F 221/2 9.8" Private collection

F 221/2

This design is the stewards' version of the members' pattern verified for **Nether Stowey 29th May Male Friendly Society** (1856 to 1913) (SOM 627), which met at the George Inn. The members' pattern (F 219 and F 220) is correctly identified and illustrated in *Happy Memories of West Somerset*, EH Smith, Bridgwater, c.1942, p.146. The largest version (c.10.8") was in the Wainwright collection, but its current location is unknown (Eunice B Overend, ed., *Catalogue of the Wainwright Collection of Friendly Society Brasses* [dispersed], The Phillips Museum [defunct], Brokerswood, Autumn 1971, p.23). Another specimen, 9.4" high, is in a private collection.

F 222 4.3" MERL / Allen / 551006

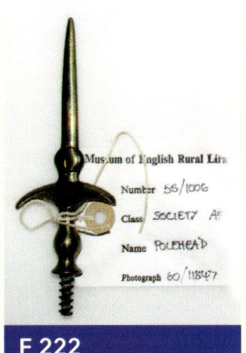

F 222

This version of F 219 and F220 has a basal spike fitting. It is verified for **Longburton Friendly Society** (1845 to 1901) (DOR 123), which met at the at the Rose and Crown Inn (1845) and at the School Room (from 1893). Two specimens on poles are in Sherborne Museum: there are slight differences in their design, but both brasses have a spike fitting rather than a hollow socket to attach the top of the pole. The 1845 rules significantly specify 'a pole painted blue with a brass spike on the top' (The National Archives FS 3/50/123).

F 223 6.3" MERL / Allen / 550959

F 223

This design is usually associated with the Anchor Inn, Hillfarrance, but no evidence has emerged in support of the claim.

F 224 6.5" MERL / Allen / 550965

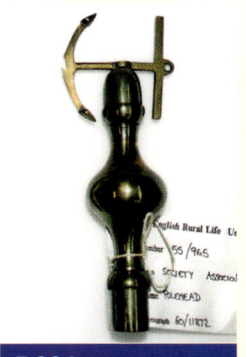

F 224

Allen attributed this design to the Watchet society meeting at the Anchor Inn, but gave no supporting evidence, and no further information has since emerged. The sign of the Anchor Inn suitably matches the pattern of F 224, but a variety of clubs existed at Watchet in the nineteenth century. Two are associated with the Anchor Inn: the Independent Union Benefit Society (1844 to c. 1873) (unregistered), and the Union Club (1817 to c.1873), but no record shows whether either carried pole heads. Two other Watchet societies, however, did carry rods, but the designs of the tops are unconfirmed. The societies were the Watchet Re-Union Friendly Society (1816 to c.1849) (SOM 310), which met at the Bell Inn, and the Watchet Equitable Friendly Society (1816 to an unrecorded end date), which met at the George Inn (The National Archives FS 1/615/310 and FS 1/615/311).

F 225 5.6" MERL / Allen / 551008

Allen attributed this design to Filton, but offered no supporting evidence. Between 1863 and 1893 the Filton Junior Benefit Society (GLOS 0817) moved from the Anchor Inn, Filton, to the Horseshoe Inn, then back, and finally again to the Horseshoe Inn. It is said to have changed emblems when moving from one to the other, but no confirmation of the claim has emerged. The other pole head associated with the club is F 112.

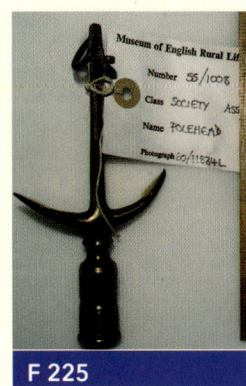

F 225

F 226

F 227

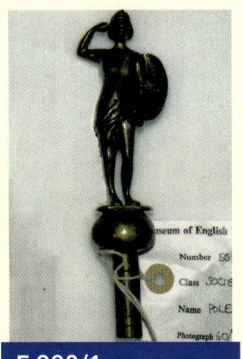

F 228/1

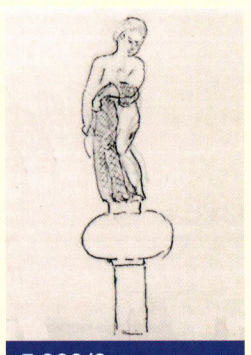

F 228/2

F 229/1

F 226   6.3″   MERL / Allen / 551003

This is a larger version of the anchor design usually attributed to Filton (F 225), possibly a steward's brass, but there is no supporting evidence. Allen did not offer a suggestion about the provenance.

F 227   8.4″   MERL / Allen / 55 / The Allen Collection list, item 'r'

The example of 'Father Time' on this precise mounting appeared in the MERL Ponsonby-Fane Notebook (p.71, no 3), and was photographed for Fuller in 1964 as part of the Allen collection at MERL, but it is now missing. Ponsonby-Fane indicated Bilton, Warwickshire (which he later altered to Staffordshire). Fuller further amended these suggestions to Bilston, Staffordshire, or Bilton, near Rugby, Warwickshire. In his second notebook Ponsonby-Fane gave Smethwick, Staffordshire, as the provenance (Plymouth City Museum and Art Gallery, museum archives, Ponsonby-Fane notebook, p.147). None of these places, however, is supported by further proof. The identical casting of the figure of 'Father Time' appears with three different mountings and sockets (F 227, F 229;1 and F 229/2), but no confirmed provenance is available for any of them.

F 228/1   6.3″   MERL / Allen / 551156

This specimen (spear missing) is only found in the Allen collection, but it was also earlier illustrated in the Ponsonby-Fane MERL notebook, p 70, no 3, there described as originating from Netherton (near Dudley), Worcestershire, albeit without evidence. No Netherton or Dudley society had any obvious connection with the symbol of a gladiator. It is possible that this specimen and the draped figure (F 228/2) may not be friendly society related.

F 228/2   c. 5″   MERL / Ponsonby-Fane notebook / p. 81, no 3, D 85/11/1

Ponsonby-Fane's MERL notebook shows the only recorded specimen of this design, and he attributed it to 'Selly Wick, Worcestershire'. The location of the draped figure shown here is unknown, and as with the gladiator (F 228/1), it is only found in the Allen Collection, and may not be friendly society related.

F 229/1   5.9″   MERL / Allen / 551097

Allen gave no provenance for this specimen, but Fuller suggested Dudley, Worcestershire, from its record in the Ponsonby-Fane MERL notebook (p. 69, no 2), albeit without supporting evidence. This figure is usually found on a ball, and the sockets are of varying design. One or other versions of 'Father Time' appear in most of the major collections. The Shickle example is of this pattern (MERL Shickle 51/1095) and is attributed without further proof to Dudley Wick.

'Time' is inscribed on the scythe.

F 229/2   5.8"   Private collection

This specimen lacks a provenance. The casting of the figure is as in the other examples (F 227 and F229/1), but the ball and the socket are different. The blade of the scythe is missing in this specimen. The mounting differs from F 227 and F 229/1, and has not been seen elsewhere.

F 229/2

F 230   5.5"   MERL / Allen / 551019

This design us usually attributed to the Williton Union Club (1800 to c.1851) (SOM 297) and (1851 to 1899) (SOM 582), which originally met at the Coach and Horses Inn (later renamed the Egremont Hotel), and then at the Wyndham Arms Inn. The rules of the early society specified a plain rod of 6 feet, but did not mention a pole head (The National Archives FS 1/615/297, 1800 rules). For the later society it was recorded that members had a brass topped pole, but the design is again unconfirmed (*West Somerset Free Press*, June 18th, 1870). No other evidence has emerged to confirm this design.

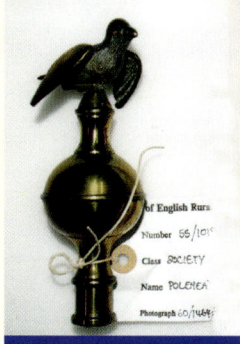

F 230

F 231   5.8"   MERL / Shickle / 511077

Shickle gave no provenance for this specimen, and no evidence has subsequently emerged. No other examples have been recorded.

F 232/1   6.6"   MERL / Jardine / 61244050

There is no confirmed provenance for this pattern, which is often associated with the name Blagdon Hill (located in the Blackdown Hills on the Somerset – Devon border, but not Blagdon, Mendips, or Blagdon Hill, Dorset). The village of Blagdon (now called Blagdon Hill) is in the parish of Pitminster, but is not recorded as ever having a friendly society of its own. The design from Pitminster is known, and is shown at F 255/1. The parishes of Culmstock, Clayhidon, Churchinford and Churchstanton, and Otterford are all quite close to Blagdon Hill, and any of them could have been the originator of this design. Nevertheless, the societies at Culmstock (suggested in the SHC Taunton Museum identification lists of the Hopkins collection, no 136) and Clayhidon (suggested by Allen) have no record of pole-carrying. The Churchinford Unity Friendly Society at Churchstanton also has a design with a bird, but it is the same as the Fivehead pattern: see F 280/1 and F 280/2, and the 1937 letter from Jonas Bloomfield, trustee, Churchinford Unity Friendly Society, who wrote that 300 dove-on-ball tops were once ordered (Museum archives, uncatalogued, Plymouth City Museum and Art Gallery [The Box]). The two varieties of this design are differentiated by possessing a ball with a central rim, as here, and a seamless ball, as in F 232/2.

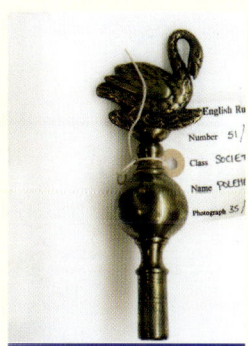

F 231

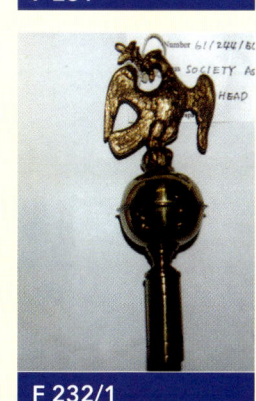

F 232/1

F 232/2   6.9"   SHC / B1537

There is no confirmed provenance for this pattern, which is often associated with the name Blagdon Hill (located in the Blackdown Hills on the Somerset – Devon border, but not Blagdon, Mendips, or Blagdon Hill, Dorset). The village of Blagdon (now called Blagdon Hill) is in the parish of Pitminster, but is not recorded as ever having a friendly Society of its own. The design for Pitminster is known, and is shown at F 255/1. The parishes of Culmstock, Clayhidon, Churchinford and Churchstanton, and Otterford are all quite close to Blagdon Hill, and any of them could have been the originator of this design. The societies at Culmstock (suggested in the SHC Taunton Museum identification lists of the Hopkins collection, no 136) and Clayhidon (suggested by Allen) have no record of pole-carrying. The Churchinford Unity Friendly Society at Churchstanton also has a design with a bird, but it is the same as the Fivehead pattern: see F 280/1 and F 280/2. The two varieties of this design are differentiated by possessing a ball with a central rim, as in F 232/1, and a seamless ball as here. The rimmed ball version of this design is more frequently found, but a plain ball, as in this example, is also common. The overall height difference between the two types is up to half an inch, the plain ball type being the larger.

F 232/2

F 233/1

F 233/2

F 233/3

F 234

F 235

F 233/1   8.7″   MERL / Shickle / 511057

Shickle gave no provenance for this design, but Ponsonby-Fane suggested Shifnal Old Dove Club, although without further evidence (MERL Ponsonby-Fane notebook, p.32, no 1). Brass doves on poles were known to have been carried at Shifnal (*Wellington Journal*, July 2nd, 1887) and Coventry (*Coventry Standard*, April 10th, 1868). The attachment to the ball below the bird is clumsy, implying that the pole head may be a marriage of top and bottom, but a second almost identical example has the same features, and is gilded (private collection). This design might alternatively have been used by Freemasons or by Oddfellows. The second image shows a variant, sold at auction September 3rd, 2021, with minor differences.

F 233/2   7″   Wells and Mendip Museum / Box 196

No provenance for this pattern has been suggested by the Wells and Mendip Museum. Brass doves on poles were known to have been carried at Shifnal (*Wellington Journal*, July 2nd, 1887) and Coventry (*Coventry Standard*, April 10th, 1868). This design might alternatively have been used by Freemasons or by Oddfellows.

F 233/3   4.5″   Private collection

No provenance has been suggested for this pattern. It is identical to MERL Shickle 511155. Brass doves on poles were known to have been carried at Shifnal (*Wellington Journal*, July 2nd, 1887) and Coventry (*Coventry Standard*, April 10th, 1868). This design might alternatively have been used by Freemasons or by Oddfellows.

F 234   8.5″   MERL / Allen / 551023

This is possibly the pole head for the Crewkerne Friendly Society, whose 1818 rules specified 'a light blue pole and a brass head', although the design has not been confirmed. Crewkerne Friendly Society, also known as The Reds, the Hand in Hand Club, and the Swan Club (1805 to after 1911) (SOM 063) met variously at the Swan Inn (recorded in 1869 and 1909), the Red Lion (1881 to 1886), and the Nags Head (1899 to 1901). The *Yeovil Times*, May 28th, 1850, mentions their 'gorgeous club sticks', which suggests an ornamental design. The Crewkerne 'Blues' Friendly Society had the same basic design (verified) but without a swan on top (see F 191). Another example with the swan was in the Wainwright collection (dispersed), and its current location is unrecorded (Eunice B Overend, ed., *The Wainwright Collection of Friendly Society Brasses* [dispersed], Phillips Museum [defunct], Brokerswood, Autumn 1971, p.24).

F 235   7.5″   Blaise Castle House Museum / T 9363

This design is verified as a steward's brass of the **Merriott King's Head Friendly Society** (1863 to after 1891) (unregistered), which met at the King's Head Inn. A letter to Jardine from the Rev SE Percival, dated September 27th, 1932, stated: 'stewards' brasses had a bird with outstretched wings' (MERL Jardine DDX / 1787).

Sprigs were attached through a hole in the beak.

F 236/1   6.9″   MERL / Shickle / 511061

No provenance was suggested by Shickle for this pattern. The specimen of this type illustrated by Fuller from the MERL Allen collection has a shorter socket, but is otherwise identical. Brass doves on poles were carried at Shifnal (*Wellington Journal*, July 2nd, 1887) and Coventry (*Coventry Standard*, April 10th, 1868). This design might alternatively have been used by Freemasons or by Oddfellows.

F 236/1

F 236/2   7.1″   Private collection

No provenance is available for this pattern, which is a variant of F 236/1, with the wings attached as a unit to the top of the back, and with a ball above the socket. Brass doves on poles were known to have been carried at Shifnal (*Wellington Journal*, July 2nd, 1887) and Coventry (*Coventry Standard*, April 10th, 1868). This design might alternatively have been used by Freemasons or by Oddfellows.

F 236/2

F 236/3   5.3″   SHC / OSFS / 750

The earliest suggestion for Shifnal is in James Kelway's notebook (no 160, p.180: SHC, Taunton Museum archives). His example, and its suggested provenance, came from Sir Spencer Ponsonby-Fane. In the MERL Ponsonby-Fane notebook, however, a similar example is labelled Dudley Port (p.61, no 2). Sir Spencer bought many examples of pole heads in the Midlands, but he left no evidence for the suggestion of Dudley Port (Tipton), Staffordshire. On the other hand there is evidence for Shifnal, although possibly not for this exact design. The Shifnal Union Benefit Society (1805 to 1899), which met at the Crown Inn, was 'commonly called the Old Dove Club', and each member carried 'a staff surmounted by a brass dove' (*Wellington Journal*, July 2nd, 1887). There are two others, on identical mountings, at SHC OSFS 751 and SHC OSFS 753, and two further examples (in private collections) with the feet of the bird in the shape of a rectangular block.

F 236/3

F 237   4.1″   MERL / Jardine / 61244208

Etherington was suggested for this design by Ponsonby-Fane (MERL Ponsonby-Fane notebook, p.96, no 2), but with no evidence. Fuller (1964) did not mention that some specimens like this one are complete: others are known with a wings unit screwed into a hole in a shallow recess on the back of the bird. In some of the latter the wings have, however, been lost. Brass doves on poles were known to have been carried at Shifnal (*Wellington Journal*, July 2nd, 1887) and Coventry (*Coventry Standard*, April 10th, 1868). Another specimen can be seen at Snowshill Manor, Gloucestershire (National Trust). This design might alternatively have been used by Freemasons or by Oddfellows.

F 237

F 238/1   5.3″   MERL / Allen / 551021

Larkhall (Bath) was suggested by Allen, following other earlier collectors, but no evidence in support has been found, apart from the design of the bird itself, which could very well be a representation of a lark.

Sprigs were often painted with green leaves and a red olive.

F 238/1

131

F 238/2

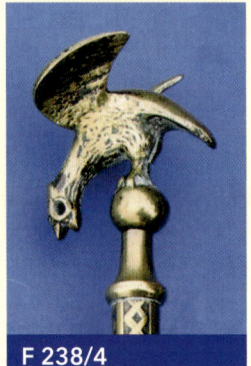

F 238/3

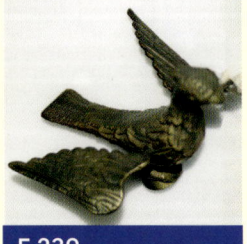

F 238/4

F 239

F 240

F 238/2   4.25″   Private collection

There is no recorded provenance for this pattern, and only this example has seen in private or public collections. This design might have been used by Freemasons or by Oddfellows. In this specimen the socket is long in proportion to the small dove on the ball.

F 238/3   4.8″   Private collection

There is no recorded provenance for this pattern, and only this example has seen in private or public collections. This design might have been used by Freemasons or by Oddfellows.

F 238/4   2.3″   Private collection

There is no recorded provenance for this pattern, and only this example has seen in private or public collections. This design might have been used by Freemasons or by Oddfellows The stem beneath the ball sits on an integral brass rod, which is 6″ tall and ornately milled. The hole seen in the beak would have had a small brass olive branch attached.

F 239   6.5″ width   MERL / Allen / 551169

Allen did not offer a provenance for this specimen. It is possible that the design was used as a pole head of a steward (on account of its large size) at the Shifnal Union Benefit Society (1805 to 1889), which was commonly known as the Dove Club, and where each member carried 'a staff surmounted by a brass dove' (*Wellington Journal*, July 2nd, 1887). Another society where brass doves were carried existed at Coventry (*Coventry Standard*, April, 10th, 1868). Brass birds of a similar design, but some with wings inserted individually either side of the body, and others with a pair of wings screwed onto the back, are found at a range of sizes, and are variously mounted on sockets or fitted by double-ended screws directly on top of their poles. This is the largest variety so far recorded. It might alternatively have been used by Freemasons or by Oddfellows.

F 240   4″   MERL / Shickle / 511070

Although the bird is the same as in F 238, Allen thought that only the latter was correct for Larkhall. With many pole heads, however, different batches, ordered at different times, came with slight variations (especially in their sockets). A no-socket version is also recorded (private collection). There is no proof that any of them were used at Larkhall.

Oakhill silk banner: colours now faded: F 242.

132

F 241　　4.7″　MERL / Allen / 550978

Allen attributed this design to Publow without giving further evidence. Pensford and Publow are both villages in the parish of Pensford, and each had a friendly society where members carried brass knobs on feast days, but their designs have not been confirmed. Publow Newly Established Friendly Society (1810 to 1895) (SOM 400 and 458) met at the George and Dragon Inn (Pensford) in 1846, and in 1853 at the Rising Sun Inn (Pensford). Pensford Old Established Friendly Society (1753 to c. 1878) (SOM 399 and 459) in 1783 had its headquarters at the King's Arms Inn (Publow). A third club in the parish of Pensford was the Chapel Club (SOM 460). The rules of both inn-based clubs specified a blue pole and a brass knob, Publow with tassels (FS 3/330/400 1846 rules), Pensford with ribbons (The National Archives FS 1/618/459, 1843 rules): there is no evidence to say which used F 241.

F 241

F 242　　7.3″　MERL / Allen / 550818

This design is verified for **Oakhill Friendly and Benefit Society** (1832 to 1908) (SOM 682), which met at the Oakhill Inn (MERL classified index 'Friendly Societies'). In an account in the *Western Daily Press*, April 9th, 1957, Mrs Elsie Hillier wrote that she had her father's brass emblem, and that a similar design could be seen outside Oakhill Inn, where the meetings were held. She also had two of the society's banners, with oak leaves on the bottom right. In 1885 members were described as carrying 'wands tipped by oak leaves and an acorn' (*East Somerset Telegraph*, May 30th, 1885). There is a great similarity between this design and that of the Stoke St Michael brass said to have been used by the stewards (F 244/1). Oakhill and Stoke St Michael are just two miles apart.

F 242

F 243/1　　5″　MERL / Allen / 551100

Allen indicated that this design was used at the Royal Oak Inn at Tiverton, Devon, but gave no further details. Alternatively a provenance from Bath seems possible: there was a Royal Oak Friendly Society at Twerton, Bath (1840 to 1864) (SOM 510), which met at the Royal Oak Inn, and on anniversary processions the members were required to carry 'a uniform staff' (The National Archives FS 1/620/510, 1840 rules). The name 'Tiverton' was often confused with 'Twerton' (Bath), which when written in italic script is virtually indistinguishable from 'Tiverton'. Moreover, the alternative spelling for 'Twerton' was 'Twiverton'. There are in addition other possible contenders for this pole head design: a 'golden acorn' on a long blue staff was carried by members of the Almondsbury Union Friendly Society (*Bristol Daily Post*, May 25th, 1877) but it is not known whether it is any of the brass designs on record or whether it was made of wood (see F 300/2). Rodney Stoke Friendly Society (1860 to 1877) (SOM 706) had a spear topped by a 'model of an acorn' (*Shepton Mallet Journal*, 15 June 1866). Again, the design is unknown.

F 243/1

F 243/2　　4.5″　Blaise Castle House Museum / T9398

No provenance is available for this specimen. It is uncertain whether this is a friendly society pole head: it could have been used by some other organisation in processions, or for some other purpose. The short socket is unusual and may indicate that this is a finial from a curtain rod or andiron. Another example is in a private collection.

F 243/2

F 243/3　　4.9″　MERL / Allen / 551151

No provenance is available for this specimen. It is uncertain whether this is a friendly society pole head: it could have been used by some other organisation in processions.

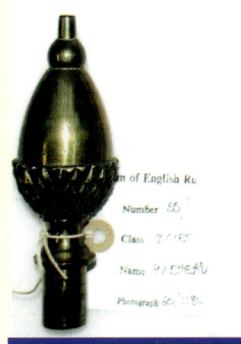

F 243/3

F 243/4

F 244/1

F 244/2

F 244/3

F 245/1

F 243/4   3.8"   Private collection

No provenance is available for this specimen. It is uncertain whether this is a friendly society pole head: it could have been used by some other organisation in processions.

F 244/1   6"   MERL / Allen / 551079

Allen suggested that this design was used by stewards at Stoke St Michael, but he provided no details in support. Three identical specimens exist in different collections: Allen (MERL 551079); Jardine (MERL 612144133); and SHC (OSFS 500). Each is on a short, octagonal, dark-green pole. The SHC specimen was purchased from Allen. Although Stoke St Michael is the only suggested origin it should be noted that there is a great similarity between this design and that of Oakhill (F 242), which is just 2 miles away.

F 244/2   5.7"   Blaise Castle House Museum / T9390

Kelway suggested that this design was used at Cullompton, but there is no supporting evidence (SHC Taunton Museum archives, Kelway Collection Notebook, p.156, no 175).

F 244/3   6"   Private collection

This pattern is said to have been carried on the poles of members of some Juvenile Druids' Lodges (UAOD), but no evidence has emerged.

F 245/1   5.9"   Wells and Mendip Museum / box 196

Stapleton (at the Masons Arms) is the usual provenance proposed for this pattern, with its distinctive double cross at the top of the crown, but with no evidence. The Allen example, shown by Fuller (1964), is slightly shorter than most, probably due to over-tightening of the central screw thread. Several provenances have been suggested for the other open crown designs (F 245/2 to F 248), including Winterbourne, Frenchay, and 'The Crown Inn, Bristol', but none have any corroborative evidence.

View of componenets of an open crown pole head.

F 245/2   5.8"   Blaise Castle House Museum / T 7594

No evidence has emerged for Winterbourne, Gloucestershire (as suggested by Jardine, MERL 61244179). Of similar height to F 245/1 are many examples with just a flat cross, ranging from 5.6" to 5.9". The numerical distribution of height measurements of all the known examples of the pattern suggests three categories, concentrated at around 5.75", 6.4" and 7". A few even larger ones are found, and are probably stewards' pole heads.

F 245/2

F 246/1   6.5"   MERL / Allen / 551002

Allen did not make a suggestion for the provenance of this design. The height and spread of these crowns depend a little on the tightness of the central screw thread. Some examples have a wide collar for the crown, others such as this one are narrow, and there are other hand crafting variations. None of the different types has a verifiable provenance.

F 246/1

F 246/2   6.9"   SHC / OSFS / 289A

This is the tallest of the three clusters of almost equal heights among the open crowns (5.75", 6.4" and 7"), except for three much larger specimens which were probably used by stewards. It came from the Kelway Collection (SHC), but no provenance was offered.

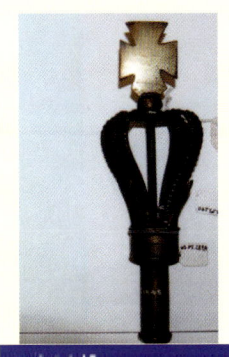

F 246/2

F 247   8.3"   MERL / Allen / 551014

Allen suggested that this design was a steward's pole head from Winterbourne, Gloucestershire, but he did not produce supporting evidence. This large specimen appears to be a steward's version of the F 246/1 design, both specimens having relatively narrow collars in relation to the width of their sockets. Other large specimens are known with heights of 8.0" (SHC OSFS 289) and 8.8" (MERL Shickle 511074).

F 247

F 248   6"   MERL / Allen / 55096

Allen left no clues as to why he attributed this specimen to Winterbourne, and yet made no such suggestion for F 246/1. This example, illustrated in good condition by Fuller (1964) as number 248, has subsequently been shortened by distortion. Some of these open crowns have the member's roll number stamped on: this one is no. 184.

Detail of ribs of open top crown: formed in one piece.

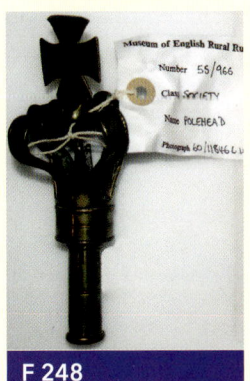

F 248

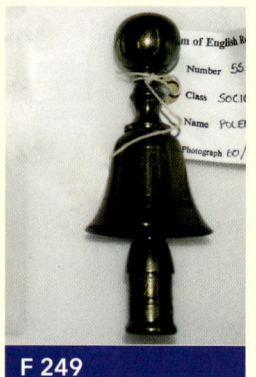

F 249

F 250

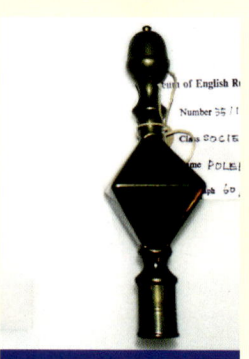

F 251

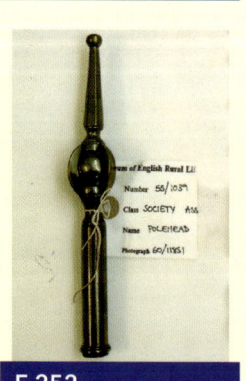

F 252

F 253/1

F 249   5.4″   MERL / Allen / 550967

Allen attributed this design to the Royal True Britons Friendly Society (1843 to 1892) (GLOS 0306), which met at the Bell Inn, Stapleton, Bristol, but he gave no supporting evidence. The society certainly had brass pole heads, but of unknown design (The National Archives FS 1/153/306, 1843 rules). The thin-necked variety of this design was used at Curry Mallet, which may mean that the thicker-necked variety shown here could be the Stapleton design. There are many other Bell Inns, however, in Bristol and Somerset.

F 250   5″   MERL / Allen / 550957

This design is verified for **Curry Mallet Friendly Society** (1836 to 1916) (SOM 041), which met at the Bell Inn. Curry Mallet had 'bell-shaped, brass-topped staves' (*Pulman's Weekly News*, June 6th, 1911). A specimen exists in nearby Ashill church (thin-necked variety). An inventory of the club possessions denoted '19 tops for club poles' (SHC D/P/cur.m 23/2 inventory).

Initials of Worthy Burt on pole of Curry Mallet Friendly Society: F 250.

F 251   5.7″   MERL / Allen / 551105

Allen repeated Ponsonby-Fane's suggestion that this design comes from Tividale in Staffordshire, but there is no supporting evidence (MERL Ponsonby-Fane notebook, p.53, no 1). No other location has been proposed. The Shickle Collection example (MERL 511143) does not have any provenance stated.

F 252   7.5″   MERL / Allen / 551039

Allen attributed this design to the Lydeard St Lawrence and Tolland Friendly Society (unregistered), which met at the Handy Cross Inn, but he did not support his attribution, and no further evidence has emerged. Nevertheless, no other location has been suggested.

F 253/1   5.6″   MERL / Allen / 551027

Allen stated that this design was used by the Wellow Friendly Society (1813 to after 1871) (SOM 320), which met at the George Inn, but his claim has not been confirmed. Wellow Friendly Society 1813 rules required each member to 'carry his pole', but the design of the pole head is not verified (SHC DDX/LW/238).

F 253/2   c.6"   Private collection

This design was used at **Clanfield, Oxfordshire**, but it is not known by which of three possible societies. Four examples are known to exist, all attached to their original painted and numbered poles. Three are in a private collection, and one is in the Swinford Museum at Filkins, Oxfordshire. One of the specimens was found in a barn at Clanfield, confirming that it was used in that village. The design is unusual in that the upper half is fitted with a downward pointing screw which fits through the top of the socket into the head of the pole.

F 253/2

F 254   5.4"   MERL Ponsonby-Fane note book

Ponsonby-Fane attributed this design to Lyme Regis, but he gave no supporting evidence, and no other information has emerged. The current location of the Ponsonby-Fane specimen is untraced: it is the only example of this design that has been recorded (MERL Ponsonby-Fane notebook p.54, no 3). There is no evidence that any Lyme Regis Friendly Society carried poles. The design may well not be a friendly society pole head.

F 254

F 255/1   10.3"   MERL / Allen / 551070

This design is verified for **Pitminster Friendly Society** (1834 to 1874) (SOM 466), which met at the Lamb and Flag Inn, and **Pitminster and Blagdon Friendly Society** (1875 to after 1900) (SOM 894). Early collectors always associated this design with the Lamb and Flag Inn (Blagdon Hill) in the parish of Pitminster, and the club banner has the lamb and flag emblem. Two specimens, engraved 'Pitminster Church', and mounted on black poles, are displayed in the church. The flag carried by the lamb on the pole head is often painted red, either entirely, or as a border, top and bottom.

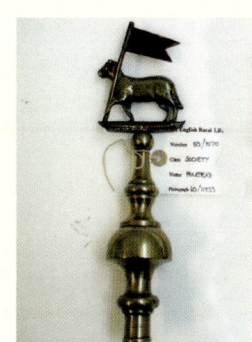

F 255/1

F 255/2   10.3"   SHC / OSFS / 023C

This design is verified for **Pitminster Friendly Society** (1834 to 1874) (SOM 466), which met at the Lamb and Flag Inn, and **Pitminster and Blagdon Friendly Society** (1875 to after 1900) (SOM 894). Early collectors always associated this design with the Lamb and Flag Inn (Blagdon Hill) in the parish of Pitminster, and the club banner has the lamb and flag emblem. Two specimens, engraved 'Pitminster Church', and mounted on black poles, are displayed in the church. The flag carried by the lamb on the pole head is often painted red, either entirely, or as a border, top and bottom. This specimen has the head of the lamb facing the viewer: it appears to be quite original, but most examples face forwards, as in F 255/1. The height shown for this pole top makes allowance for the flag, which has been accidentally bent down.

F 255/2

F 256   6.5"   MERL / Allen / 550939

This design is verified for **Sturminster Newton Castle Friendly Society** (1811 to 1844) (DOR201), which met at the Crown Inn. *The Sherborne, Dorchester and Taunton Journal*, June 18th, 1835, in a report about the club anniversary, referred to a "new club pole with a handsome brass top in the form of a globe, surmounted with a crown, [inscribed] on a raised band round the ball 'Sturminster Friendly Society'". It was a gift from the President, the Rev J Michel.

F 256

F 257/1

F 257/2

F 258

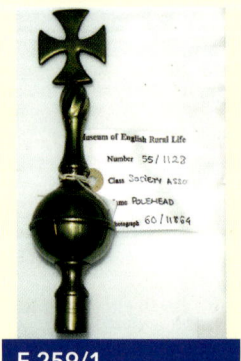

F 259/1

F 259/2

F 257/1   6.3″   MERL / Allen / 550947

Allen stated that this design was a steward's brass from West Bagborough, but he gave no further evidence. Ordinary members of West Bagborough Friendly Society (1871 to after 1924) (unregistered), which met at the Rising Sun Inn, carried a 'brass-topped staff' (*Taunton Courier*, May 27th, 1908), but the design is unknown. The pole head shown here was used by **Crowcombe Friendly Society** (1858 to 1913) (SOM 696), as identified by Kelway. In his notebook he included alongside his sketch the comment 'Crowcombe - bought direct' (Kelway notebook, p.126, SHC Taunton Museum archives). As Allen observed, it is probably a steward's emblem, as a member's design from Crowcombe is almost certainly F 041, a flat spear type. The crown in this specimen is the same as that of Sturminster Newton (F 256), but there is no inscription around the ball.

F 257/2   5.5″   SHC / OSFS / 284

This specimen is attributed to Tolpuddle, Dorset, but no supporting evidence has emerged. At first sight the design here is similar to F 257/1, but, unlike the latter, it has a rimless ball, a shorter socket, and a quite differently modelled crown.

F 258   7.9″   Private collection

This design is verified for **Stalbridge Union Society of Foresters** (1846 to 1906) (DOR 050), which met at the Red Lion Inn, and on anniversaries at other inns in rotation. The 1846 rules required members to have 'a pole' and 'proper ensigns' (The National Archives FS 3/49/50, rules, 1846). The specimen was described by the last secretary of the society as 'the deer' in his recollection of the varied pole heads carried in procession by the Stalbridge Friendly Society (see note opposite p.50, Ponsonby-Fane notebook at MERL: the deer pole head is illustrated on p.51). For other pole heads carried by the Stalbridge Union of Foresters see F 060/1, F060/2, F 076, and F 077. This specimen was obtained by Lady Guest from Charles Stanbrook, the last secretary of the Stalbridge Union Society of Foresters, upon its demise in 1906.

F 259/1   7.5″   MERL / Allen / 551128

Allen did not offer a suggestion for this pattern, and there is no evidence for Wednesfield, Staffordshire. No other example is recorded. Fuller (1964) probably retrieved the suggestion of Wednesfield from the Ponsonby-Fane notebook at MERL, p.71, no 1. Ponsonby-Fane also showed a second quite different design (p.71, no 2) for the same location.

F 259/2   6.5″   MERL / Shickle / 511084

Shickle gave no provenance for this specimen. No other examples are known. It is not clear whether it was used by a friendly society or by some other organisation, or whether, like several other pole heads in the Shickle collection, it is a marriage of unrelated components.

F 259/3   15″   Private collection

No other example of this specimen is known, and it has no recorded provenance: it may have been used by an Oddfellows lodge. Its function is self-evident, the quill pens (on a 17.3″ pole) indicating the office of a club secretary: for example, in an Oddfellows grand parade of several lodges to Cullompton Church in 1845 the secretaries and their assistants carried 'cross pens' (*Western Times*, May 17th, 1845).

F 259/3

F 260   7.4″   Private collection

Allen's attribution of this design to the Skerrid Mountain Inn Club, Abergavenny, and to nearby Gilwern or Llandover, is not supported by any evidence, but no other locations have been suggested. The design may be from a Druid Society. Many examples are recorded.

F 260

F 261   6.3″   MERL / Allen / 550878

This design is verified for **Cullompton**. Few other friendly society brass pole heads have the heavy quality of this hollow casting, with its heart in hand Oddfellows' symbol. Between 1842 and 1844 two Oddfellows (IOOFMU) lodges were established in Cullompton, the Brotherly Compact Lodge and the Loyal Peace and Concord Lodge, both of which, according to Oddfellows' directories, failed at some date between 1846 and 1850. Shortly afterwards in July 1850, **Cullompton Benefit Friendly Society** (1850 to 1912) (unregistered) was instituted, and became known as the Heart and Hand Club, with the club symbol as a hand and heart (*Western Times*, April 19th, 1858). Each member carried this emblem in brass on a stave (*Western Times*, May 28th, 1912). A similar description of the club pole head was given to Jardine in 1932 in a letter from the Rev HS Bunny, who was repeating what he had heard from J James, the club secretary of 1899 (MERL, Jardine notes, letter dated November 11th, 1932). There can be little doubt that the Cullompton Benefit Society arose out of the failure of the two Oddfellows' lodges, and that it adopted the brass heart and hand pole heads from this source.

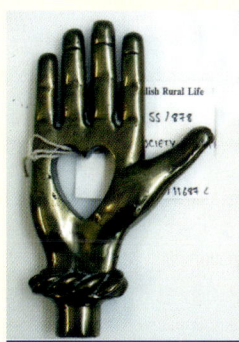

F 261

F 262   8″   MERL / Allen / 550964

This design was used by male members of **Combe St Nicholas Male and Female Friendly Society** (unregistered), which met at the Green Dragon Inn, and later at the George Inn. In a letter to Jardine dated October 27th, 1932, the Rector (unnamed) confirmed that Jardine's sketch was correct (MERL DDX/1787). At the club anniversaries the females wore white dresses and sashes, and the males carried 'poles with brass heads' (*Chard and Ilminster News*, May 30th, 1896). At the funeral of Mrs Coate in 1892 the poles of the members had 'brass star mountings, draped in black' (*Western Gazette*, April 22nd, 1892). The Combe St Nicholas Friendly Society (Males), 1840 to 1869, co-existed for many years with the Combe St Nicholas Male and Female Friendly Society (1860 to 1902), but the former is not recorded as carrying poles.

F 262

F 263   9.6″   MERL / Allen / 550962

Halse Friendly Society, sometimes known as the Halse Sociable Society (1811 to 1931) (unregistered), which met at the New Inn, had brass pole tops, but the design is unconfirmed. Nevertheless, the 1866 rules (SHC Tite collection) specify a staff and the *West Somerset Free Press*, May 14th, 1870, refers to 'blue club staves with brass tops and red, white and blue ribbons attached'.

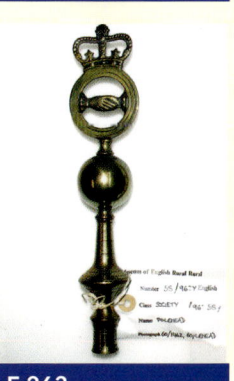

F 263

F 264/1

F 264/2

F 264/3

F 265

F 266

F 264/1   11.6"   MERL / Allen / 550951

This design is verified for **Bishops Lydeard Friendly Society** (also known as the **Old Club** or the **True Blues**) (1807 to 1896) (unregistered), which met at the Gore Inn. The *West Somerset Free Press*, June 3rd, 1871, refers to a 'club staff with a brass top and blue ribbons'. In a letter to Jardine dated October 22nd, 1932, the Rev FC Fitch of Bishops Lydeard stated: 'your sketch is definitely Bishops Lydeard' (MERL Jardine Index). A similar silver-plated version exists (F 264/3), but there is no evidence that the Bishops Lydeard brass pole heads were silver-plated for use at the Bishops Lydeard club.

F 264/2   14.5"   MERL / Ponsonby-Fane notebook, insert page, no 3, D85/11/1 and SHC / Du Cann Collection / 20189

This design is verified as a steward's brass from **Bishops Lydeard Friendly Society** (also known as the **Old Club** or the **True Blues**) (1807 to 1896) (unregistered). It is illustrated in the MERL Ponsonby-Fane notebook, as a Bishops Lydeard design. After the sale of the Ponsonby-Fane collection the specimen reappeared in the Du Cann collection, now in the SHC.

F 264/3   11.8"   SHC / OSFS / 111

The silver-plated version of F 264/1 is verified for **North Curry**, but its use by the Bishops Lydeard Friendly Society is unrecorded. **North Curry Friendly Society** (before 1803 to c.1910) (unregistered) met at the Bird in Hand Inn and later at the Assembly Rooms. The pole heads came into the possession of the North Curry Friendly Society, already silver-plated, after July 1897. Why these brasses were silver-plated is unknown. Col. W Barrett succeeded his father, great-uncle and another relative as fourth President of the North Curry Friendly Society; he carried this particular silver-plated pole head in procession there, and donated it to Taunton Museum in 1922 (SHC Taunton Museum archives, accession notes). Other specimens are recorded. The *West Somerset Free Press*, July 3rd, 1897, reported that three dozen [silver] plated pole heads were to be sold from the estate of the late Thomas Hobbs of Ash Priors, formerly an honorary member of the Bishop's Lydeard friendly society, which had ceased in 1896. Some, or all, were probably sold to the Barretts in 1897. The use of these silver-plated pole heads before 1896 is unrecorded.

F 265   9.7"   MERL / Shickle / 510984

This design is verified for **Axbridge Union Society** (1801 to before 1876) (SOM 005). In a letter to Jardine, September 9th, 1932, the Rev Owen Thomas identified the design, and wrote that It was carried by the high stewards and the low stewards, and that the son of one of the stewards still had the pole head in 1932 (MERL DDX 1787). *The Wells Journal*, June 12th, 1858, reported that members of the Axbridge Union Society were 'bearing staves and other insignia'.

F 266   9.6"   MERL / Allen / 550943

Two Milverton Clubs carried poles, but the designs have not been confirmed. The Milverton Young Men's Reform Benefit Society (before 1850 to after 1893) (unregistered) met at the School Room; it processed with 'poles, ribbons [and] brass appendages (design unstated) (*Western Flying Post*, June 18th, 1867). The Milverton Reform Benefit Society started in 1815, became the Victoria Friendly Society in 1867, and ended by 1878 (unregistered). It also met in the School Room, and it processed with 'gay poles, ribbons and flowers' (*Taunton Courier*, June 7th, 1871). Its 1854 rules specified the carrying of a staff (Bristol Central Library GC7 197, 1854 rules). A third society, the United Benefit Society (or Friendly Society), 1847 to 1913, meeting at the Globe Inn, appears not to have had poles. It is not known if the earliest club, the Society of Artificers and Labourers (1787 to c. 1815) (SOM 406) had any regalia.

F 267   8.3"   MERL / Allen / 550974

F 267

This design is verified for **Halberton New Inn Friendly Society,** which was also known as the **Old Agricultural Society** (1817 to 1912) (DEV 410), and which met at the New Inn. The members had new staffs in 1862 (*Tiverton Gazette*, May 10th, 1862). In 1871 the members were reported as carrying 'a long blue staff with a brass ball and, on top of the ball, a crown' (*Western Times*, June 6th, 1871). The other Halberton friendly society had a swan on top of the brass ball (F 278). The SHC Taunton Museum Friendly Society lists of the Hopkins collection, compiled by HStG Gray, includes the comment: 'Halliday, Antique dealers of Taunton, in October 1910, had the New Inn Benefit Society Minute and Account Book (1819 - 1837), besides a very large number of their brasses, mostly on navy blue poles (with red numbers) and their banner marked 'Agricultural Society', a blue sash, and a hat'.

F 268/1   7.1"   MERL / Allen / 550941

F 268/1

Allen attributed this design to **Ashcott**, although in the Fuller list (1964) the provenance was extended also to Aller. The SCH Taunton lists added Boroughbridge and Othery, although for Othery there is no supporting evidence. The Aller, Ashcott, and Boroughbridge patterns differ in detail. **Ashcott Friendly Society** (also known as the **Union Society,** and from 1858 as the **New Friendly Society**) (1772 to 1858, and 1858 to 1919) (SOM 002 and SOM 728), latterly met at the Old Schoolroom. The members were recorded in 1880 as carrying 'brass spears', a reference more to their having poles topped with a metal device rather than to the design of the pole head itself, which hardly resembles the outline of a spear (*Western Gazette*, June 4th, 1880). A specimen in a private collection was obtained from a descendant of the original owner, a club member. Heights range from 7.1" to 7.5", sockets show differences, and the shapes of the knops may be bi-conical, as here, or almost round, as in F 268/4. Such differences may relate to batches being ordered at different times.

F 268/2   7.1"   Private collection

F 268/2

This design is confirmed for **Aller,** where a similar pole head to the one shown here is preserved at St Andrew's Church. **Aller Friendly Society** (1849 to 1940) (unregistered) met at various times at the Bear Inn, the White Lion Inn, and the Old Schoolroom. Members were recorded in 1871 as carrying 'poles with brass tops and streamers' (*Western Gazette*, June 4th, 1871). Heights range from 7.1" to 7.5", the sockets show differences, and the knops may be bi-conical, as here, or almost round, as in F 268/4.

F 268/3   8"   Aller Church

F 268/3

This design is verified as a banner top of **Aller Friendly Society** (1849 to 1940) (unregistered), which met at various times at the Bear Inn, the White Lion Inn, and the Old Schoolroom. St Andrew's Church, Aller, retains the banner of the society. The banner top is a village-made adaptation of the members' design, with large 'paddles' soldered to the sides and a lamb finial bolted to the top. An example of the member's smaller brass is also preserved in the church (F 268/1).

F 268/4   7.5"   SHC / OSFS / 004

F 268/4

This general design was used by **Boroughbridge Ten Year Friendly Society** (from 1863 or before to 1881 or later) (unregistered), which met at the King Alfred Inn. The pattern was confirmed by the Rev JM Chadwick, Rector of Boroughbridge, c.1920 (SHC Taunton Museum Friendly Society lists of the Hopkins collection, compiled by HStG Gray) and by the press report of 1866 where it was recorded that the members of the friendly society carried a 'club staff ornamented on top with a crown of brass' (*Western Gazette*, May 18th, 1866). The bulbous knop type, as shown here, was not necessarily the variant used at Boroughbridge. Heights range from 7.1" to 7.5", the sockets show differences, and the shapes of the knops may be bi-conical, as in F 268/1, or almost round, as here.

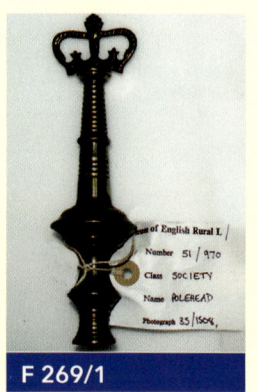

F 269/1

F 269/2

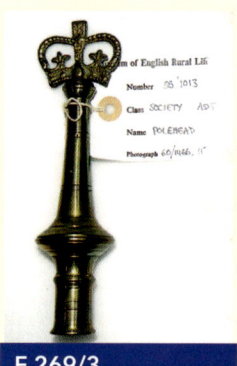

F 269/3

F 270

F 271

F 269/1   7"   MERL / Shickle / 510970

This design is verified for **Cannington Friendly Society** (also known by 1771 to 1822 as the **Loyal Union Friendly Society**, and after 1822 as the **13th of May Club** or **Blues** until its demise c.1887) (SOM 025 until it 1874, when it became unregistered), which met at the Old Blue Anchor Inn (or simply the Anchor Inn). The pattern was verified for the 13th of May Club in a letter to Jardine dated September 15th, 1932, by the Rev P Brocklesby Davis (MERL Jardine DDX/1787). As with pole heads from some other places, significant variations in detail exist, such as the shape of the knop and the proportions of the sections. Nevertheless, all have three distinctive bands of ridged rings: two above the knop, and one below. There was also a 29th of May Club at Cannington, with a different brass head, topped by a bird with outstretched wings, but the design has not been identified (letter to Jardine, 1932, from Rev P Brocklesby Davis, MERL Jardine DDX/1787).

F 269/2   7.2"   Blaise Castle House Museum / T9342

The specimen is attributed to Cannington: it has the same protruding ring on the stem between the crown and the knop, as in F 269/1, but it lacks the distinctive three bands of ridged rings usually associated with the Cannington pattern. Another example is in a private collection. There is no evidence to confirm that this is a Cannington brass.

F 269/3   6.9"   MERL / Allen / 551013

Several examples exist of a design very similar to that of the Cannington 13th May Friendly Society (F 269/1), but without the distinctive three bands of ridged rings, and with the stem between the crown and the knop lacking the central protruding ring. The Allen Collection has a second very similar example, 7.1" (551016). The provenance is unknown.

F 270   7.3"   SHC / OSFS / 069A

This design is verified for **Enmore Friendly and Union Society** (1803 to c.1893) (SOM 092), which met at the Castle Inn and later at the Tynte's Arms Inn. The Rev EH Smith, Rector of Enmore, illustrated the pole head in *Happy Memories of West Somerset*, Bridgwater, 1945, pp 146 - 148. In a reply to Jardine, dated September 7th, 1932, he wrote that the latter's sketch of the design was correct, and that the Enmore Club was succeeded by the Goathurst Club (MERL Jardine DDX 1787).

F 271   7.1"   MERL / Allen / 551015

Allen did not justify his attribution, but there is some evidence that this design was used at **High Ham**. Notes made by Dom Ethelbert Horne, Prior of Downside, with a drawing of this design, indicated that the owner's family (from High Ham) claimed to have possessed the specimen for 200 years (SHC Taunton Museum archives). Although the length of time is clearly an exaggeration, the gist of the attribution is plausible. Nevertheless, no reports have emerged of pole carrying by either of the societies that met in the village. The School House Friendly Society is generally associated with the design at F 079, but no evidence has emerged to confirm that the King's Head Society used the pattern shown here, or, indeed, that they had any pole heads. In common with several similar designs, this pole head was made in separate pieces which screw together, and the crescent arms can easily be re-assembled either way up: it is not known which is correct, and specimens in collections vary in this respect.

F 272   9.1"   MERL / Allen / 550949

Allen attributed this design jointly to Williton, Broadway and Donyatt, but without evidence. Fuller (1964) arbitrarily reduced this to just Broadway. The Williton design appears to be F 273/3: Broadway is F 273/2. Poles with a gilt head were specified in the 1802 rules of Donyatt Friendly Society (before 1791 to c. 1818) (SOM 081), and poles with a brass head in the 1818 rules of Donyatt Independent Society (1818 to 1906) (SOM 082). In 1876 members paraded, each carrying a brass-mounted club pole (*Bridgwater Mercury*, May 17th, 1876), but the design is unknown. Other contenders for this pattern include Bathpool, North Petherton (the 'Reds' society), and West Monkton.

F 272

F 273/1   9.5"   MERL / Allen / 550955

Allen suggested West Monkton but without evidence. West Monkton Friendly Society (1822 to 1892) (SOM 442 and SOM 930), which met at the Vestry Room, mustered 100 members 'each with a black crape rosette attached to his pole' at the 1879 funeral of the club secretary (*Taunton Courier*, February 12th, 1879) but the pole head escaped description. Members of nearby Bathpool Friendly Society (1859 to after 1892) (unregistered) also carried pole heads, design unknown, but probably similar to West Monkton (*Somerset County Gazette*, May 19th, 1883).

F 273/1

F 273/2   c. 9"   Private collection

Broadway Friendly Society and the later **Broadway Friendly Union Society** (1798 to 1836, and 1836 to 1936) (SOM 258 and SOM 266: unregistered after 1912), which met at the Bell Inn, specified in 1836 a 'pole and brass knob' (FS15/590 1836 rules) and the pole head of George Warry, secretary of the club from 1836, was still owned a descendant in 2000. A steward's Broadway pole head, height 16", was in the Wainwright collection, location now untraced (Eunice B Overend, *Catalogue of the Wainwright Collection of Friendly Society Brasses* [dispersed], The Phillips Museum [defunct], Brokerswood, Autumn 1971, p.24). This type has a broad based crown (1.25"). The other suggested locations are: Bathpool, Donyatt, North Petherton, West Monkton, and Williton.

F 273/2

F 273/3   9.6"   Private collection

This variant of the column, ball and crown design is c.9.6" in height, and is distinguishable by the narrow base of the crown (only 1"), and the c. 0.5" bands of fine engine turning on the socket, above the knop, and below the ball. The milling of the outstanding rims of the socket, knop, and lower ball attachment gives further distinction. Early collectors attributed this variant to the **West Somerset Friendly Society** (1860 to 1879 and 1879 to 1896) (SOM 810 and SOM 901), which met in Williton at the Lamb Inn (later named the Railway Hotel). One newspaper report specifically referred to the members' 'wands.... surmounted by a globe and crown' (*West Somerset Free Press*, June 7th, 1884). The other suggested locations are: Bathpool, Broadway, Donyatt, North Petherton, and West Monkton.

F 273/3

F 273/4   9"   SHC / OSFS / 959

Only one example of this double crown version of the crown-on-ball column pole head has been recorded. WB Broadmead of Enmore donated it to Taunton Museum in 1906, and it appears not to have been altered in any way. It is not known which society used it. The suggested locations are: Bathpool, Broadway, Donyatt, North Petherton, West Monkton, and Williton.

F 273/4

F 274

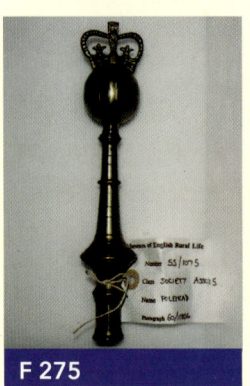

F 275

F 276

F 277

F 278/1

F 274   5.8"   MERL / Allen / 551009

This design is verified for **Stoke St Gregory Friendly Society** (1849 to c.1913) (SOM 703, but unregistered from 1870), which met at the Royal Oak Inn. Photographs of Stoke St Gregory Friendly Society anniversary (c.1910) show this design (SHC A/ CKP 140). Members carried poles with blue ribbons (*Somerset County Gazette*, May 19th, 1900). Mrs F French, 'Some Old Village Customs', *Somerset Men in London, 13th annual report*, 1914, p 14, included a small sketch of the pole head.

F 275   8.8"   MERL / Allen / 551075

Fuller (1964), following the Allen listing, attributed this design to the North Petherton 'Blues' Friendly Society, but the evidence does not support this claim. The Rev J Addy, in a letter to Jardine dated September 13th, 1932, wrote that the North Petherton Blue Club had a pole head topped with an acorn surrounded by four leaves, and this description fits the design shown at F 291. It would seem that if the North Petherton provenance for the specimen illustrated here is correct (F 275), then the design must have belonged to **North Petherton Red Society** (MERL Friendly Society Index Card Notes). The Vicar of North Petherton in 1837 is known to have sold brass pole heads to the members of the Red society, but the design is unspecified (Fuller, Margaret, West Country Friendly Societies, Reading, 1964, p.113). Members certainly carried 'staffs' at their anniversary processions (*Bridgwater Mercury*, May 31st, 1871). Many variations exist in the detail of this design, suggesting production batches for different times or locations. The six proposed locations are: Bathpool, Broadway, Donyatt, North Petherton, West Monkton, and Williton (see F 273/1, F 273/2, F 273/3, and F 2763/4).

F 276   9.5"   MERL / Allen / 550956

No evidence has emerged for an association of this design with either Hele and Bradninch in Devon or Bradford (on Tone) with Hele in Somerset. The term 'Hele and Bradninch' was not used in any of the titles of Bradninch clubs, and none of them had records of pole heads. The term may be a misreading for Bradford (on Tone) which also has a hamlet Hele in its parish. Bradford Union Friendly Society members had 'poles with a brass top' (*Western Gazette*, May 25th, 1866), but the design is unknown.

F 277   11.5"   MERL / Allen / 550952

No suggested location has been offered for this design in the MERL Allen collection. It appears to be a one-off specimen and, if genuine (rather than a marriage), might be a steward's emblem. The pattern of the bird is unusual, however, for a friendly society pole head.

F 278/1   8.5"   MERL / Allen / 550954

This design is verified for Halberton, Devon. There is no evidence for Wembdon, which is also a location sometimes suggested. **Halberton Hearts of Oak Friendly Society** (1859 to after 1891) (unregistered) met at the Swan Inn, and it had 'a long blue staff with a brass ball, and on top of the ball... a swan' (*Western Times*, June 6th, 1871). No other known pole top matches this description. The design of this pole head appears to be identical for all specimens, whether F 278/1 or F 278/2.

F 278/2   8.5"   MERL / Shickle / 511065

This design is verified for **Kentisbeare Friendly Society** (1843 to 1948) (DEV 0642, but unregistered from 1945), which met at the Wyndham Arms. The Kentisbeare society had 'staves, decorated red. white and blue and surmounted by a small brass swan', (*Western Times*, June 5th, 1925). New brass pole heads for the society were recorded in 1862 (*Tiverton Gazette*, June 17th, 1862). Members carried their staves at the funeral of the Rev Edwin Chalk, as he had requested (*Western Times*, August 28th,

1936). Unlike the members with their 'brass-mounted staves', the stewards carried 'other staves surmounted by fleur-de-lis', but their exact design is not recorded (*Exeter and Plymouth Gazette*, May 28th, 1926).

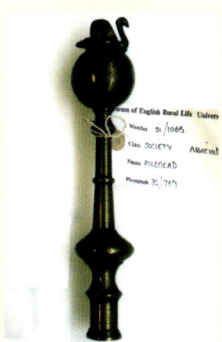

F 278/2

F 279   7.9″   MERL / Allen / 551018

This design has not been verified for the Wembdon Friendly Society (1855 to c.1907) (SOM 658 but unregistered after 1868), which met at the Rest and be Thankful Inn and later at the Cottage Inn. Although Wembdon seems to be the only location suggested by early collectors, no evidence has emerged to support the claim. Wembdon Friendly Society members carried 'a staff mounted with brass' (*Axbridge and Cheddar Gazette*, May 18th, 1866), but the design is not recorded.

F 279

F 280/1   9″   MERL / Allen / 550948

This design is verified for **Fivehead Friendly Society** (1832 to 1865) (unregistered) and **Fivehead New Friendly Society** (1865 to 1939) (unregistered), which met at the Crown Inn, Drayton, and from 1865 at the School Room. *The Langport Herald*, June 2nd, 1866, described the members' 'blue poles with a brass head surmounted by a dove'. A pole with its pole head now in a private collection is marked 'JG', and it belonged to a member of the club named John Gridley, 1885 – 1950. A former secretary's pole head is now held in the SHC Taunton Museum collection (OSFS/349A). The pole heads of this society are usually found with the wings of the brass birds deliberately flattened against the body, as seen in a photograph labelled 'Club Day at Standerswick' (1930s) (SHC A/B/WL1). Why the wings of the pole head dove were bent down by members is unknown. In at least one extant example the process of bending has snapped the wing off.

F 280/1

F 280/2   8.8″   MERL / Shickle / 511067

This design is verified for **Churchingford Unity Society** (1878 to c.1927), which met at Churchstanton at the York Inn until 1898, then at the Kings Arms (1899). There were several earlier clubs here, and they may have used the design as well. A trustee verified the Churchstanton (Churchingford) design as 'a dove with outstretched wings, on a ball and with an olive branch in its mouth' (Bromfield letter, May 27th, 1937, Plymouth City Museum and Art Gallery archives). In 1932 a specimen was still owned by a member's descendant (MERL Jardine notes, letter Rev EH Smith, 27/10/1932). This design appears in a photograph in *Country Life*, July 31st, 1958, p. 236, accompanied by a letter from 'Autolycus', confirming the pattern as coming from Churchstaunton [Churchstanton] and owned by person living locally. The pattern is identical to the Fivehead pole head.

F 280/2

F 281   8.5″   MERL / Allen / 550945

The design has not been adequately verified for Middlezoy, although it is probable that it was used by the Middlezoy Seven Year Friendly Society (1858 to 1879) (unregistered) and the Middlezoy New Friendly Society (1879 to c.1893) (unregistered). Early collectors gave Middlezoy as the provenance of this design, and certainly poles were in evidence. Honorary members carried white poles, and free members blue poles with brass tops (*Western Gazette*, May 22nd, 1868). The 1879 rules required each member to have a blue sash and a light blue pole with brass mountings and orange and blue ribbons (Bristol Central Library, BL16B2/GC6986). This actual design was verified by Charles Wainwright, who had a specimen with the owner's initials on, but the supporting details were then lost. (Eunice B Overend, ed., *Catalogue of the Wainwright Collection of Friendly Society Brasses* [dispersed], The Phillips Museum [defunct], Brokerswood, Autumn 1971, p.26).

F 281

F 282/1

F 282/1   8.5"   MERL / Shickle / 511071

No location has been suggested for this design. It appears to be a one-off specimen and, if genuine, might be a steward's emblem. The pattern of the bird is unusual, however, for a friendly society pole head.

F 282/2   c. 11"   Private collection

No location has been suggested for this design. It appears to be a one-off specimen and, if genuine, might be a steward's emblem. The pattern of the bird is unusual, however, for a friendly society pole head.

F 282/2

F 283/1   c. 9.5"   MERL / Allen / 551053

Allen suggested that this design was used at Creech St Michael, also Bradninch (Devon), but there is no evidence for either.

F 283/2   7.3"   Private collection

This specimen appears to be a marriage: it is lacking the usual upper section of the column, but in its place a bird has been attached later. No other examples have been seen.

F 283/1

F 284   5.8"   MERL / Allen / 551050

This design may have been used by the Kingsbury Episcopi Male Friendly Society (the Old Friendly Society) (1861 to 1909) (unregistered), which met at the School Room, but there is no confirmation. A specimen visible in a photograph in *The Way We Were*, Kingsbury Episcopi History Group, Crewkerne, 1997, p.26, appears to show F 284, but it is not sufficiently distinct for identification. Kingsbury Episcopi Friendly Society males carried 'brass-headed staves' but the design was not specified (*Sherborne Mercury*, May 31st, 1864). There are several versions of this design: the main variable is the top. In some specimens the underneath of the arms is patterned, and in others it is smooth on the underside and red-painted on the top: but there are no distinct simple categories. Hardington Mandeville, Kingsbury Episcopi, Montacute, Odcombe, Norton sub Hamdon, and Stogursey have all been stated to have used the general design of the members' pole head, but all lack supporting evidence.

F 283/2

F 284

Detail of moulded pattern: F288.

F 285   7.1″   SHC / OSFS / 137A

This design is verified for **Odcombe Friendly Society** (1834 to 1895) (SOM 450), which met variously at the Odcombe Inn, the Pye Corner Inn, the Rising Sun Inn and the School Room. As this specimen was donated to Taunton Museum in 1904 by Dr RH Walter, whose father Dr WW Walter was club surgeon to Odcombe Friendly Society, the attribution to Odcombe seems to be correct (SHC: Exercise Book of Friendly Society Brasses). The elongated leaves appear to denote that this was a steward's or flag-pole brass. No other examples have been recorded with the elongated leaves.

F 285

F 286   5.8″   MERL / Allen / 551047

There is no confirmation that this was the precise pattern that was used by members of the Odcombe Friendly Society (1834 to 1895) (SOM 450), which met variously at the Odcombe Inn, Pye Corner Inn, Rising Sun Inn and the School Room. The club certainly possessed pole heads, but the design is uncertain: Odcombe Friendly Society paid 6/6d for 'club knobs' in 1845 (SHC DD\X\MNC/1, club accounts) and poles are specified in the 1844 club rules (The National Archives FS 1/618/450).

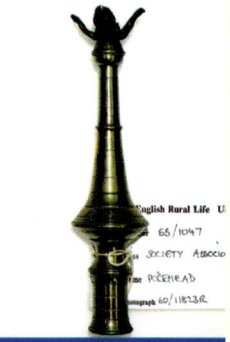

F 286

F 287   6.2″   MERL / Allen / 551034

There is no confirmation that this was the precise pattern that was used by members of the Norton Provident Society (1885 to after 1961) (SOM 964), which met at the Reading Room. Members at Norton sub Hamdon paraded 'carrying their poles' (*Western Gazette*, 12 June 1891), but the design is unknown.

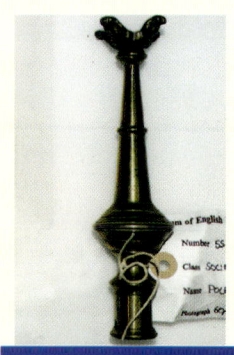

F 287

F 288   5.9″   MERL / Allen / 551017

No evidence has been found to confirm that brass pole heads were used at Montacute, although the location has often been associated with pole heads of this general design.

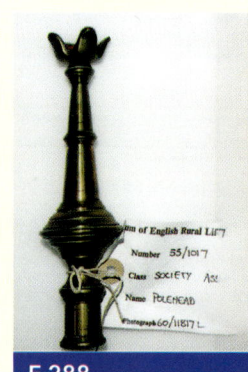

F 288

F 289   5.3″   MERL / Allen / 551048

There is no confirmation that this was the precise pattern that was used by members of the Hardington Mandeville United Friendly Society (1873 to after 1911) (unregistered), which met at the School Room. The 1888 club rules make mention of poles, requiring them to be all alike (SHC T/OH/dns/3). The society membership included both males and females, but only the males carried 'brass-headed wands with blue streamers' (*Western Gazette*, June 17th, 1874).

Detail of plain pattern: red paint on upper side: F 289.

F 289

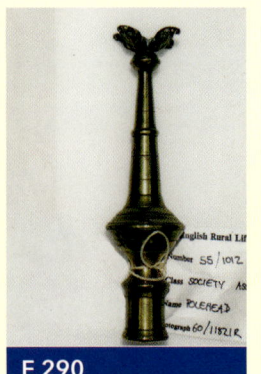

F 290

F 291

F 292/1

F 292/2

F 293

F 290   6.3"   MERL / Allen / 551012

Two designs of pole heads have been attributed to the Stocurcy (Stogursey) New Friendly Society (1845 to 1952), which met at the New Inn, but with no evidence for either. One is as here, and the other is similar to that of the Nether Stowey George Inn Friendly Society (F 219 or 220). The society sold poles, tassels and brass tops to members between 1846 and 1864 (SHC D\P\stogs/23/1), but the design was unspecified. Staves with ribbons were carried (*West Somerset Free Press*, June 1st, 1907).

F 291   8"   MERL / Allen / 551074

The column brass shown here has two main varieties, one with three leaves (F291 and F 293), and the other with four (F 292/1 and F 292/1). Allen and Fuller (1964) both wrongly attributed this three leaf design to the North Petherton Red Club. The Rev J Addy, in a letter to Jardine dated September 13th, 1932, clearly stated that the four leaf variety belonged to North Petherton, and that the club was the Blues, not the Reds (MERL Jardine Index). The three leaf variety shown here has also been attributed to Bawdrip, but with no evidence. The heights of the different types depend on how far the acorn spindle is screwed in.

F 292/1   8.1"   MERL / Allen / 550944

This design has two main varieties, one with three leaves (F291 and F 293), and the other with four (F 292/1 and F 292/2). Allen attributed this four leaf design to Goathurst, and a letter to Jardine from the Rev EH Smith, dated September 27th, 1932, confirms the suggestion (MERL DDX/1787). Nevertheless, there are two varieties of the four leaf type: one with two ridged rings around the column above the knop, as here, and the other with only one (F 292/2). Goathurst Male Friendly Society (1863 to 1913) (unregistered) met at the School Room, and paraded with staves, but it is not clear if the pole tops were like F 292/1 or F 292/2 (*Bridgwater Mercury*, June 10th, 1891). The other society which used the four leaf variety was North Petherton Blue Club (The Rev J Addy in a letter to Jardine dated September 13th, 1932), but again it is not clear if this was version F 292/1 or F 292/2. This pattern is also attributed to Puriton, but without evidence. The heights of the different types depend on how far the acorn spindle is screwed in.

F 292/2   8.8"   Blaise Castle House Museum / T7517

The column brass with an acorn surrounded by leaves has two main varieties, one with three leaves (F291 and F 293) and the other with four (F 292/1 and F 292/2). The type here has four leaves and a single ridged ring around the column above the knop. The Rev J Addy of North Petherton confirmed to Jardine in a letter dated September 13th, 1932 (MERL DDX/1787), that the four leaf variety was used there by the North Petherton Tradesmen's Friendly Society (the Blue club) (1816 to c. 1892) (SOM 463), which variously met at the Swan Inn and the George Hotel, and in 1871 were reported as parading with staffs (*Bridgwater Mercury*, June 31st, 1871). Nevertheless, it is not known whether the pole head was the four leaf variety shown here or the one shown in F 292/1. The four leaf variety has also been confirmed for Goathurst (see F 292/1) and suggested, also without evidence, for Puriton. The heights of the different types depend on how far the acorn spindle is screwed in.

F 293   8.1"   MERL / Allen / 551073

The column brass with an acorn surrounded by leaves has two main varieties, one with three leaves (F291 and F 293) and the other with four (F 292/1 and F 292/2). The type here is a three leaf variety which Allen attributed to Bawdrip, but without any further evidence. Bawdrip certainly had a friendly society in the 1870s, but with no evidence that the members carried poles or that such poles had brass pole heads (*Somerset County Gazette*, June 1st, 1878). The heights of the different types depend on how far the acorn spindle is screwed in.

F 294/1   c. 9.8″   Ponsonby-Fane collection (dispersed), location unknown

Langport New Friendly Society (1815 to 1827) and Langport New Friendly Permanent Society (1827 to 1856) (SOM 175), which met at the Black Swan, had red poles topped with brass knobs, but not of the design shown here (SHC Q/RSf6). Ponsonby-Fane is the sole source for this attribution: his notebook and article show the only recorded specimen attributed to Langport (Ponsonby-Fane notebook, p.83 [drawing], MERL D85/11/1, and Sir Spencer Ponsonby-Fane, 'Somerset Friendly Society Pole Heads', *The Connoisseur*, extra Christmas number, 1913, photograph, p.69). The pole head in these sources and in Fuller's drawing (1964), plate XLIX, no 294, is a one-off and a marriage: the column is correct, but the top is a brass needle holder for a knitting belt. The 9.8″height has been scaled from the image on p.69 of his article. The proper Langport design is unknown, but may be as shown at F 117/1.

F 294/1

F 294/2   5.9″   SHC / 9727

This design is verified as a banner top used by **Barrington Friendly Society** (1797 to 1915) (SOM 254), **Barrington Friendly and Insurance Society** (1912 to 1915) (SOM 254), and **Barrington 5 year Burial Society** (1915 to 1945) (unregistered). Members met at the Royal Oak Inn, and from 1912 at the School Room. The Rev Prebendary J Hamlet, Vicar of Barrington, who ran Barrington Friendly Society for many years, gave this specimen to Taunton Museum. The red pole has a brass ferrule at the bottom, with two attached rings. It was originally painted blue according to the Rev Hamlet. He wrote that the 10ft red pole with this top was carried by the two senior stewards. The one here was apparently cut down from 10ft to its current height of 7ft 10in. The President and clerk carried simple white wands without heads (Rev J Hamlet, *History of Barrington Friendly Society*, Centenary 1907, SHC D/P/barr/23/2). The members' brass is shown at F 210.

F 294/2

F 295   2.7″   Private collection

Fuller (1964) attributed this design to Shapwick and Polden Hill, but did not specify a particular society. Her claim was based on the drawing in the Ponsonby-Fane notebook (MERL D85/11/1, p.36), which clearly attributes the pole head to [Somerset] javelin men. The latter were used to provide a judge's official escort, and to keep order in court. The pole head had no connection with a friendly society, nor any necessary link with Shapwick. It is unclear why Fuller included it in her 1964 list.

F 295

F 296   7.3″   MERL / Allen / 551035

This design was used by **Kingston Union Friendly Society** (1819 to 1836) and by **Kingston Friendly Society** (1836 to c. 1912), which first met at the House of Mr George Fearncombe, and later at the Farmer's Arms at Kingston St Mary. In a letter to Jardine, n.d., D Lench of Manor View, Kingston St Mary, wrote: 'your sketch is an exact copy of [a pole head belonging to an] old member's widow' (MERL, Jardine Index). The 1820 and 1836 rules both specify poles with a brass (FS1/690B/163: 1820 rules; SHC Tite Collection: 1836 rules). Examples of the design are in the church. The three sets of rings on these specimens vary in detail. In the verified version they are distinctly grooved. In other examples claimed to have originated at Kingston St Mary (e.g. Torquay Museum and a private collection) they are only lightly scribed.

F 296

F 297   c. 4.4″ MERL / Allen / 551054

This design is verified for **Stoke St Michael**. The pole has gold and red stripes, and the wooden acorn top is painted yellow. An example is in each of the Allen and Jardine Collections. The MERL Jardine Index indicates that Allen 'purchased the Deputy Steward's gilt acorn from Mr Frank Griffin of Stoke St Michael'. They were said to have been carried by the deputies of the Young Men's Club (Joyce Jefferson, ed., *A History of Stoke St Michael*, 2006, p76), but the source of this claim is unconfirmed.

F 297

F 298

F 299/1

F 299/2

F 299/3

F 299/4

F 298   3.8"   MERL / Allen / 550931

The design is verified for **Glastonbury Friendly and Benefit Society** (1817 to 1912) (SOM 128), which met at the Town Hall. The example at SHC (5/1989/684A) is inscribed 'Jas Lawrence Glastonbury 1817 No 5'. He was the first Secretary to the club. Many of the other brass acorn tops are also engraved with the member's name or initials, the date he joined the club, and his membership number: the one shown here is marked 'JL 1818 no. 4'. Only the top of the pole head is brass: the base is wooden and carved into the pattern of an acorn cup.

The pole head of James Lawrence: F 298.

F 299/1   6.5" (book only: acorn missing from top) SHC / 197.1993

The design is verified as an officer's pole head of **Glastonbury Friendly and Benefit Society** (1817 to 1912) (SOM 128), which met at the Town Hall. For this specimen an ordinary member's pole head was fixed on top of a tin-plated book, painted black and with the inscription 'G. F. & B. S' (standing for the name of the society). The reverse side has the inscription 'Estd 1817'. The pole head served as either the Secretary's or the Treasurer's emblem. In the specimen shown here the top 'acorn' has become detached, but the fixing hole remains on the upper edge of the book. When complete, the attachment should resemble that in F 299/2. The drawing in Fuller (1964), plate L, no 299, erroneously omits the acorn fitment at the top.

F 299/2   9"   Private collection

The design is verified as an officer's pole head of **Glastonbury Friendly and Benefit Society** (1817 to 1912) (SOM 128), which met at the Town Hall. The tin-plated book has a mottled painted exterior, inscribed 'Glastonbury Friendly and Benefit Society', in full. As there are two similar specimens (F 299/1 and F299/2), it would appear that one was for the secretary and the other was for the treasurer.

F 299/3   4.4"   Blaise Castle House Museum / T7582

From the evidence of the member's brass at F 298 the design shown here is verified for **Glastonbury Friendly and Benefit Society** (1817 to 1912) (SOM 128), which met at the Town Hall. The larger specimens of the Glastonbury pole head were probably used by the stewards. Two examples at 4.4" and 5.1" are known.

F 299/4   7.8"   Private collection

From the evidence of the members' brass at F 298 the design shown here is verified for **Glastonbury Friendly and Benefit Society** (1817 to 1912) (SOM 128), which met at the Town Hall. The very large versions of the Glastonbury design (F 299/4 and F 299/5) were probably banner tops. The one of 7.8" height, as shown here, is wooden throughout, with the acorn gilded, whereas the 7.5" specimen (F 299/5) has a brass top. Both have the diagonal chasing on the acorn, as with the smaller members' pole heads.

F 299/5   7.1"   Private collection

From the evidence of the members' brass at F 298 the design shown here is verified for **Glastonbury Friendly and Benefit Society** (1817 to 1912) (SOM 128), which met at the Town Hall. The very large versions of the Glastonbury design (F 299/4 and F 299/5) were probably banner tops. The one of 7.8" height (F 299/4) is wooden throughout, with the acorn gilded, whereas the 7.5" specimen, shown here, has a brass top. Both have the diagonal chasing on the acorn, as with the smaller members' pole heads.

F 299/5

F 300/1   3.5"   MERL / Allen / 551055

Allen suggested that this wooden specimen was a steward's pole head from the Wookey Ring O' Bells club, but he did not provide any supporting evidence, and no further details have emerged.

F 300/2   c. 3.1" MERL / Ponsonby-Fane notebook, p.35, No 1, D 85/11/1

The current location of this specimen is unknown following the sale of the major portion of the Ponsonby-Fane Collection at Brympton in 1956. It was attributed to Almondsbury by Ponsonby-Fane in an uncoloured drawing with no supporting detail of provenance. In 1877 a 'golden acorn' on a long blue staff was carried by the members of the Almondsbury Union Friendly Society (*Bristol Daily Post*, May 25th 1877), but it is not known if the top was of wood, as here or of brass (see F 243/1)

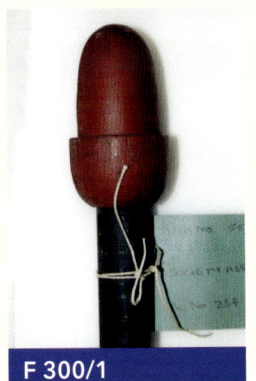
F 300/1

F 300/3   6.2"   Blaise Castle House Museum / T9373

This wooden specimen has no recorded provenance. It appears from its size that it is a flag pole top, but there is no evidence that it was used by a friendly society.

F 301   2.75"   Salisbury Museum / 1935.144

Britford, Wiltshire, has been suggested as the provenance of this wooden pole head, but no evidence has emerged to support the claim.

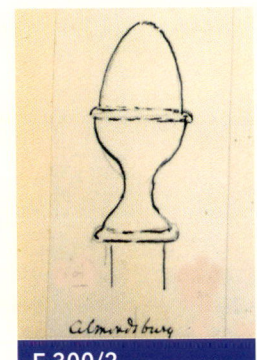
F 300/2

Glastonbury officer's pole head detail: F 299/2.

F 300/3

F 301

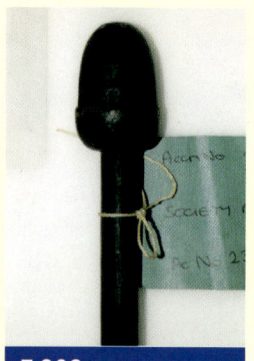

F 302

F 303

F 304/1

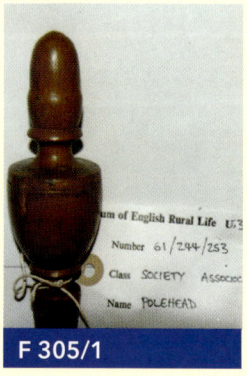

F 304/2

F 305/1

F 302   2″   MERL / Allen / 551029

Allen provided no confirmation for this wooden pole with top, and no reliable evidence has emerged. Another identical specimen is in Taunton Museum (SHC acc 8789), where it is attributed to Hatch Beauchamp, but again with no supporting evidence (given by CH Greed). Hatch Beauchamp Friendly Society had blue poles, but it is not clear if there were pole tops, and, if there were, whether they were wooden or brass (*Langport Herald*, June 28th, 1866).

F 303   3.75   Salisbury Museum / 1996R2120

This wooden specimen has no verified provenance, but it has been attributed to Berwick St John.

F 304/1   7″   Blaise Castle House Museum / T9372

Shepton Montague has been suggested as the source of this wooden pole head, but there is no supporting evidence.

F 304/2   4.9″   Blaise Castle House Museum / T4070

The design is verified for **Corsley, Wiltshire**, but it is not clear which of several nineteenth century societies at the location is the relevant one. The staff belonging to this wooden specimen has the painted inscription 'Corsley Friendly Society'. Members' and stewards' brasses have been attributed to Corsley, but without supporting evidence (F 063/1 and F 063/2).

F 305/1   7″   MERL / Jardine / 61244253

This wooden pole head is attributed to Kingston Deverill, but there is no supporting evidence.

Acorn finials in use by members of the UAOD (Druids).

F 305/2   4″   Wiltshire Museum (Devizes) / 2004.539 to 541

Of the three staffs attributed to Bromham, only the one illustrated here has retained its wooden top, unusually painted with a lattice pattern to suggest the cup of the acorn. There is no supporting evidence to confirm the provenance.

F 306   4.8″   MERL / Allen / 551057

The three wooden pole heads illustrated as F 306 to F308 by Fuller are attributed to Stratton-on-the-Fosse, but Allen, the collector, provided no supporting evidence.

F 307   7.3″   MERL / Allen / 551056

The three wooden pole heads illustrated as F 306 to F308 by Fuller are attributed to **Stratton-on-the-Fosse**, but Allen, the collector, provided no supporting evidence, but this design (F 307) was shown in a photograph of the 1892 Stratton club anniversary (Library Archives, Downside Abbey).

F 308   5.1″   MERL / Allen / 551058

The three wooden pole heads illustrated as F 306 to F308 by Fuller are attributed to Stratton-on-the-Fosse, but Allen, the collector, provided no supporting evidence.

F 309   6″   MERL / Allen / 551030

The wooden pole head attributed to Broadwindsor, Dorset, is attached to a hexagonal pole painted with alternating dark green and red vertical stripes. It is thought to be a steward's emblem, but there is no supporting evidence to confirm either this or the provenance.

Acorn finials at Edford near Lichfield: material not known.

F 305/2

F 306

F 307

F 308

F 309

F 310/1

F 310/2

F 310/3

F 310/4

F 310/5

F 310/1   5.5"   MERL / Allen / 550997

The Hilton Benefit Society has been suggested as the provenance for this wooden pole head, but there is no supporting evidence. The rules of the 1835 Hilton Benefit Society (1835 to 1895) (DOR 056), which met at the Fox Inn, required members to have 'a rod with a vase' (the architectural term for part of a column), but the precise design has not been established (The National Archives FS 1/108/056, rules 1835).

F 310/2   5.3   Dorset Museum, Dorchester / 1914.9.1

This design is verified for **Milton Abbas, Dorset**, but the society is not confirmed. On the pole is painted 'J Butt - Delcombe', and the location appears to be in the parish of Milton Abbas, Dorset, but there is no evidence as to which society in the parish had wooden pole heads of this pattern.

F 310/3   4.2"   SHC / OSFS / 608

Stratton-on-the-Fosse was suggested for this wooden pole head, but there is no supporting evidence. The date when the attribution was made appears to be later than the date of donation of the specimen. The specimen illustrated was given to Somerset County Museum in memory of E Harold Caley by his widow in 1940.

F 310/4   8.2"   Blaise Castle House Museum / T4071

This is one of a pair of wooden pole heads, 8.2" high (the other is 6.3" and of similar shape and colouring, but of slightly different dimensions due to hand crafting). Both are on long darkened blue poles with red and white spiral stripes. There is no evidence for the provenance.

F 310/5   c. 8"   Stoke Abbott Church

This design is verified for **Stoke Abbott Friendly Society** (before 1840 to after 1929) (unregistered), which met at the Anchor Inn. The Stoke Abbott Sick Club Walk was revived after the club terminated, and has been held intermittently since then. A member's wooden pole head is seen at F 313/2. The one illustrated here is a steward's version, missing its top, but in better condition than its pair. The pole head is attached to a pole, mostly painted white, with a red base and some blue ornamentation.

The replacement poles at Stoke Abbott church: F 310/5.

F 311 9″ MERL / Allen / 551036

This wooden pole head appears to have been used on a flagpole, and it is attributed to Leigh, near Yetminster in Dorset, but there is no supporting evidence.

F 312 4.3″ Salisbury Museum / 1937.123

This wooden pole head has been attributed to Fonthill Gifford, but there is no supporting evidence.

F 313/1 c. 6″ Gloucestershire Museum

This pattern for a wooden pole head was attributed by Fuller (1964) to the Coaley Hill Benevolent Society, Gloucestershire, but no evidence was provided in support of the suggestion.

F 313/2 7″ Dorset Museum, Dorchester / 1991.528

This design is verified for **Stoke Abbott Friendly Society** (before 1840 to after 1929) (unregistered). A collection of over twenty Stoke Abbott members' staves with wooden tops is held in the church. They were made by Canon Roger W H Dalison, Hon. Canon of Rochester 1928 to 1934, and were presented to the club in 1929 (*Western Morning News*, June 10th, 1929). The design of the new set may not have completely matched earlier ones. In 1863 there is a newspaper reference to 'blue poles with gilt tops' (*Western Gazette*, May 23rd, 1863). A few older specimens, in poor condition, have also survived. The Stoke Abbott Sick Club Walk was revived after the club terminated, and has been held intermittently since then.

F 314/1 c. 3.5″ Location unknown

Fuller (1964) stated that this wooden pole head and its pole were held by the Salisbury Museum, but their current location has not been traced, and the attribution to Melbury Abbas, Wiltshire, has no supporting evidence.

Coloured ribbons as streamers were commonly attached to pole heads: F 310/5.

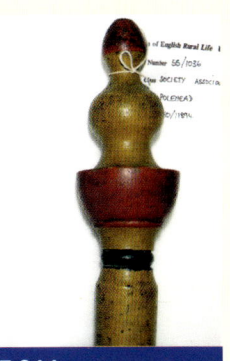

F 311

F 312

F 313/1

F 313/2

F 314/1

F 314/2

F 314/3

F 315/1

F 315/2

F 315/3

F 314/2   3"   Wiltshire Museum, Devizes / 2004.535

This wooden pole head is described as a steward's emblem used at Great Bedwyn, but no supporting evidence has emerged. The Great Bedwyn Friendly Society had its own crested earthenware meat dishes, plates and mugs.

F 314/3   4"   Wiltshire Museum, Devizes / 91.1978

This wooden pole head is described as a steward's emblem used at Poulshot, but no supporting evidence has emerged. For the reputed version for members, see F 316/2.

F 315/1   6.8"   MERL / Allen / 550995

This wooden pole head is attributed to High Ham, but no supporting evidence has emerged. The colours, which have darkened over time, are alternating red and green, thus differing from the specimen at Wells (F 315/2). There were two concurrent societies at High Ham: this specimen could be from either.

F 315/2   6.2"   Wells / 668

This wooden pole head is attributed to High Ham, but no supporting evidence has emerged. The colours, which have darkened over time, are alternating red and white, thus differing from the specimen at MERL (F 315/1). There were two concurrent societies at High Ham: this specimen could be from either.

F 315/3   8.2"   SHC / Du Cann collection / 201894

No comparable design of this wooden pole head is recorded, and the item has no known provenance.

Great Bedwyn FS (F 314/2) owned a dinner service for their anniversary feast: the Old Cleeve Female FS had crockery to serve members tea for their celebration.

F 316/1   7.2"   SHC / OSFS / 160B

This design is verified as an example of the old wooden pole heads of **Shepton Beauchamp Loyal Brothers Friendly Society** (1802 to 1899) (SOM 384), which met at the New Inn, and after 1856 at the School Room. This particular specimen was purchased by Taunton Museum through the negotiations of the Rev Prebendary J Hamlet, in 1909. Originally it belonged to George Newis, who died in 1855, aged 70, and it is of a pattern that was used by club until c.1860. After 1860 the club members had brasses (SCM Accessions, vol II, 1909), but their design has not been verified. The 1802 rules required members to carry a pole on the feast day (The National archives FS 1/617B/384).

F 316/1

F 316/2   4"   Wiltshire Museum, Devizes / 91.1978

This wooden pole head is described as a member's emblem from Poulshot, but there is no supporting evidence (see F 314/3 for the reputed version for stewards).

F 316/2

F 317/1   9.3"   Dorset Museum, Dorchester / 1953.20.6 (Richard Hine Collection)

This design is verified as having been used by a steward of **Beaminster Friendly Society** (1762 to 1827) (not registered), (1827 to 1862) (DOR 111) and (1862 to 1892) (DOR 135), which met at the Town Hall. On the closing of Beaminster Friendly Society the staves with wooden tops were bought by Richard Hine, who illustrated them and described the society in his 1914 *History of Beaminster*.

F 317/1

F 317/2   unknown   Location unknown

This design is verified as having been used by a members of the **Beaminster Friendly Society** (1762 to 1827) (not registered), (1827 to 1862) (DOR 111) and (1862 to 1892) (DOR 135), which met at the Town Hall. On the closing of Beaminster Friendly Society the staves with wooden tops were bought by Richard Hine, who illustrated them and described the society in his 1914 *History of Beaminster*.

F 317/2

F 317/3   6.2"   Dorset Museum, Dorchester / 1953.20.8

There is no evidence to support the claim that this highly decorated wooden pole head came from Halstock: it bears a strong resemblance to F 317/2 from Beaminster.

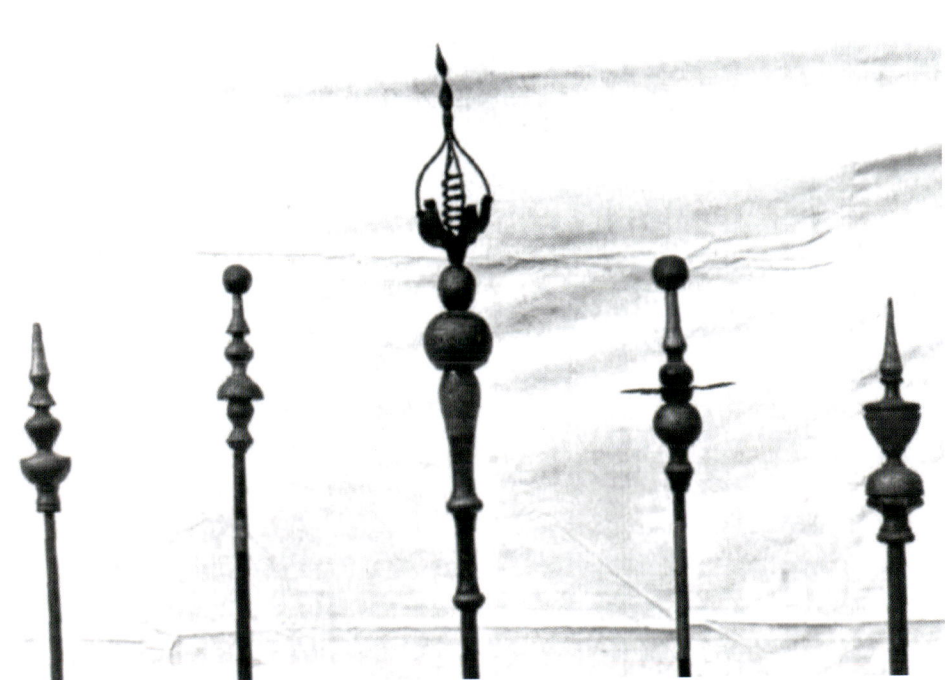

Beaminster Friendly Society committee pole heads.

F 317/3

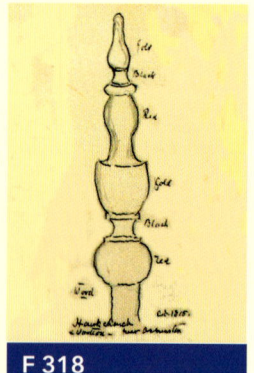

F 318

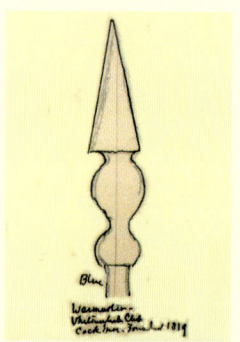

F 319/1

F 319/2

F 320

F 321

F 318   c. 6.8″ MERL / Ponsonby-Fane notebook, p.40, no 3, D 85/11/1

No evidence has emerged to confirm that this highly decorated wooden pole head was used at Hawkchurch. The current location is unknown, following the sale of the major portion of the Ponsonby-Fane Collection at Brympton in 1956. Another pole head, reputedly from the same club, is at F 321. Hawkchurch had a very large friendly society.

F 319/1   c. 5.4″ MERL / Ponsonby-Fane notebook p.99, no 3, D 85/11/1

No evidence has emerged to confirm that this wooden pole head was used at Warminster. The current location of the one shown is unknown, following the sale of the major portion of the Ponsonby-Fane Collection at Brympton in 1956.

F 319/2   4.6″   MERL / Shickle / 511150

The Shickle list (V and A catalogue register number M 555 to 809 – 1928) provides no provenance for this wooden flag pole top. It closely resembles the pole top in F 319/1.

F 320   –   Salisbury Museum / no recorded accession number

No supporting evidence has emerged for the suggestion that this pole threaded with streamers was used by the Adelphi Club at Chute Standen, Wiltshire.

F 321   12.1″   SHC / Du Cann collection / 201897

No evidence has emerged that this wooden pole head was used at Hawkchurch. The specimen was originally in the Ponsonby-Fane collection (Ponsonby-Fane notebook, MERL D 85/11/1, p.58) and reappeared in the Du Cann collection. Another pole head, reputedly from the same club, is at F 318.

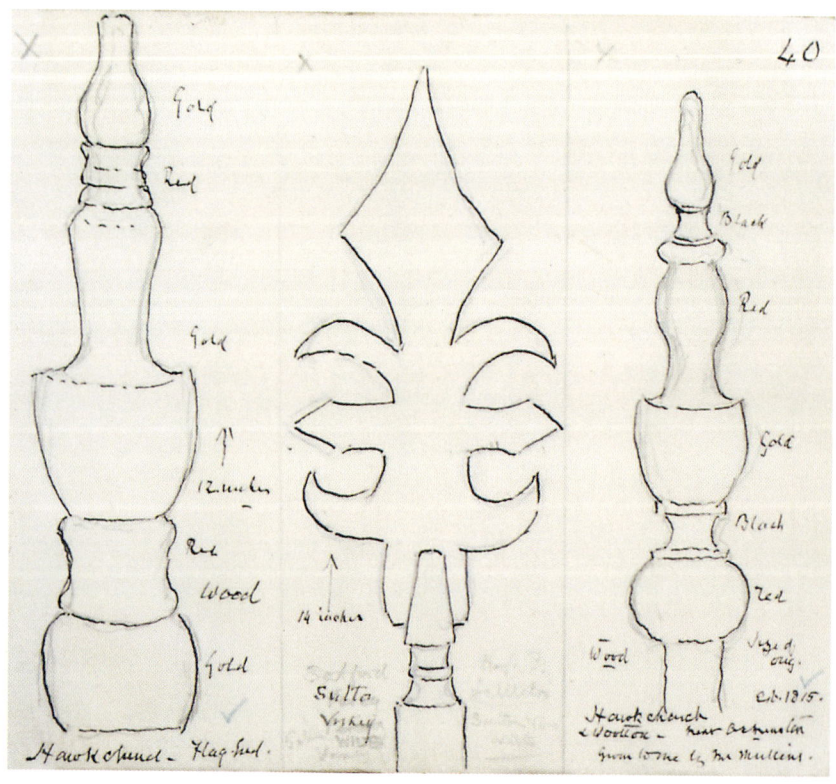

Ponsonby-Fane drawings of Hawkchurch pole heads.

F 322/1   6.1″   Ponsonby-Fane notebook, p.44, no 3, D 85/11/1

No evidence has emerged to confirm that this wooden pole head was used at Halstock, Dorset. The current location of the specimen is unknown, following the sale of the major portion of the Ponsonby-Fane Collection at Brympton in 1956.

F 322/2   6.3″   Blaise Castle House Museum / T4073

There is no provenance for this wooden pole head, except a suggestion that it was used in Wiltshire.

F 323/1   c. 7.3″ MERL / Ponsonby-Fane notebook, p.58, no2, D 85/11/1

No evidence has emerged to confirm the suggestion this wooden pole head was used at Yeovil. The current location is unknown, following the sale of the major portion of the Ponsonby-Fane Collection at Brympton in 1956.

F 323/2   4.1″   SHC / OSFS / 609

This design is confirmed for **Warminster Friendly Society** (1829 to 1872), which met at the Cock Inn. It appears to be the specimen offered by WE Edwards, a resident of Warminster, to Taunton Museum in 1914. His letter to HStG Gray, the Curator, explains that he obtained it from the proprietor of the Cock Inn (SHC Taunton Museum archives).

F 324   8.7″   SHC / Du Cann collection / 201895

No evidence has emerged to confirm Ponsonby-Fane's view that this wooden pole head was used at North Perrott. The specimen reappeared in the Du Cann collection following the dispersal of the Ponsonby-Fane collection (Ponsonby-Fane notebook, MERL D 85/11/1, p.37).

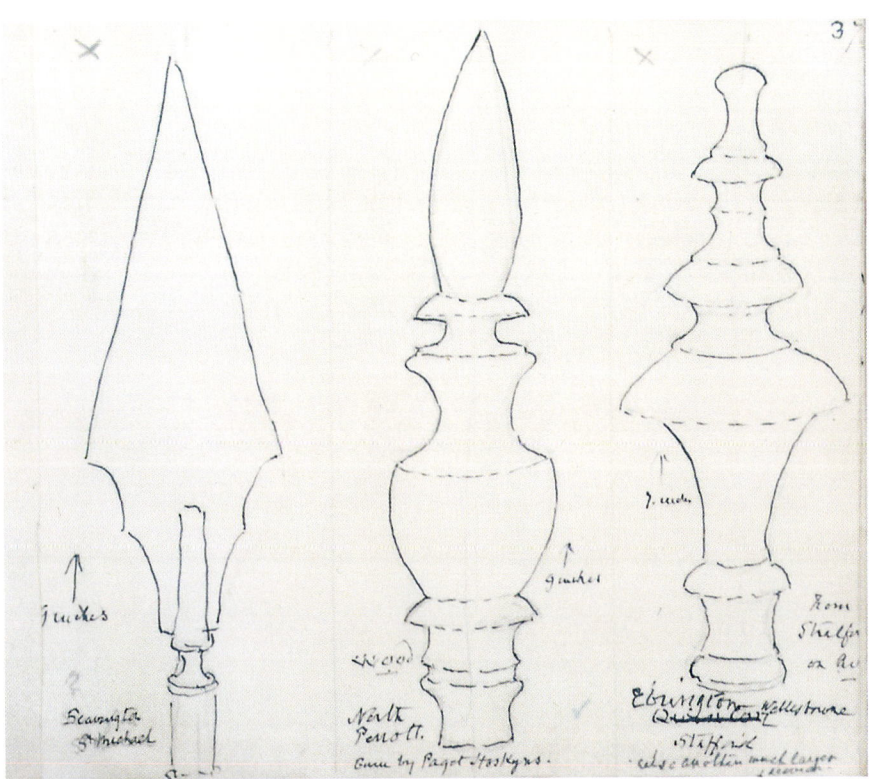

Ponsonby-Fane drawing of F 234 reputedly from North Perrott.

F 322/1

F 322/2

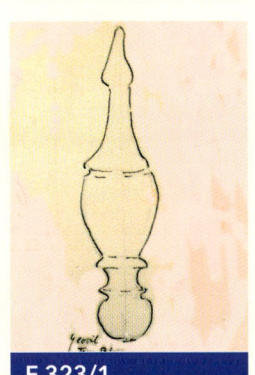

F 323/1

F 323/2

F 324

F 325

F 326

F 327/1

F 327/2

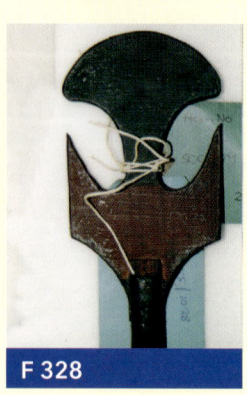

F 328

F 325   5.5″   SHC / Du Cann collection / 201893

No evidence has emerged to confirm that this wooden pole head was used at Merriott as was claimed by Ponsonby-Fane (MERL D 85/11/1 Ponsonby-Fane notebook, p.96). The specimen reappeared in the Du Cann collection following the sale of the Ponsonby-Fane collection.

F 326   10″   MERL / Jardine / 61244108

This design has been confirmed for Ullesthorpe, Leicestershire. The society was probably the Ullesthorpe Men's Friendly Society, also known as the Red, White and Blue Club (*Rugby Advertiser*, May 5th, 1888). In a letter to Jardine dated September 24th, 1932, CA Martin, Agent for Viscount Feilding, verified that this wooden pole head was used by a steward, and stated that a member's version was of the same pattern, but smaller (MERL, Jardine Index).

F 327/1   8.45″   SHC / Du Cann collection 201896

No evidence has emerged to confirm that this wooden pole head was used at Winsham. Members of Winsham Friendly Society (1782 to c. 1848) (SOM 135), which met at the King's Arms, were required by their 1811 rules to carry 'a deep blue pole with blue and white ribbons', but there was no mention of a pole head (The National Archives FS 1/615/315). The later society, the Winsham Male and Female Friendly Society (1865 to 1913) (SOM 790), which met at the National School Room, had brass pole heads, as seen in a 1909 postcard photograph, but the scale is too small to identify the pattern. The only recorded specimen of the wooden pole head, shown here, was in the Ponsonby-Fane collection, later reappearing in the Du Cann collection (MERL D 85/11/1 Ponsonby-Fane notebook, p.43, no 2).

F 327/2   7.8″   Dorset Museum, Dorchester / 1953.20.7

There is no evidence that this wooden pole head was used at Corscombe. Nevertheless, members of Corscombe Friendly Society (1780 to after 1888) (unregistered), which met at the School Room, carried staffs with brass tops (*Western Gazette*, May 24th, 1878), and the staffs were 'many-coloured' (*Western Gazette*, May 23rd, 1873). The design of the brass tops is unrecorded.

F 328   5.5″   MERL / Allen / 551028

This design is verified as a steward's pole head of **Timberscombe Friendly Society** (1815 to 1948) (SOM 405, and from 1912 a NHI Approved Society), which met at the School Room. Photographs in private collections show the Timberscombe Friendly Society procession, c.1935, with the pole heads shown at F 328 and F329/1 in use, but also visible are other officers' poles with heads of a more simple design. Members had plain poles which were adorned with large bunches of flowers. This pole head and F 329/1 are each made from a thin flat piece of wood, cut into the required outline shape, and slotted into the top of the pole.

Timberscombe steward's pole F 328 carried by man on left.

F 329/1   7"   MERL / Allen / 551061

This design is verified as a steward's pole head of **Timberscombe Friendly Society** (1815 to 1948) (SOM 405, and from 1912 a NHI Approved Society), which met at the School Room. Photographs in private collections show the Timberscombe Friendly Society procession, c.1935, with the pole heads shown at F 328 and F329/1 in use, but also visible are other officers' poles with heads of a more simple design. Members had plain poles which were adorned with large bunches of flowers. This pole head and F 328 are each made from a thin flat piece of wood, cut into the required outline shape, and slotted into the top of the pole.

F 329/1

F 329/2   5.5"   MERL / Shickle / 511149

Shickle offered no suggestions for the provenance of this iron pole head.

F 330   c. 17"   Current location unknown

This design is confirmed as a committee member's pole head of **Beaminster Friendly Society** (1762 to 1827) (not registered), (1827 to 1862) (DOR 111) and (1862 to 1892) (DOR 135), which met at the Town Hall. On the closing of the society the staves were purchased by Richard Hine, and Illustrated in both Ponsonby-Fane's notebook (MERL D 85/11/1) and Richard Hine's *History of Beaminster*, 1914, where he also described the society. The metal portions of F 330 and F 331/1 alternate with wooden sections that slot into one another.

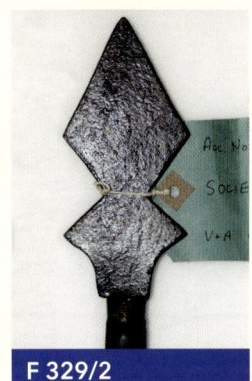
F 329/2

F 331/1   c. 14"   Current location unknown

This design is confirmed as a committee member's pole head of **Beaminster Friendly Society** (1762 to 1827) (not registered), (1827 to 1862) (DOR 111) and (1862 to 1892) (DOR 135), which met at the Town Hall. On the closing of the society the staves were purchased by Richard Hine, and Illustrated in both Ponsonby-Fane's notebook (MERL D 85/11/1) and Richard Hine's *History of Beaminster*, 1914, where he also described the society. The metal portions of F 330 and F 331/1 alternate with wooden sections that slot into one another

F 330

F 331/2   c. 11"   Current location unknown

This design is confirmed as a committee member's pole head of **Beaminster Friendly Society** (1762 to 1827) (not registered), (1827 to 1862) (DOR 111) and (1862 to 1892) (DOR 135), which met at the Town Hall. On the closing of the society the staves were purchased by Richard Hine, and Illustrated in both Ponsonby-Fane's notebook (MERL D 85/11/1) and Richard Hine's *History of Beaminster*, 1914, where he also described the society.

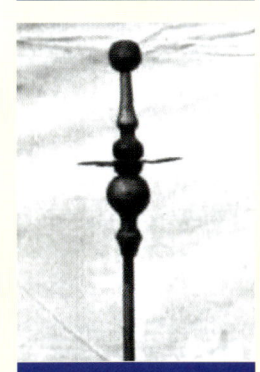
F 331/1

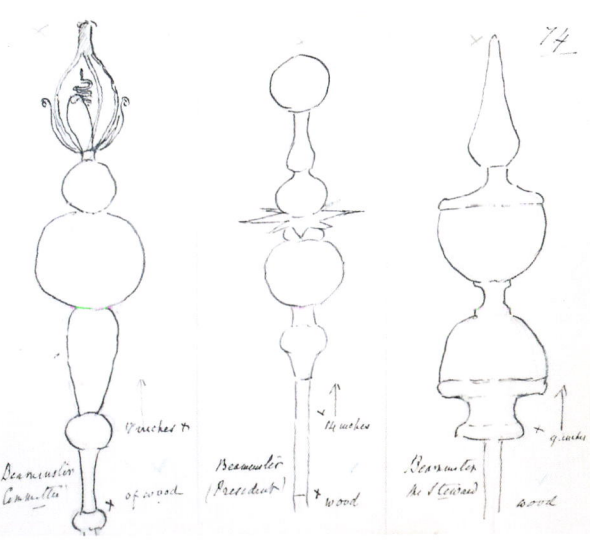

Ponsonby-Fane drawings of Beaminster committee pole heads.

F 331/2

F 332

F 332   8.8"   Salisbury Museum / no recorded accession number

No evidence has emerged that this design was used at Berwick St John, Wiltshire.

F 333/1   9.6"   MERL / Allen / 550920

The Drayton and Muchelney Men's Friendly Society is the only society mentioned for this design by early collectors, but no conclusive evidence has emerged to confirm this statement. There are several references to the members carrying poles with blue and buff or white streamers (for example *Langport Herald*, May 8th, 1869), and a few specify that the staves are 'spear-headed' (*Langport Herald*, May 22nd, 1866), but a 'gilt ornament' is also mentioned (*Western Gazette*, May 21st, 1864). Although the 1866 description of the poles as 'spear-headed' may seem conclusive proof of the Drayton shape, reports in newspapers at the time used the term 'spear' to represent many of the more complicated designs of flat brasses. The 1864 reference to a gilt ornamental head is curious for a plain iron pole head.

F 333/1

F 333/2   7"   Salisbury Museum / 1996R2123a

There are two of these hand-made iron pole heads, but they have no provenance details. It was suggested that they were used for the tops of banner poles (letter from Cyril Fox to Frank Stevens, September 9th, 1932: Salisbury Museum archives), but the society and the location were not mentioned.

F 333/3   9.7"   Trowbridge Museum / 1977.897

Trowbridge Museum has six of these tin pole heads, on modern staves, and they resemble the description of the early Keevil Friendly Society specimens referred to in a letter to Jardine from the Rev FM Weller, Keevil, 1932, who wrote that members carried 6 ft staves surmounted by a tin battle axe, later replaced by brass emblems (MERL, Jardine Index). These items are believed to be funerary staves. Although such staves were known to have been used at Keevil, it is uncertain whether the specimen shown here came from that source.

F 333/2

F 333/4   13.4"   Blaise Castle House Museum / T9396

There is no verified provenance for this iron pole head, although it is catalogued under Kingston Deverill. The cross-bar and the blade resemble the Yeomanry pole top illustrated at M/Javelin/05 (SHC). There is no evidence that this is a friendly society pole head. The dimension excludes the screw at the base.

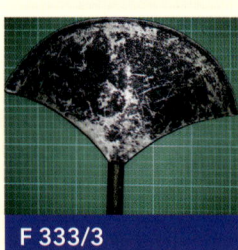

F 333/3

F 333/4

Court Pride of the Valley, AOF (Foresters), Lodsworth: four spears, possibly metal.

F 333/5   7.8"   Blaise Castle House Museum / T9365

There is no confirmed provenance for this iron pole head. The dimension excludes the screw at the base. Another specimen (9.1", although the blade is of the same length as this example) is in the Holburne Museum (VE037), described as originating in Market Lavington, Wiltshire, but without any supporting evidence.

F 333/5

F 333/6   8.5"   Blaise Castle House Museum / T4068

This is one of four near-identical blacksmith-made iron pole heads, with a top portion of twisted metal inserted into a red-painted wooden ball with woollen fringe, which surmounts a dark blue pole with a white painted spiral stripe. The top metal portions slightly vary in height. The set of four has no known society association. This specimen was illustrated in the set of 8 photographs taken at the 1911 Taunton Castle exhibition of the Philip Le Gros' collection (SHC, Museum archives). The four pole heads of this design and their poles are in the photograph showing the entire display.

F 333/6

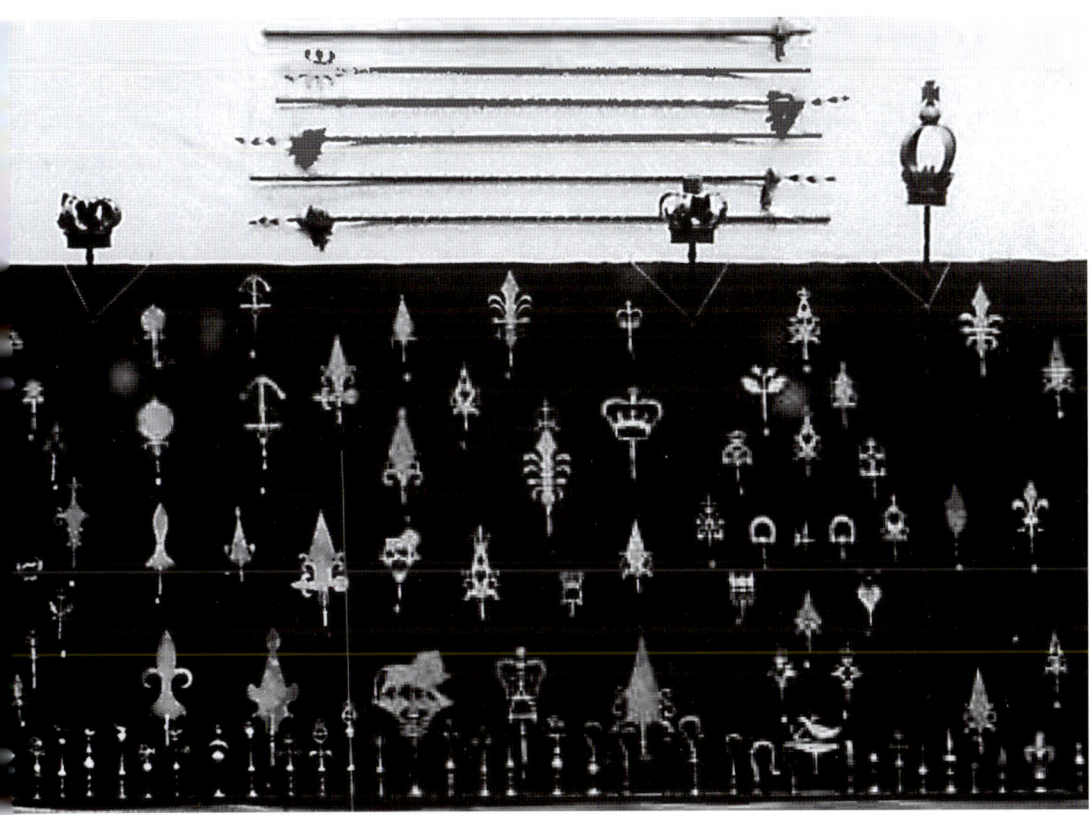

Le Gros collection on show at Taunton Castle: four F 333/6 designs are above the main display.

M/Axe/01

M/Axe/02

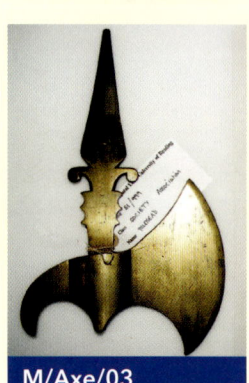

M/Axe/03

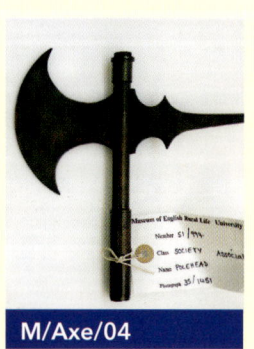

M/Axe/04

Axes: The Ancient Order of Foresters had officers called woodwards, who carried axes, variously decorated and sometimes made of wood: so, too, did the lodge-keepers in the short-lived Bristol-based Order of Sherwood Rangers, but the design is unrecorded.

M/Axe/01   9.5″   MERL / Allen / 551094

No provenance has been suggested for this pattern of ornamental axe. Versions have also been seen with shaped wooden handles fitted into a shorter socket than the one illustrated.

M/Axe/02   5.25″   MERL / Allen / 551102

No provenance has been suggested for this pattern of ornamental axe. This example is one of a pair, each with a short turned wooden handle.

M/Axe/03   11.4″   MERL / Shickle / 510999

Shickle suggested Bristol Ancient Order of Foresters for this ornamental axe, but provided no evidence in support. Several examples exist, including a version with a short wooden handle. The SHC specimen was illustrated in the Kelway Collection Notebook, p.120, with the caption: 'Taken from the Hatchet Public House, Denmark Street, Bristol, about 1850. Two were crossed over the chairman's seat: Marshal's emblem'. Kelway did not record which organisation owned them.

M/Axe/04   7.1″   MERL / Shickle / 510994

No provenance has been suggested for this pattern of ornamental axe. This specimen may be lacking a spike at the top.

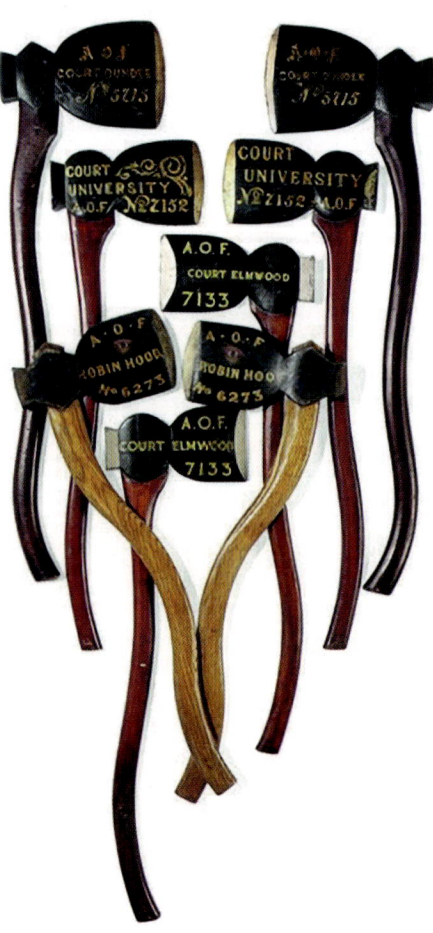

Pairs of axes from three Foresters' Courts (AOF).

164

M/Axe/05   5.4″   SHC / OSFS / 716

No provenance has been suggested for this pattern of ornamental axe. An ornate geometrical pattern has been engraved on the face of the axe.

M/Axe/06   12.4″   Blaise Castle House Museum / T 9394

No provenance has been suggested for this pattern of ornamental axe. The MERL Ponsonby-Fane notebook (MERL D 85/11/1, p. 82, no 3) illustrates a similar, but slightly more ornate specimen, with the stem pierced by a central diamond. He attributed it to Langford, Wiltshire, but offered no supporting evidence. Its current location is unknown.

M/Axe/07   20″ above the screw thread   Private collection

This very large banner top was used by the Oddfellows (IOOFMU), **Liverpool**. It is ornately inscribed on one side of the blade 'Presented to the **Royal Peace Lodge No 976** of the Independent Order of Odd Fellows of the Manchester Unity of the Liverpool District by Brother Richard Smith'. On the other side are Oddfellows symbols and the motto 'Amicitia, Amor et Veritas'. The axe has been very roughly repaired. There is a large screw attachment to fix it to the top of a large pole.

M/Axe/08   11.5″ wide   Private collection

The specimen is a typical wooden painted axe as used in many Courts of the Ancient Order of Foresters. JW stands for the office of Junior Woodward. On the reverse is the register number of the Court. An axe used by a Senior Woodward would have the initials SW.

M/Axe/05

M/Axe/06

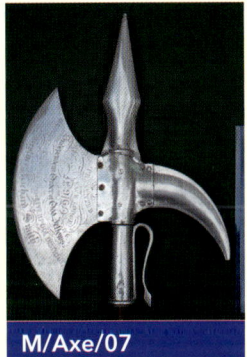
M/Axe/07

M/Axe/08

Detail of inscription on Oddfellows' presentation axe M / Axe / 07 (IOOF-MU).

M/Crook/01

M/Crook/02

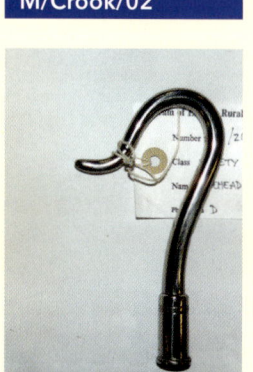

M/Crook/03

M/Crook/04

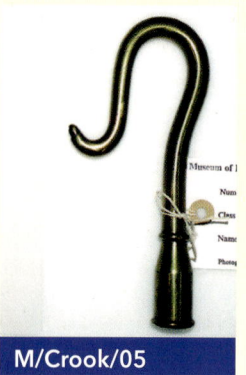

M/Crook/05

Crooks were widely used throughout Somerset and the Bristol area, and elsewhere, especially by the Loyal Order of Ancient Shepherds, Ashton Unity (LOAS AU), and to some extent by the Ancient Order of Shepherds (second degree of the Ancient Order of Foresters, but later independent of them), and by the Oddfellows.

M/Crook/01   4.6″   MERL / Allen / 551149

The provenance is unknown. This example has a plain tip, a plain crook, and a plain socket integral with the crook.

M/Crook/02   6.5″   Wells and Mendip Museum / box 196

The provenance is unknown. This example has a plain tip, a plain crook, and a plain socket integral with the crook.

M/Crook/03   5.75″   MERL / Jardine / 61244066

The provenance is unknown. This example has a plain tip, a plain crook, and a ringed socket.

M/Crook/04   6.4″   Private collection

The provenance is unknown. This example has a plain tip, a plain crook, and a ringed socket.

M/Crook/05   6.6″   MERL / Allen / 551148

The provenance is unknown. This example has a plain tip, a plain crook, and a ringed socket.

Shepherds' Hall, Bath, poles with crooks painted on wall (LOAS).

M/Crook/06   8.4″   MERL / Shickle / 511156

Shickle suggested that this example came from a Junior Shepherd (Bristol) Club, but provided no supporting evidence. Another example (30″ long, including shaft) was shown in the SHC Kelway Notebook, p.96, but the whereabouts of the specimen is unrecorded. This example has a plain tip, a plain crook, and a ringed socket.

M/Crook/07   6.75″   Private collection

The provenance is unknown. This example has a plain tip (bent), a plain crook, and a ringed socket. Unusually, it is made of pewter.

M/Crook/08   7.2″   MERL / Allen / 551144

The provenance is unknown. This example has a plain tip, a plain crook, and a ringed socket.

M/Crook/09   9.5″   Holburne Museum / VE 112

The provenance is unknown. This example has a plain tip, a plain crook, and a very elaborate ringed socket.

M/Crook/10   6.9″   Holburne Museum / VE 010

The provenance is not known for this particular example, but it was a general issue design used by the Loyal Order of Ancient Shepherds (LOAS). One location where this pattern was reputed to have been used was **Chilcompton** (SHC 7/2003/2), and another example was attributed to a lodge of the LOAS in **Ashton** or **Hotwells**, where it was used by the grandfather of JH Jones of Keynsham (SHC Taunton Museum archives, notes and drawing by AE Stephens, 1936). Crooks of this type were widely used throughout Somerset and the Bristol area, and elsewhere. The design consists of a plain tip, a fluted and barbed crook, and a ringed socket.

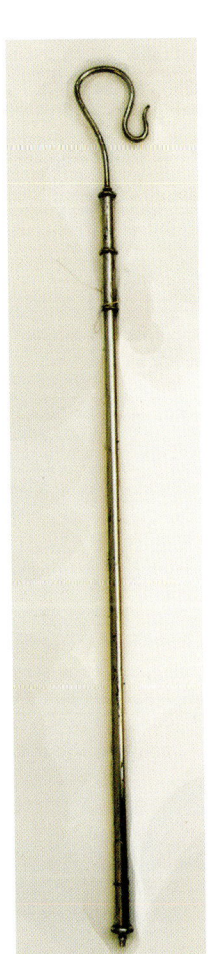

*LOAS (Shepherds) unkown Lodge: an unusual metal pole
M / Crook / 06.*

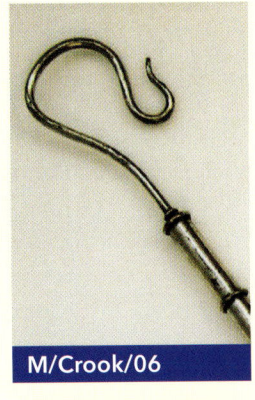

M/Crook/06

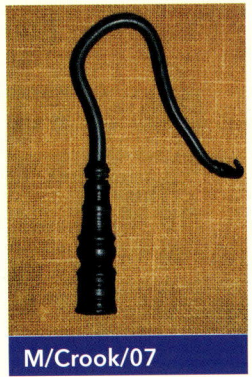

M/Crook/07

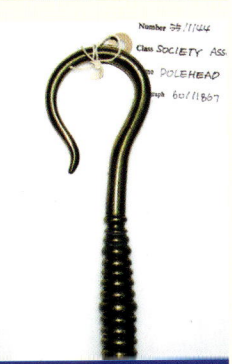

M/Crook/08

M/Crook/09

M/Crook/10

M/Crook/11

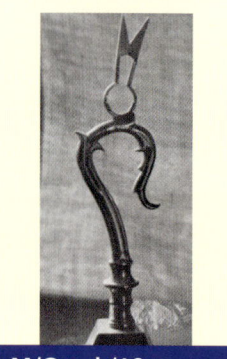

M/Crook/12

M/Crook/13

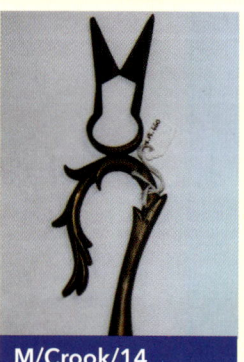

M/Crook/14

M/Crook/15

M/Crook/11   8.9″   Private collection

The provenance is not known for this design, but the main part of this pole head is the same as in M/Crook/10, and can therefore be attributed to one or more lodges of the Loyal Order of Ancient Shepherds, in or beyond the West Country. This example has a plain tip, a fluted and barbed crook, and a ringed extended socket.

M/Crook/12   c. 9.6″   Location unknown

This image appeared in *Country Life,* July 31st, 1958, p.236 (the letters section). The author did not know the provenance of the pole head, and its current location is unrecorded. In early lodges the officers called Guardians carried shears (Edwin Crew, *LOAS(AU) Centenary Souvenir 1826-1926*, Manchester, p.18). The design has a plain tip, a fluted and barbed crook surmounted with shears, and a ringed socket.

M/Crook/13   5.6″   Holburne Museum / VE 065

This pattern is generally described as having been used by Juvenile Branches of the LOAS, but there is no supporting evidence. It is similar to M/Crook/14, but lacks the shears. This example has a plain tip, a fluted and barbed crook, and a ringed socket.

M/Crook/14   8.3″   SHC / OSFS / 660

This pattern is generally considered to have been used by Juvenile Branches of the LOAS, but no supporting evidence has emerged. In early lodges the officers called Guardians carried shears (Edwin Crew, *LOAS(AU) Centenary Souvenir 1826-1926*, Manchester, p.18). This example has a plain tip, a fluted and barbed crook surmounted by sheep shears, and a ringed socket. It is a more slender construction than the design shown at M/Crook/12.

M/Crook/15   6.25″   Wells and Mendip Museum / box 196

Early collectors, including Allen (MERL 55/1025), ascribed this pattern to Pucklechurch, and nowhere else has been suggested. It is likely that it was used by the Shepherds meeting there, rather than by the independent friendly society. The Royal Oak and Acorn Lodge, 1184, LOAS (1865 to before 1943) (GLOS 0943), at Pucklechurch, had 'shining crooks' (*Bristol Mercury*, July 20th, 1872), and the pattern of the pole head fits the name of the lodge. The lodge met at the White Hart Inn, and later at the Temperance Hotel, Patchway. The design has a stub tip, low relief ornamentation with leaves and tendrils, and a plain short socket.

Detail of moulding on Shepherd society crook possibly from Pucklechurch.

M/Crook/16   6.8"   Private Collection

This design was for general issue to lodges of the LOAS or AOS, but there is no record of which particular lodges adopted it. The crook is stamped 'G Tutill & Co', who were makers of regalia and banners for friendly society orders and trade unions. The design has a pointed tip and low relief ornamentation all over, including an ornamented socket.

M/Crook/16

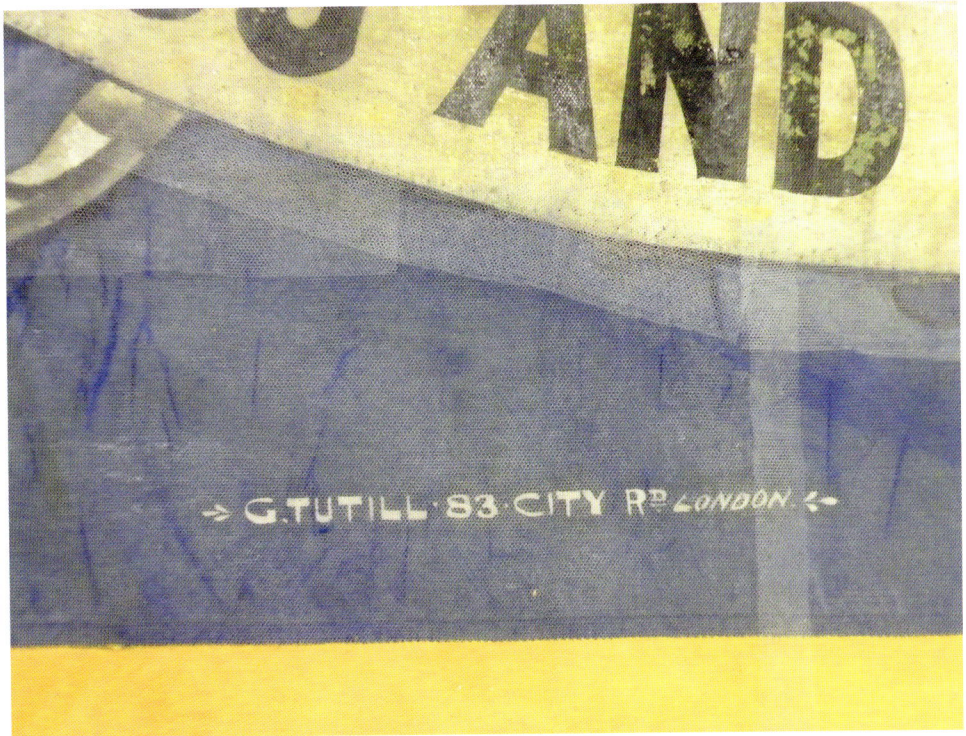

G Tutill supplied banners (this one for Dulverton Friendly Society) besides crooks (M / Crook / 16) and metal banner tops.

M/Crook/17

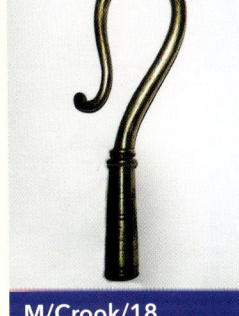

M/Crook/18

M/Crook/17   6.25"   Holburne Museum / VE 120

The provenance is unknown. The design has a stub tip, a plain crook, and a ringed socket.

M/Crook/18   8.2"   Holburne Museum / VE 101

The provenance is unknown. The design has a stub tip, a plain crook, and a ringed socket.

M/Crook/19   9.75"   Private collection

The provenance is unknown. The design has an acorn tip, low relief flowers along top edge (not visible in this image), and a ringed socket.

M/Crook/19

M/Crook/20   6.5"   Private collection

The provenance is unknown. The design has an acorn tip, a plain crook, and a plain socket integral with crook. Another example has been seen with a suggested Glasgow provenance.

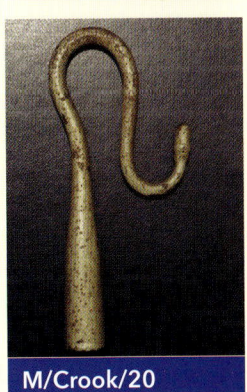

M/Crook/20

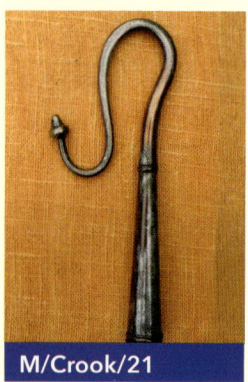

M/Crook/21

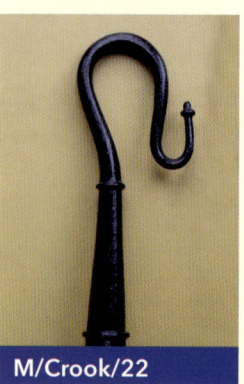

M/Crook/22

M/Crook/23

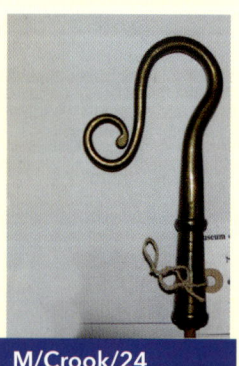

M/Crook/24

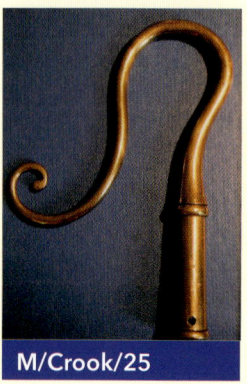

M/Crook/25

M/Crook/21   8.3″   Private collection

The provenance is unknown. This design has an acorn tip, a plain crook, and a ringed socket.

M/Crook/22   8″   Private collection

The provenance is unknown. The design has an acorn tip, a plain crook, and a ringed socket.

M/Crook/23   4.8″   Torquay Museum / V 521

The provenance is unknown. The design has a flat pad tip, a plain crook, and a ringed socket.

M/Crook/24   6.25″   MERL / Forster / 55257

The provenance is unknown. This design has a flat pad tip, a plain crook, and a ringed socket.

M/Crook/25   7.6″   Private collection

This design is verified for the **Rose of Somerset Lodge, Loyal Order of Ancient Shepherds, no 1806,** (1877 to after 1952), which met at the Rising Sun Inn, **Pensford**, and later at the George and Dragon Inn. An example of this pattern, together with a sash and membership book, was sold in 2014, once the property of a member of this lodge. It is very probable that other lodges also used this pattern of crook. The design has a flat pad tip, a plain crook, and a ringed socket. The crook of this specimen has been bent down: others may be 8″ to 8.25″.

LOAS (Shepherds) regalia from member 664, Rose of Somerset Lodge no 1806, Pensford.

M/Crook/26   9.5"   MERL / Jardine / 61244258

The provenance is unknown. This design has a flat pad tip, a plain crook, and a ringed socket which has been extended.

M/Crook/27   10.4"   Holburne Museum / VE 036

The provenance is unknown. This design has a flat pad tip, a plain crook and a ringed socket which has been extended.

M/Crook/28   1.7"   Plymouth City Museum and Art Gallery / 1907.11.2545

The provenance is unknown. This design has a flat pad tip, a plain crook, and a ringed socket which has been extended.

M/Crook/29   8.1"   Blaise Castle House Museum / T 9347

The provenance is unknown. This design has a flat pad tip, a plain crook, and a ball socket.

M/Crook/30   7.3"   Torquay Museum / V 508

The provenance is unknown.. This design has a spear tip, a plain crook, and a ringed socket.

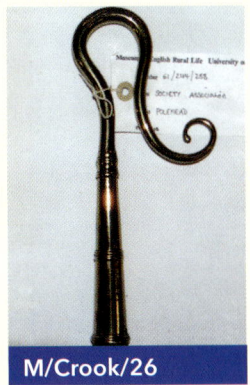

M/Crook/26

M/Crook/27

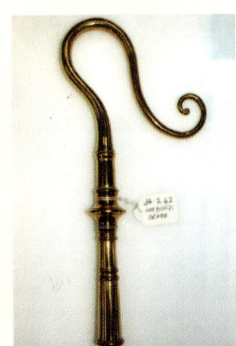

M/Crook/28

M/Crook/29

M/Crook/30

A Scottish Shepherds Friendly Society.

M/Crook/31

M/Crook/32

M/Crook/33

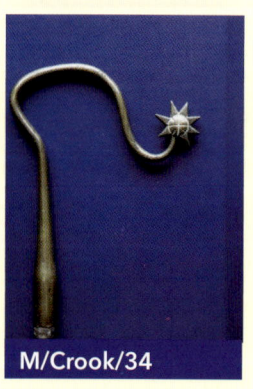

M/Crook/34

M/Crook/31   9"   Wells and Mendip Museum / box 196

The provenance is unknown. This design has a spear tip, a plain crook, and a ringed socket which has been extended.

M/Crook/32   5.9"   SHC / OSFS / 501

Blaise Castle House Museum identify their example as 'Taunton St James's Society', but there is no supporting evidence. In the private collection assembled by Mr Trickey of Bishops Lydeard (c.1925), this pattern was ascribed to Rowbarton (Juveniles), again without evidence. The design has a spear tip, a plain crook surmounted by brass lamb, and a ringed socket.

M/Crook/33   7.7"   SHC / 183 / 1989 / 1

The provenance is unknown. This design has a spear tip, a plain crook with a flat cross-section, and a ringed socket.

M/Crook/34   7.25"   Private collection

The provenance is unknown. This design has a star tip, a plain crook, and a ringed socket.

LOAS banner from Shepherds Glee Lodge 997, Bristol.

M/Crook/35   6.25"   Private collection

The provenance is not known for this design. This design has a ball tip, a plain crook, and a ringed socket.

M/Crook/36   7"   Private collection

The provenance is not known for this design. This design has a ball tip, a plain crook, and a ringed socket.

M/Crook/37   8.2"   MERL / Shickle / 511047

The provenance is not known for this design. This design has a ball tip, a beaded crook, and a ringed socket.

M/Crook/38   10.25"   Private collection

The provenance is not known for this design. This design has a cross tip, a plain crook, and a plain socket integral with crook.

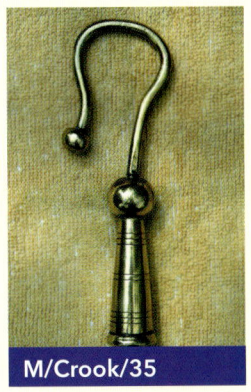

M/Crook/35

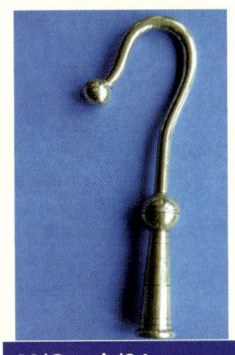

M/Crook/36

M/Crook/37

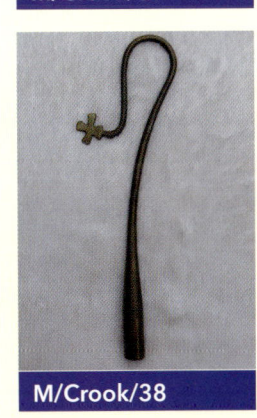

M/Crook/38

Turned wooden poles were commonly used by the LOAS (Shepherds) lodges.

M/Crown/01

M/Crown/02

M/Crown/03

M/Crown/04

M/Crown/01   6.8"   Blaise Castle House Museum / T7595

This gold painted metal open crown with red highlights is no longer on a pole. It is said to have belonged to a Tintinhull Juvenile Society, but there is no supporting evidence.

M/Crown/02   17.5"   Blaise Castle House Museum / T4060

This crown has been attributed to Horningsham, Wiltshire, but there is no supporting evidence. The metal open crown has faded gold and red paint, and around the rim of the crown is the motto 'God Save the Queen'. The darkened blue pole has red and white spiral stripes. The crown was collected by Philip Le Gros of Frome, and was illustrated in the set of eight photographs taken of Philip Le Gros' collection in 1911 (copies are held in the Somerset Heritage Centre Museum archives).

M/Crown/03   19"   Blaise Castle House Museum / T4061

This crown has been attributed to Horningsham, Wiltshire, but there is no supporting evidence. The metal open crown has faded gold, blue and red paint, and around the rim of the crown is the motto 'God Save the Queen'. The darkened blue pole has red and white spiral stripes. The crown was collected by Philip Le Gros of Frome, and was illustrated in the set of eight photographs taken of Philip Le Gros' collection in 1911 (copies of the photographs are held in the Somerset Heritage Centre Museum archives).

M/Crown/04   9" (and 9" wide) Blaise Castle House Museum / T4062

This crown has been attributed to Horningsham, Wiltshire, but there is no supporting evidence. The metal open crown has muted gold, blue and red paint, and around its rim is a faded motto, now illegible. The crown is still attached to a darkened blue pole. The crown was collected by Philip Le Gros of Frome, and was illustrated in the set of eight photographs taken of Philip Le Gros' collection in 1911 (copies of the photographs are held in the Somerset Heritage Centre Museum archives).

M/Crown/05   8" (and 8" wide) Blaise Castle House Museum / T4063

This crown has been attributed to Horningsham, Wiltshire, but there is no supporting evidence. The metal open crown with muted gold, blue and red paint is lacking its original top finial. Around the rim of the crown is a faded motto, now illegible. A darkened blue pole is still attached. The crown was collected by Philip Le Gros of Frome, and was illustrated in the set of eight photographs taken of Philip Le Gros' collection in 1911 (copies of the photographs are held in the Somerset Heritage Centre Museum archives).

M/Crown/05

M/Crown/06   6.5"   MERL / Allen / 551152

This metal open crown has no recorded provenance.

M/Crown/07   c.15"   Wainwright Collection (dispersed): location untraced

This metal open crown was reputedly from Maiden Bradley, Wiltshire, but no evidence has emerged in support, and its current location is unknown. It was in the Wainwright Collection (Eunice B. Overend, ed., *Catalogue of the Wainwright Collection of Friendly Society Brasses* [dispersed], The Phillips Museum [defunct], Brokerswood, Autumn 1971, p.28).

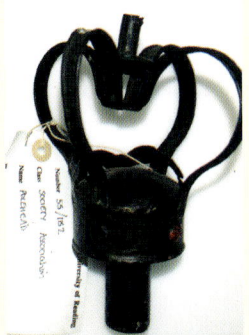

M/Crown/06

M/Crown/08   8.6"   SHC / Du Cann Collection / 201896

The drawing of a metal open crown, originally from the Ponsonby-Fane Collection (dispersed), but later in the Du Cann Collection, shows a slightly different pattern from the one in the Wainwright Collection (M/Crown/07), although both were reputed to have come from Maiden Bradley (MERL Ponsonby-Fane notebook, D 85/11/1, p.195). The provenance, however, is unconfirmed. The Ponsonby-Fane drawing (M/Crown/08b), while slightly out of proportion compared with the photograph of the actual specimen (M/Crown/08a), shows the vibrancy of the original paint, now much faded.

M/Crown/07

M/Crown/08a

M/Crown/08b

M/Crown/09   31.5"   Blaise Castle House Museum / T4064

No evidence of provenance for this open metal crown has emerged. It has muted gold, blue, and red paint, and the top flat cushion and crown have the mottoes 'V.R.' and 'Friendship' (obverse), and 'V.R.' and 'God Save the Queen' (reverse). The supporting twisted metal shaft is fixed to a dark blue wooden pole with red and white spiral stripes.

M/Crown/10   31.5"   Blaise Castle House Museum / T4065

No evidence of provenance for this open metal crown has emerged. It has muted gold, blue, and red paint, and the top flat cushion and crown have the mottoes 'V.R.' and 'A Friendly Society' (obverse), and 'V.R.' and 'Love and Unity' (reverse). The supporting twisted metal shaft is fixed to a dark blue wooden pole with red and white spiral stripes.

M/Crown/09

M/Crown/10

M/glass/01

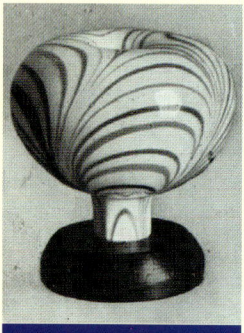

M/glass/02

M/glass/03

M/glass/01   12"   Current location unknown

This pole head is made of glass and was in the Ponsonby-Fane collection (MERL Ponsonby-Fane notebook D 85/11/1, p.92 no 2), but no provenance was recorded for it. The current location of this specimen is unknown, following the sale of the Ponsonby-Fane Collection in 1956 (Sale Catalogue of the contents of Brympton d'Evercy House, 1956: MERL D35/11 no 4). There is no indication accompanying the drawing to show how it was attached to the staff.

M/glass/02   6"   Current location unknown

In 1911 this glass specimen was in the collection of Mrs CE Challicombe of Clevedon. It is verified as originating from Nailsea, where it was used by a member of the Nailsea Glass Makers' Guild, which met at the Glass Makers' Arms. Glass manufacture took place at Nailsea between 1788 and 1873. The guild was not a registered friendly society. The two glass pole tops (M/glass/02 and M/glass/03) were illustrated as fig. V in H St George Gray's article 'Nailsea Glass', *The Connoisseur*, Vol XXX, no 118, June 1911, p.88. The pole top was made of opaque white glass streaked with pink and royal blue. Mrs Challicombe's collection is now in the SHC, Taunton Museum, but these glass pole heads have not been found among the pieces of glassware.

M/glass/03   12.5   Current location unknown

In 1911 this glass specimen was in the collection of Mrs CE Challicombe of Clevedon. It is verified as originating from Nailsea, where it was used by a member of the Nailsea Glass Makers' Guild, which met at the Glass Makers' Arms. Glass manufacture took place at Nailsea between 1788 and 1873. The guild was not a registered friendly society. The two glass pole tops (M/glass/02 and M/glass/03) were illustrated as fig. V in H St George Gray's article 'Nailsea Glass', *The Connoisseur*, Vol XXX, no 118, June 1911, p.88. The pole top was made of opaque white glass streaked with pink and royal blue. Mrs Challicombe's collection is now in the SHC, Taunton Museum, but these glass pole heads have not been found among the pieces of glassware.

M/Javelin/01

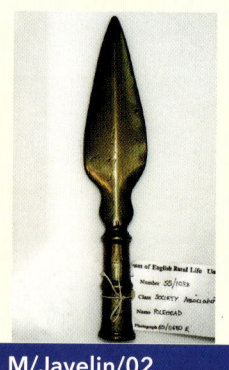

M/Javelin/02

M/Javelin/03

M/Javelin/04

M/Javelin/05

M/Javelin/01   c. 9″   SHC / OSFS / 607

Although this specimen has no recorded provenance, the javelin top and pole with woollen tassel resemble those seen in the photograph of the Judge's Escort at the Wells Court House, c.1863, carried by the Somerset Javelin Men (D. Bromwich and R. Dunning, *Victorian and Edwardian Somerset from old Photographs*, 1997, p.108).

M/Javelin/02   9.9″   MERL / Allen / 551037

Allen did not give any provenance for this specimen. It may not have originated from a friendly society: the blade of the javelin is of varying thickness unlike the sheet brass of most spear-like friendly society pole heads.

M/Javelin/03   10.9″   SHC / B 1808

The top of this specimen is made of iron, painted yellow, and mounted on a pole. It was originally in the Kelway Collection, but no provenance is given in his notebook alongside the drawing (SHC Taunton Museum Archives, Kelway notebook, p.159).

M/Javelin/04   13.75   SHC / Du Cann Collection / 201870

No provenance for this specimen has emerged. It is probably a flag-pole top, but not necessarily from a friendly society.

M/Javelin/05   c. 15″   SHC / Walter Collection 1901

This pole head is catalogued as the top of the standard of the **Stoke and Martock Yeomanry**. The company helped to suppress Reform Riots at Yeovil in 1830. The entire length of the pole and head is 131.3″.

M/Javelin/06   7.25″   Private collection

In the MERL Ponsonby-Fane notebook a similar specimen was included as a friendly society pole head, but the design was actually the standard top to the colours of a **Militia** unit (MERL D 85/11/1, p.85, no3). Laid-up colours with this top exist in churches at Cullompton, Taunton, and Exeter, besides Malta, Gibraltar and other British military bases. The pattern shown here appears to be a regular issue design, and is the one most commonly seen, but there are other variants with slightly different 'cut-outs', and there are several varieties of socket (see M/Javelin/07).

M/Javelin/07   7.3″   MERL / Shickle / 510933

This specimen appeared without a stated provenance in the Shickle Collection when it was presented to the V and A Museum, and remains catalogued in Shickle's Collection of Friendly Society pole heads at MERL, but it is a **militia** pole head (see M/Javelin/06).

M/Javelin/08   12.25″   SHC / Du Cann Collection / 201869

This specimen has no recorded provenance, and it is by no means certain that it is of friendly society origin. The material is silver plate on copper.

M/Javelin/09   16.3″   MERL / Acc 2001/5

This specimen was used at **Bishop Sutton**, but not by a friendly society. The steel pole head is fixed above a tassel on a varnished pole covered with suede at the top. In 1941 Fred Elson, antique dealer, Christmas Steps, Bristol, wrote that the poles were kept at Sutton Court, home of Strachey family, and the servants used them on the Bishop Sutton Friendly Society parades (SHC, Taunton Museum archives). There are examples at MERL and Blaise Castle House Museum.

M/Javelin/10   15.4″   Private collection

This is an example of a country house brass ornamental halberd, but the provenance is unknown. The crest is included in Fairbairn's illustrations.

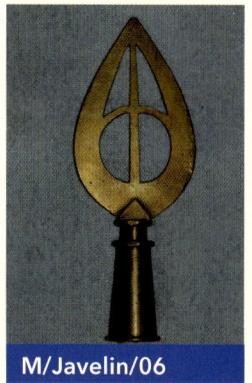
M/Javelin/06

M/Javelin/07

M/Javelin/08

M/Javelin/09

M/Javelin/10

M/Mace/01

M/Mace/06

M/Mace/11

M/Mace/02

M/Mace/07

M/Mace/12

M/Mace/03

M/Mace/08

M/Mace/13

M/Mace/04

M/Mace/09

M/Mace/14

M/Mace/05

M/Mace/10

M/Mace/15

Oddfellows maces were noted at **Bristol** (*Bristol Mercury*, February 22nd, 1845), **Exeter** (*Western Times*, August 16th, 1845), **Cullompton** (*Western Times*, May 17th, 1845), and **Yeovil** (*Sherborne Mercury*, August 1st, 1846}. No doubt there were many others. An example of a collection of these in use at the Pride of Clapham Lodge is illustrated in Daniel Weinbren, Th*e Oddfellows 1810 - 2010*, Lancaster, 2010, p.219. In addition to the ones shown here (M/Mace/01 to M/Mace/15) the Clapham set includes a mace with an hourglass top. The different designs were carried by the various lodge officers. There are many variants on the patterns illustrated here.

M/Mace/01   25.25″ MERL / Allen / 551174 Unknown provenance.

M/Mace/02   31.4″   MERL / Allen / 551176 Unknown provenance.

M/Mace/03   26.6″   MERL / Allen / 551173 Unknown provenance.

M/Mace/04   28.6″   MERL / Allen / 551175 Unknown provenance.

M/Mace/05   27.5″   MERL / Allen / 551026 Unknown provenance.

M/Mace/06   34″   MERL / Allen / 551024 Unknown provenance.

M/Mace/07   28.8″   MERL / Allen / 551140 Unknown provenance.

M/Mace/08   22.8″   MERL / Allen / 550922 Unknown provenance.

M/Mace/09   16.7″   MERL / Allen / 551177 Unknown provenance.

M/Mace/10   26″   MERL / Allen / 551180 Unknown provenance.

M/Mace/11   16.2″   SHC / B 1902 (Kelway Notebook p. 112) Unknown provenance.

M/Mace/12   26.3″   MERL / Allen / 551182 Unknown provenance.

M/Mace/13   27″   MERL / Allen / 551131 Unknown provenance.

M/Mace/14   25.7″   MERL / Allen / 551179 Unknown provenance.

M/Mace/15   16.4″   MERL / Allen / 551178 Unknown provenance.

M/Sickle/01

M/Sickle/02

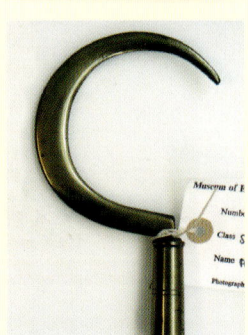

M/Sickle/03

M/Sickle/04

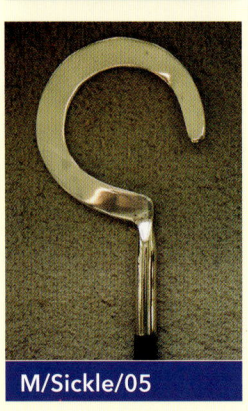

M/Sickle/05

M/Sickle/01   6.25"   MERL / Jardine / 61244168

Jardine listed this pattern as belonging to the Golden Sickle (or Hook) Society, Coalpit Heath, Gloucestershire, but the outline of those sickles seems to have been more ovoid, whereas this outline is semi-circular. He offered no supporting evidence.

M/Sickle/02   6.3"   SHC / OSFS / 222A

This pattern is generally ascribed to the Golden Hook Society at **Coalpit Heath, Gloucestershire**. HJ Hooper in 1909 presented this specimen to Taunton Museum and wrote that it came from the oldest inhabitant of Coalpit Heath, whose father was a member. Hooper claimed that it was not a Druids' Society. In the catalogue of the Wainwright Collection the drawing of the pattern is labelled 'Wheatsheaf Golden Hook Club' (Eunice B. Overend, ed., *Catalogue of the Wainwright Collection of Friendly Society Brasses* [dispersed], The Phillips Museum [defunct], Brokerswood, Autumn 1971, p.21).

M/Sickle/03   6.5"   MERL / Allen / 550876

Allen gave no suggestion of provenance for this pattern, and no further details have emerged.

M/Sickle/04   9.1"   SHC / OSFS / 600

No details of provenance are recorded for this pattern, and no further information has emerged.

M/Sickle/05   10.8"   Private collection

No details of provenance are recorded for this pattern. Several are known to have existed as a set.

UAOD (Druids) meeting at Stonehenge 1905.

M/Sickle/06   11″   MERL / Allen / 551142

Allen gave no provenance for this specimen. Two examples are recorded: their large size suggests that they were stewards' brasses, and the pattern strongly resembles the smaller version which is usually associated with the Golden Hook Society of Coalpit Heath, Gloucestershire. In the catalogue of the Wainwright Collection the drawing of the pattern is labelled 'Wheatsheaf Golden Hook Club'. (Eunice B. Overend, ed., *Catalogue of the Wainwright Collection of Friendly Society Brasses* [dispersed], The Phillips Museum [defunct], Brokerswood, Autumn 1971, p.21).

M/Sickle/06

M/Sickle/07   7.8″   MERL / Shickle / 511051

Shickle made no suggestions for the provenance of this pattern. No others are recorded. Unlike the pole head shown at M/Sickle/08, there is no raised ornamental acorn and leaves at the top of the socket.

M/Sickle/08   7.9″   Private collection

This specimen is stamped 'G Kendall Lodge 827', showing that it was used by the **George Kendall Lodge**, **No 827, United Ancient Order of Druids**, **Nottingham**. The members met at the Dog and Bear Inn, Bridlesmith-Gate (*Nottinghamshire Evening Post*, February 23rd, 1896). An example with an identical pattern has been ascribed to Wirksworth or Cromwell in Derbyshire, but without supporting evidence (Wirksworth Parish Records 1608 - 1899: www.wirksworth.org.uk, retrieved 15/05/2016). How widely the pattern was used by other UAOD lodges is unknown.

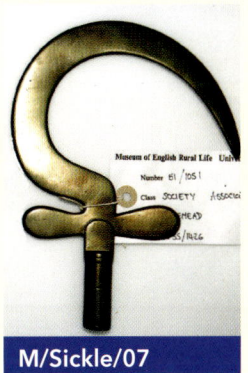

M/Sickle/07

M/Sickle/09   8″   Blaise Castle House Museum / T7509

No details of provenance have emerged for this specimen, the only one of its pattern so far recorded.

M/Sickle/10   10.8″   Private collection

No details of provenance have emerged for this specimen: several examples have been recorded.

M/Sickle/08

M/Sickle/11   9.75″   Private collection

This design is verified for the **United Ancient Order of Druids**, Bristol district (UAOD), but not for any particular local lodge. In the second annual Bristol UAOD parade some of the officers from local lodges carried 'wands tipped with the harp and golden sickle' (*Bristol Mercury*, October 11th, 1887). The design was probably also used elsewhere.

M/Sickle/11

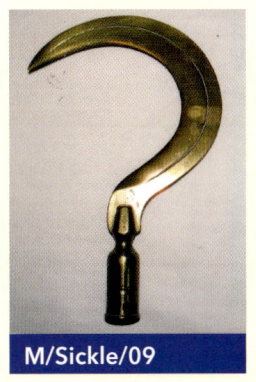

M/Sickle/09

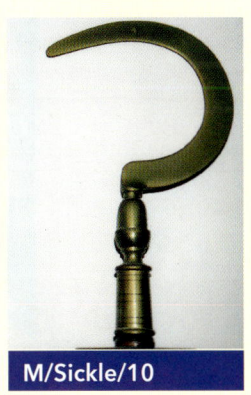

M/Sickle/10

M/01

M/02

M/03

M/04

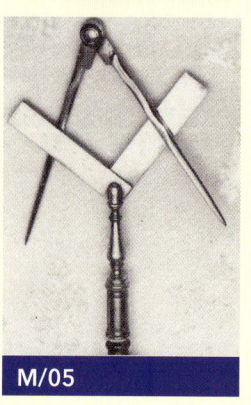

M/05

M/Various Masonic or Orders pole heads/01   4.4"   Private collection

Similar tops for wands, with the dove and olive branch, were available for purchase (in 2022), as part of **Craft Freemasonry** regalia. This particular specimen was obtained in North Devon, but the exact provenance and age are unknown. The specimen shown at M/Various Masonic or Orders pole heads/12 is from the same source.

M/Various Masonic or Orders pole heads/02   4.5   MERL / Allen / 551170

This specimen is similar to the illustration on p.146 of Victoria Solt Denis, *Discovering Friendly and Fraternal Societies*, 2005, showing regalia of the **Grand Order of Total Abstinent Sons and Sisters of the Phoenix,** but the provenance of this particular pole head is unknown. Bristol had seven lodges of the Order, and Bath had two, but it is not known if any of them used this symbol.

M/Various Masonic or Orders pole heads/03   5.7"   Private collection

No provenance has emerged for this design. The heart in hand (or just the hand or the heart) on a ball is often found on pole heads, varying in size and detail. They are associated with Oddfellows' Lodges. Bristol and its surrounds had 69 Oddfellows' lodges, while Somerset had 139, but details of their regalia have mostly been lost. The surface of the hand on this specimen is plain whereas some examples have the outline of a heart on the palm. The socket here may be a replacement.

M/Various Masonic or Orders pole heads/04   8.8"   Private collection

As there is no recorded provenance for this design (this particular specimen is one of a pair) it is not possible to say whether it originated from Freemasons, Oddfellows, or Rechabites, all of whom used pole heads in the form of a moon in their rituals.

M/Various Masonic or Orders pole heads/05   c. 14" - 17" Wainwright Collection (dispersed)

This specimen is probably of Masonic origin but the provenance is unknown. Several examples of The Square and Compasses design of pole head have been recorded, but currently there are none among any of the major museum collections of friendly society pole heads. The Kelway Collection specimen was listed as originating from Lancashire, but without any supporting evidence, and it is not known what became of the examples in the Kelway Collection or in the Wainwright Collection (SHC: Kelway Collection Notebook, p.110, where the full-size drawing measures some 14". The Wainwright image shown here comes from the Christie's 1974 dispersal sale catalogue).

M/Various Masonic or Orders pole heads/06   14.4"   Private collection

This design was used by lodges of the **Order of Free Gardeners**, but the precise provenance of this specimen is unknown. There were only a few branches of Free Gardeners in the West Country: six were established in Bristol, but none in Somerset. This specimen is one of a pair from Northern Ireland, probably banner tops on account of their size. The square is crossed not just with compasses but also with a pruning knife, symbolic of the Order of Free Gardeners.

M/06

M/Various Masonic or Orders pole heads/07   15.55"   Private collection

This design was used by lodges of the **Order of Free Gardeners**, but the precise provenance of this specimen is unknown. There were only a few branches of Free Gardeners in the West Country: six were established in Bristol, but none in Somerset. The square is crossed not just with compasses but also with a pruning knife, symbolic of the Order of Free Gardeners. The eyelet half-way up the socket indicates the use of this pole head as a finial for a flag or banner.

M/07

M/Various Masonic or Orders pole heads/08   10.7"   SHC / OSFS / 293

The Kelway Collection Notebook suggested a Lancashire Masonic Lodge as the provenance of this pole head, but there is no supporting evidence. For a five-pointed star of similarly unverified origin see F 165/3, which was originally in the HJ Hooper Collection, and is now in the Holburne Museum, Bath.

M/08

M/Various Masonic or Orders pole heads/09   8.2"   SHC / OSFS / 720

Taunton Museum obtained this specimen from AW Allen, but he supplied no provenance for it. The sun symbol on a staff was used in some lodges of Freemasons, Oddfellows, and Rechabites.

M/09

M/Various Masonic or Orders pole heads/10   12"   MERL / Allen / 551082

Allen gave no provenance for this specimen. The sun symbol on a staff was used in some lodges of Freemasons, Oddfellows, and Rechabites.

Freemasons, Rechabites or Oddfellows sun pole head.

M/10

183

M/11

M/12

M/13

M/14

M/15

M/Various Masonic or Orders pole heads/11 4.8" Private collection

Several examples of this design have been recorded, but their origin is not verified. The symbol may have been used by the United Patriots Order, but evidence has not been found to associate their branches with the carrying of poles topped with this design. Bristol and its surrounds had 23 branches of the Order, and Somerset had 75.

M/Various Masonic or Orders pole heads/12 5.2" Private collection

The term 'Assistant' is cast in on the ribbon. Similar tops for wands are still available for purchase (in 2022), as part of **Craft Freemasonry** regalia. This particular pole head was obtained in North Devon, but the precise provenance and age are unknown. The specimen shown at M/Various Masonic or Orders pole heads/01 is from the same source.

M/Various Masonic or Orders pole heads/13 9.1" Private collection

This is a pole top made for general use made by **Tutills of London:** it is not specific to a particular society. Bradford Abbas Friendly Society (Dorset), for example, used these tops on its banner, as illustrated in a 1926 club day photograph (Eric Garrett, *Bradford Abbas - The History of a Dorset Village*, Yeovil, 1989, p 223). Many friendly societies also purchased their painted silk banners from George Tutill of London, a regalia specialist, as did several different types of organisation, not just friendly societies. The pole top shown here was made in two halves, front and back, which were stamped in low relief. The maker's details, G Tutill 83 City Road London, were embossed each side of the spear on the edges of the two lower projections. The entire finial is hollow and is attached to the top of its pole by a threaded spike. Tutills produced more than one pattern of banner top.

M/Various Masonic or Orders pole heads/14 c. 15" Private collection

These two pole tops were designed to go on banner poles, and were made by the manufacturers **Kenning of London**. As with Tutill products (M/Various/13), they were used by several different types of organisation, not just friendly societies. The top was made in two halves, front and back, which were stamped in low relief. The maker's details, 'Kenning - London', are embossed each side of the spear on the edges of the two lower projections. This type is provided with a socket.

M/Various Masonic or Orders pole heads/15 11.25" Private collection

This design of pole head was produced not for friendly society use, but for the various lodges of the **Orange Order**. The precise origin of this particular specimen is unknown. Although the button top and general appearance are reminiscent of friendly society pole heads these tops are of heavier duty brass than was used in friendly societies. The Orange Order lodges also use other designs, including a five-pointed star in a circular border, and halberds.

Select bibliography: history of the friendly society movement

Beveridge, Lord (1948), *Voluntary Action*, George Allen and Unwin

Beveridge, Lord, and Wells, A F, eds (1949), *The Evidence for Voluntary Action*, George Allen and Unwin

Brabrook, Edward W (1881, 3rd edition, revised and enlarged), *The Law of Friendly Societies (Tidd Pratt's Law of Friendly Societies)*, Shaw and Sons, Fetter Lane

British Parliamentary Papers (1874 [c.995 – c.998]), *Reports of the Assistant Commissioners on Friendly and Benefit Building Societies*, George Edward Eyre and William Spottiswoode (HMSO)

Carpenter, Kenneth E, ed (1972), *Friendly Societies: Seven Pamphlets, 1798 – 1839*, Arno Press, New York

Cordery, Simon (2003), *British Friendly Societies, 1750 – 1914*, Palgrave Macmillan

Davis, Paul (1926), *The Old Friendly Societies of Hull*, A Brown and Sons, Hull

Dennis, Victoria Solt (2005), *Discovering Friendly Societies: Their Badges and Regalia*, Shire Publications, Princes Risborough

Eden, Frederick Morton (1797), *The State of the Poor*, 3 volumes, J Davis

Fuller, Margaret D (1964), *West Country Friendly Societies*, Oakwood Press for the University of Reading

Garton, J A (1936), *Glowing Embers from a Somerset Hearth*, Clare, Son & Co. Ltd., Wells

Gorsky, Martin (1999), *Patterns of Philanthropy*, The Royal Historical Society – The Boydell Press, Woodbridge

Gosden, P J H J (1961), *The Friendly Societies in England 1815 – 1875*, The University Press, Manchester

Gosden, P J H J (1973), *Self-Help ; Voluntary Associations in Nineteenth-century Britain*, B T Batsford

Green, David G (1993), *Re-inventing Civil Society: The Rediscovery of Welfare Without Politics*, IEA Health and Welfare Unit

Hardwick, Charles (1880, 3rd edition), *The History, Present Position, and Social Importance of Friendly Societies (Hardwick;s Friendly Societies' Manual)*, John Heywood, Manchester

Hoffman, Frederick L (1920), *National Health Insurance and the Friendly Societies*, Prudential Press, Newark, NJ

Ismay, Penelope (2018/9), *Trust Among Strangers: Friendly Societies in Modern Britain*, Cambridge University Press

Morley, Shaun, ed (2011), *Oxfordshire Friendly Societies, 1750 – 1918*, vol 68, The Oxfordshire Record Society, Chipping Norton

Neave, David (1991), *Mutual Aid in the Victorian Countryside 1830 – 1914*, Hull University Press

Robinson, M Fothergill (1913), *The Spirit of Association*, John Murray

Stead, T B (1880), *A Short History of the Chief Affiliated Friendly Societies*, Fred. R Spark, Leeds

Weinbren, Daniel (2010), *The Oddfellows 1810 – 2010*, Carnegie

Wilkinson, John Frome (1886), *The Friendly Society Movement*, Longmans, Green, and Co

Wilkinson, John Frome (1891), *Mutual Thrift*, Methuen and Co

INDEX OF PLACES

ALPHABETICAL LIST OF PLACES WITH POLE HEADS OF KNOWN DESIGN, OR WHERE THERE WERE POLES WHICH EITHER DID NOT HAVE POLE HEADS OR THE DESIGN OF THE POLE HEADS WAS UNKNOWN

Key

Places with pole head designs that have been suggested, whether verified or not, are found in the main catalogue. Their position in the catalogue is indicated in the index below by the references shown in bold type. For example, the design claimed for Abergavenny is shown below as **F260**.

Places which have either references just to poles or even also to pole heads (but the design is unknown) do not feature in the main catalogue, but they are shown below with the appropriate reference source and the detail. Thus for Alderton, Glos., there is a reference to club sticks in the *Cheltenham Chronicle 15 June 1901*, but as there is no detail of the design there is no mention of Alderton in the main catalogue.

The sources include material from The National Archives, and in such cases the reference is prefixed by the initials TNA. For example, Almondsbury has a reference to a staff in its 1846 rules, a copy of which is to be found in The National Archives under (TNA) FS 1/164/330.

Source materials quoted in this index also include press reports, books, and journals, as specified in relevant entries, together with some archival matter from Bristol Central Library and the Somerset Heritage Centre at Taunton (designated SHC).

Clutton: **F003/3, F005/2, F007/2, F009/4, F116**

Coaley, Glos: **F313/1**

Coalpit Heath, Glos: **M/Sickle/01**

Cockhill, Warks: **F178/1**

Combe Florey: **F041**

Combe Hay: **F096**

Combe St Nicholas: **F262**

Combwich: **F144. F145**

Compton Bishop: Compton Bishop Friendly Society – staff - Rules 1803 - (TNA) FS 1/605/15

Compton Martin: **F086, F088/1**

Congleton, Cheshire: **F191/4**

Corscombe, Dorset: **F327/2**

Corsley Heath, Wilts: **F063/2**

Corsley, Wilts: **F063/1, F304/2**

Corston: **F116**

Coughton, Warks: **F191/4**

Coventry, Warks: unknown society - club staves with brass doves to be sold off dissolution - *Coventry Standard April 10th 1868*; **F237**

Cranmore: **F083**

Creech St Michael: Pride of Creech Lodge LOAS - sash and crook (pattern not described) - *Taunton Courier May 22nd 1929*; **F283/1**

Crewkerne: Hand in Hand Club, alias Swan Club or the Reds - light blue pole and brass head - Rules 1815 - (TNA) FS!/606/63; Royal Old True Blues Friendly Society - black pole and brass head - Rules 1864 - SHC Tite Collection; **F191/1. F203/1, F216, F234**

Croscombe: **F099/3, F218/4**

Crowcombe: **F041, F257/1**

Cullompton, Devon: **F244/2, F261**

Culmstock, Devon: **F232/1, F232/2**

Curry Mallet: **F249, F250**

Curry Rivel: **F211, F213**

Dawley, Shropshire: Morning Star Lodge No 1, Working Men's FS - blue sticks with brass heads and blue ribbons - *Shropshire Examiner July 11th 1874*

Ditcheat: **F094/1, F094/2, F094/3**

Donyatt: **F272, F273/1, F273/2, F275**

Doulting: **F081**

Dowlish Wake: **F042**

Downend: **F107**

Downside **F167**

Drayton: **F333/1**

Dudley Port, Staffs: **F236/3**

Dudley, Worcs: **F227, F229/1, F229/2**

Dunkerton: **F005/2, F007/1, F007/2**

East Chinnock: East Chinnock Friendly Society - blue pole with yellow head (perhaps brass, but no detail) - Rules 1863 - (TNA) FS!/623/655; **F138**

East Coker: East Coker Union Friendly Society - club pole, brass mounted - *Western Gazette June 2nd 1876*

East Haddon, Northants: **F217/2**

East Harptree: **F058/1, F058/2**

Ebbw Vale, Glam: Ebbw Vale New Town Friendly Society - brass-mounted pole - *Merthyr Telegraph Aug 19th 1865*; **F028**

Ebrington, Glos: **F187**

Edgington: **F102**

Edington, Wilts: Edington Friendly Society - javelin - Rules 1817 - (TNA) FS 1/722/038

Enmore: **F270**

Etherington: **F237**

Evercreech: Triumph Lodge, Ancient Order of Druids - crooks (pattern not described, but probably a sickle) - *Shepton Mallet Journal July 12th 1935*; **F064**

Evershot, Dorset: Evershot Friendly Society - poles - *Western Gazette 8 June 1883*

Exton: Exton Friendly Society – pole - *Tiverton Gazette 1 June 1876*

Failand: **F108, F109/1**

Farmborough: **F009/1**

Farrington Gurney: **F103, F104**

Felton: **F181**

Filton, Bristol: **F100, F101, F108, F109/1, F112, F225, F226**

Fishponds, Bristol: **F164/1, F164/2, F165/1**

Fivehead: **F280/1**

Fonthill Gifford, Wilts: **F312**

Frampton Coterell, Glos: **F015**

Frome: **F026, F094/1, F094/2, F094/3**

Gillingham, Dorset: Gillingham Seven-year Friendly Society - garlands on poles - *Sherborne, Dorchester and Taunton Journal 29 May 1860*

Gilwern, Mon: **F260**

Glastonbury: **F135, F298, F299/1, F299/2, F299/3, F209/4, F299/5**

Goathurst: **F270, F292/1, F292/2**

Halberton, Devon: **F267, F278/1**

Hall Green, Birmingham: Bull's Head Inn Benefit Friendly Society - club sticks with brass tops: 100 for sale (dissolution) - *Birmingham Mail Aug 29th 1887*

Halse: **F263**

Halstock, Dorset: **F317/3, F322/1**

Hambridge: Hambridge Male Friendly Society - blue poles with brass heads - *Western Gazette June 8th 1866*

Hambrook, Bristol: **F151, F152, F153/1**

Misterton: **F208/2**

Monkton Farleigh, Wilts: **F098**

Montacute: Montacute Female Society at the Kings Arms - wand - Rules 1836 - (TNA) FS 1/618/425a; Montacute Female Society at the Phelips Arms – wand- Rules 1837 - (TNA) FS 1/618/425b; **F284, F288**

Moorlinch: Moorlinch Friendly Society - blue pole and brass head - Rules 1845 - (TNA) FS 1/617B/407; **F102**

Moreton, Dorset: **F218/1**

Mosterton, Dorset: Red, White, and Blue Friendly Society - poles - *Pulman's Weekly News 21 June 1891*

Muchelney: Muchelney Friendly Society - blue pole and gilt ornaments (wood? brass?) - *Western Gazette May 21st 1864*; F333/1

Nailsea: **F048, F049, M/Glass/01, M/Glass/02, M/Glass/03**

Nether Stowey: **F124, F219, F220, F221/1, F221/2**

Netherbury, Dorset: Netherbury Friendly Society club poles - *Bridport News 2 Aug 1872*

Netherton, Worcs: **F228/1**

Nettlebridge: **F167, F172/5**

Newton St Loe: Friendly Society of Gentlemen, Traders, and Others – staff - Rules 1835 - (TNA) FS 1/618/429

Nibley, Glos: **F140/1, F140/2, F140/3**

North Brewham: **F009/6, F062**

North Cadbury: **F048, F049**

North Coker: **F198/2, F199, F202**

North Curry: **F211, F264/3**

North Perrott: North Perrott Male and Female Friendly Society - poles and blue streamers (men only) - *Western Gazette 3 June 1887*; **F324**

North Petherton: **F272, F273/2, F273/3, F273/4, F275, F291, F292/1, F292/2**

Northleach, Glos: Friendly Society at the Wheatsheaf Inn – staves - *Cheltenham Chronicle 17 June 1862*; Red Lion Benefit Society – staves - *Cheltenham Chronicle 17 June 1862*

Norton Fitzwarren: **F208/1**

Norton St Phillip: **F086, F088/1**

Norton sub Hamdon: **F284, F287**

Nottingham: **M/Sickle/08**

Nunney: **F167**

Nuttall (unidentified place): **F200/6**

Oakhill: **F242**

Odcombe: **F284, F285, F286**

Old Cleeve: Old Cleeve Roadwater Friendly Society - staffs - *West Somerset Free Press 29 May 1875*: Blue Anchor Friendly Society - club staff - *West Somerset Free Press 4 June 1870*; Old Cleeve and Nettlecombe Friendly Society - club staff - *West Somerset Free*

Press 11 June 1870

Othery: **F268/1**

Panborough: **F154/1, F154/2, F155**

Paulton: **F002/3, F013/4, F014, F068/3, F082/1**

Pawlett: **F212**

Paxton: **F214/2**

Pensford: **F241, M/Crook/25**

Pilton: **F081**

Pitminster: **F232/1, F255/1, F255/2**

Plymouth, Devon: **F203/1**

Porlock: New Friendly Society - staffs - *West Somerset Free Press 13 July 1861*; Union Society (Old Society) - staffs - *West Somerset Free Press 13 July 1861*

Portishead: **F006**

Poulshot, Wilts: **F314/3, F316/2**

Priddy: **F179, F180/1**

Publow: **F241**

Puckington: **F214/1**

Pucklechurch, Glos: **F157/2, M/Crook/15**

Puddletown, Dorset: **F218/1**

Puriton: **F292/1, F292/2**

Quinton, Warks: **F172/3**

Radstock: **F029/1**

Redhill: **F071, F072**

Redlands, Bristol: **F148/1, F148/2, F148/3**

Rhayader, Radnorshire: Rhayader Friendly Society - long poles with brass tops - *Radnor Express Oct 12th 1905*

Rode (Road): **F067, F068/1**

Rodney Stoke: Rodney Stoke Friendly Society - spears on top of which is a model of an acorn - *Shepton Mallet Journal June 15th 1866*

Seavington: **F/004/1, F004/2, F004/3**

Selly Wick, Warks: **F228/2**

Shapwick: **F295**

Shepton Beauchamp : **F174/1, F209, F316/1**

Shepton Montague: **F304/1**

Sherborne, Dorset: **F025/1, F025/2, F195/2, F199, F202, F205, F206**

Shifnal, Shropshire: Shifnal Union Benefit Society (Dove Club) - staff surmounted by brass dove - *Wellington Journal July 12th 1887*; **F233/1, F233/2, F233/3, F236/1, F236/2, F236/3, F237, F239**

Shipham: **F030/1**

Shipston on Stour, Warks: **F184/1**

Shirehampton: **F033**

Siston, Bristol: **F108, F109/1**

Somerton: **F050, F052, F053/1, F053/2**

Soundwell, Bristol: **F128, F129. F130**

West Bagborough: Bagborough Friendly Society - members each carrying a brass-topped staff - *Taunton Courier 27th May 1908*

West Coker: **F198/2, F199, F202**

West Cranmore: **F008**

West Monkton: **F272, F273/1, F273/2, F273/3, F273/4, F275**

West Pennard: **F056, F057**

West Stour, Dorset: **F095/1, F095/2**

Westbury on Trym, Bristol: **F017, F119, F120/1, F120/2**

Westbury sub Mendip: **F031, F032**

Westonzoyland: **F045/1, F045/2, F045/3**

Weymouth, Dorset: Weymouth Friendly Society - staves with black cloth (for a funeral) - *Dorchester, Sherborne and Taunton Journal 30 Dec 1819*

Whitchurch: **F192, F193, F194/1, F195/1, F195/2, F196, F197/1, F197/7**

Wick, Glos: **F031, F034/3, F133/1, F133/2**

Wickwar, Glos: Wickwar Friendly Society - sale of club sticks - *Bristol Mercury 17 Mar 1879*

Williton: **F230, F272, F273/2, F273/3, F273/4**

Willoughby, Warks: **F217/1**

Willsbridge, Bristol: **F147**

Wincanton: **F089/1, F089/2, F090**

Winchcombe, Glos: Unicorn Sick Club - club sticks - *Gloucester Citizen 1 May 1933*

Winford: **F101**

Winfrith, Dorset: Winfrith Friendly Benefit Society - wands tipped with a brass spear - *Southern Times June 5th 1852*

Winsham: Loyal Brothers Friendly Society - gilded wands (wood? brass?) - *Somerset County Gazette May 19th 1883*; F327/1

Winsley, Wilts: **F027**

Winterbourne, Glos: **F245/1, F245/2, F247, F248**

Witham Friary: **F037**

Withington, Glos: Withington Friendly Society - club staff - *Cheltenham Chronicle 21 Oct 1871*

Woodend, Worcs: **F201/3**

Wookey: **F300/1**

Wool, Dorset: Wool Friendly Society - coloured staves, white fringe, ornamental gilded top (wood? brass?) - *Dorset County Chronicle June 7th 1842*

Woolavington: **F102**

Wraxall: Wraxall Friendly Society - staff, clean and perfect - Rules 1832 - (TNA) FS 1/615/299

Wrington: **F192, F193, F194/1, F195/1, F196, F197/1**

Writhlington: **F070/1, F070/2**

Wroughton, Wilts: Wroughton Primitive Methodist Benefit Society - club staves - *Swindon Advertiser 28 May 1866*

Wyke Regis, Dorset: Wyke Regis Friendly Society - wands ornamented with a brass device - *Dorset County Chronicle June 2nd 1825*

Yatton: **F011/1, F011/2**

Yeovil: **F188, F323/1, M/Javelin/05**

Zeals, Wilts: **F043**